Cree's
Dictionary of Latin
Quotations

EDITOR, VIRGINIA LOUISE ULRICI

Cree's Dictionary of Latin Quotations

Compiled by

Anthony Cree M.A.

Oxford University

Pronunciation guide by Simon Jones

NEWBURY BOOKS

EDITIO PRIMUS

Copyright © 1978 by Anthony Cree

Published in the United States of America in 1978
by Newbury Books, Topsfield, Massachusetts 01983

Sole distributor for the United Kingdom
J. Hannon & Company, 36 Great Clarendon Street, Oxford, England

Library of Congress Catalog Card Number 78–51482
ISBN 0-912728-12-4

Printed in the USA

DEDICATION TO R.B.S.

Introduction

My complete dictionary is a continuation of the work commenced several years ago with my earlier dictionary (Cree's Shorter Dictionary of Useful and Familiar Latin Quotations published by Hannon, Oxford, England). I have endeavoured to retain the essential simplicity of the earlier book but at the same time it is perhaps the most thorough and complete book of its type. Naturally the vast majority of quotes must come from a classical source, however, I have introduced a considerable number of modern, religious, medical and legal latin tags. It has been my intention that every latin quotation that a student is likely to find in the course of his 'non-classical' readings, will be found in this volume. For this reason I have been content to retain the alphabetical format, and every effort has been made to provide an accurate account of the quotes source as well as the translation and author.

I am indebted to Simon Jones, ex-Classics Scholar of Balliol College, Oxford, who has devised the ingenious, but simple system of pronunciations presented in this volume. The importance of pronunciation of the spoken quotation cannot be over-emphasised, and it is my hope that this present revival of interest in classical languages will result in a situation arising, where the more famous and useful quotations are once again used orally by educated people.

Finally, I should like to thank all those who have helped me over the past years, and without whose aid this book would not have been possible.

Nil Possee creari de niho

Anthony Cree

Foreword

The felicitous phrase is a joy for ever. It is a strong and noble joy, neither diminished by repeated savouring nor impaired by the collective appreciation of the whole world. And this is especially true of those Latin quotations which posterity has judged worth preserving, perhaps more worth preserving than even the Latin language itself. For we live today in difficult and turbulent times, when for the most part man's thoughts and energies are increasingly directed to his immediate concerns and when it becomes increasingly unreasonable to expect everybody to learn Latin.

Yet everybody will sooner or later be confronted by some — and those some significant — memorials of the ancient language, if not on the lips of speakers, then in the pages of literature and in the traditions of the law, or embalmed in the majesty of a stone inscription. These are not casual survivals. They represent human speech at its wisest and most memorable, comprising more than the sum of its constituent parts. Here is the quintessence of the language of the Romans, much better apprehended by means of jewels such as these than from the most heroic attempts at translation; here is lit up the long perspective of the past (for Latin was a long-lived language) from the twilight of legend to the late Middle Ages and beyond. How admirably suited is this lapidary tongue to produce the perfectly chiselled expression, whether the poignant *sunt lacrimae rerum* or the happy cadence of *mens sana in corpore sano* or, at a distance of over 1500 years, the vigour of *si monumentum requiris, circumspice*!

In these pages, whether he comes in quest of some elusive or enigmatic utterence or wanders randomly among treasures that wait on his discovery, the reader may be sure of beholding a multitude of brilliant stars shining forth with lustre still undimmed out of the darkening firmament that is Latin.

G. P. Goold

Acknowledgments

We are grateful to our many friends for their enthusiasm, genuine interest and help in the preparation of this book. A.C.

G. Courtenay, M.B.A.O.T., S.R.O.T.   P. McLaughlin, B.A.   Hassan Ascari, B.A.
M. Junata, B.A.   Roy Dinsdale, B.A.   Edward Holden, B.A.   Richard O'Sullivan, B.A.
Damian Green, B.A.   Neil Livingstone, B.A.   Helen Yanacek, B.A.   Fiona Skrine
Nicola Skrine, B.A.   Lorna Good   C. Boydell   S. Odell, S.R.O.T.   C. Burton, S.R.O.T.
Murrey Bracey, B.A.   Penny Howe, B.A.   Alicia Collinson, B.A.   Patrick Roche, B.A.
B. Margolis, B.A.   Nick Trent   C. Mainprice, B.A.   V. Hardman-Lea, B.A.   Nick St.
Aulbyn, B.A.   G. Davies, B.A.   Edward Edwards, B.A.   David Soskin, B.A.   Yan
Karpinski, B.A.   Frank Lilley, B.A.   Caroline Hunt, B.A.   Peter Chappell, B.A.
Peter Carvoso, B.A.   Martin Havelock, B.A.   R. Farquarson, B.A.   D. Lee, B.A.
J. Pugh-Smith, B.A.   Richard Pelley, B.A.   B. Longley, B.A.   M. Hudson, B.A.
D. Hutchence, B.A.   D. Warren, B.A.   P. Shirley, B.A.   Count Thomas Rogowski,
B.A.   D. McDonagh, B.A.   S. Walker, B.A.   L. Gort, Dip.Relig.   R. Bremener, B.A.
P. Green   D. Kirk, B.A.   N. Reynolds, B.A. (Brown University, USA)   C. Bush, B.A.
J. Burnett-Rae, B.A.   David Milne, B.A.   The Hon. Richard Norton, B.A.   W. England,
B.A.   R. Bridges, B.A.   R. Fleming, B.A.   K. Hutchence, B.A.   B. Longley, B.A.
M. Hamer, BSc.(Melbourne)   V. Van Amerongen, B.A.   Jos Passey   S. Goodhard,
Dip.Soc.   C. Schaeffer, B.A.   A. Johnson, B.A.   Rev. Dr. D. Macguffie, M.A.
B. Langston, M.A.   S. Steed, B.A.   L. Barker, B.A.   T. Fitzalan-Howard, B.A.
R. Fitzalan-Howard, B.A.   C. Newman, B.A.   C. Yapp, B.A.   R. Rendell, B.A.
N. Hughes, B.A.   R. Pelley, B.A.   L. Valdez   G. Jones, B.A.   J. Lofthouse, B.A.
D. Tregelgis, B.A.   R. Codrington, B.A.   K. Tudor, B.A.   A. R. McM. Bell
S. Beatty, B.A.   A. Didsbury, B.A.   Dr. Leofranc Holford Stevens   D. Dales, M.A.
M. Young, B.A.   R. Turner, B.A.   D. Howard, B.A.   S. Swift, B.A.   The Grand
Duchess Maria Romanov   A. Morris, B.A.   Victoria Schofield, B.A.   G. Davies,
B.A.   R. Stanley, B.A.   C. Raeburn, B.A.   C. Hogarth, B.A.   H. Bugler, B.A.
J. Thomas, B.A.   V. Dinham, B.A.   S. Barwick, B.A.   C. Tharp, B.A.   T. Toohey,
B.A.   M. Soole, B.A.   A. Bell, B.A.   G. Hunter   Rajava Wijesinda, B.A.
C. London, B.A.   A. Martinez, B.A.   Chas. Wood, B.A.   C. Clifford, B.A.
J. Egerton, B.A.   K. Gregory, B.A.   D. Matthew, B.A.   N. Hopkins, B.A. M. Taylor,

B.A.   N. Turner, B.A.   J. Savin, B.A.   J. Holdsworth, B.A.   J. Brazier, B.A.
K. Pearson, B.A.   D. Thomas, B.A.   G. Downing, B.A.   M. Gourley, B.A.   S. Revell,
B.A.   W. Fetherby, B.A.   A. Russel, B.A.   A. Amos, B.A.   A. Elliot, B.A.   C. Pitt-
Lewos, B.A.   J. Evans, B.A.   J. Oughton, B.A.   R. Pine, B.A.   R. Corbett, B.A.
A. Hindell, B.A.   T. Longford, B.A.   B. Langston, M.A.   N. Field-Johnson, B.A.
Giles Bowring, B.A.   M. Bachus, B.A.   G. Mather, B.A.   F. M. C. M. Bell, B.A.
Freya Darvell, B.A.   Robert Scoble, M.A.(Syd.)   S. Lamb, B.A.   S. Lovick
A. Sebesta, B.A.   V. Samson, M.B.A.O.T.   R. Scott-Fox, B.A.   B. Bhutto, B.A.
R. Hyder, B.A.   Mark Morris, B.A.   N. Coulshed, B.A.   P. Hayden, B.A.   C. Low,
B.A.   Ross McInnes, B.A.   H. Byers, Dip.Educ.   Laurence Gormley, B.A.
N. Perrin, B.A.   R. Smith, B.A.

Abbreviations

> The abbreviations in this list represent most of the abbreviations in current use. The system of latin abbreviation is simple if one remembers that the first syllable (or syllables) of the latin word has remained intact, the reduction being achieved by removing the remaining part of the word, which in this list appears in brackets.

ACAD(EMICAE) QUAEST (IONES) *(Academic Disputations)*
AEN(EID)
AMPH(ITRUO)
APOL(OGIA)
ARS AMAT(ORIA) *(The Art of Love)*
AUG(USTUS CAESAR) *(Life Of)*
CAES(AR) *(Life of Julius)*
CARM(EN) *(Poem)*
CATIL(INE)
CONSUL(ATUS) HONOR(II) *(On the Consulate of Honorius)*
CONTRA EPIST(ULAM) PARMEN(II) *(Against the Letter of Parmenius)*
1,2 COR(INTHIANS)
DE ARTE POET(ICA) *(On the Art of Poetry)*
DE BEWEF(ICIIS) *(On Benefits)*
DECLAM(ATIO) *(On Declamation)*
DE DIVINAT(IONE) *(On Divination)*
DE FIN(IBUS) *(On the Ends of Good and Evil Men)*
DE IMIT(ATIONE) CHRISTI *(On the Imitation of Christ)*
DE LAUDIBUS STIL(ICHONIS) *(In Praise of Stilicho)*
DE NAT(URA) DEORUM *(On the Nature of the Gods)*
DE OFF(ICIIS) *(On Duties)*
DE PARTITIONE ORAT(ORIA) *(On the Division of Oratory)*

DE RER(UM) NAT(URA) *(On the Nature of Things)*
DE GEN(ECTUTE) *(On Old Age)*
ECL(OGVES)
EL(EGIES)
EP(ISTULAE) AD ATT(ICUM) *(Letters to Atticus)*
EP(ISTULAE) EX PONT(O) *(Letters From the Black Sea)*
EPIG(RAMS)
EP(ISTLES)
FAB(LES)
FAST(I) *(Calendar)*
FRAGM(ENT)
GAL(ATIANS)
GEORG(ICS)
HEAUT(ONTIMORUMENOS) *(The Self-Tormentor)*
HIST(ORIES)
IMIT(ATIO)CHRISTI=DE IMIT.CHRISTI, Q.V.
IN JOANN(EM) *(Commentary on St. John)*
IN SOMN(IUM) SCIP(IONIS) *(The Dream of Scipio)*
INST(ITUTA) JUR(IS) CIV(ILIS) *(Institutes of Civil Law)*
MET(AMORPHOSES)
MOSTELL(ARIA)
N(ATURAL) H(ISTORY)
NAT(URALES) QUAEST(IONES) *(Disputations on Nature)*
OR(ATIO) IN CATIL(INAM) *(Speech Against Catiline)*
PANEG(YRICUS) TRAJ(ANI) *(Danegyric of Trajan)*
PHARS(ALIA)
PHIL(IPPICS)
PRO RAB(IRIO) POSTUMO *(Speech for Rabirius Postumus)*
PRO REGE DEJOT(ARO) *(Speech for King Dejotarus)*
PR(QUERBIAL)
PS(ALMS)
REM(EDIUM) AMOR(IS) *(The Remedy for Love)*
ROM(ANS)
SAT(IRES)   ST. MATT(HEW)
THEB(AID)
2 THESS(ALONIANS)
TRUC(ULENTUS) *(The Truculent Man)*
TUSC(ULANAE) QUAEST(IONES) *(Tusculan Disputations)*
VESP(ASIANUS) AUG(USTUS) *(Life of Vespasian)*

Pronunciation

The quotations given in this volume may be pronounced in three ways, according to their provenance and date. Those from classical authors (i.e. up to c.400 A.D.) are nowadays pronounced in the so-called 'classical' pronunciation, i.e. approximately as their authors would have pronounced them. Those from ecclesiastical and medieval sources are commonly spoken in the ecclesiastical pronunciation, which differs from the classical mainly in some consonant sounds. Short phrases of everyday occurrence, like *vice versa*, *nisi prius*, etc., are normally pronounced as if they were English words; this I call the English pronunciation.

CONSONANTS. The following letters are pronounced similarly in all three systems: b, d, f, k, l, m, n, p, q, r, t, x, z. They have the same values roughly as the English letters in *book, dog, fast, keep, leap, make, not, pat, quick, run, take, axe,* and *haze*. Q in Latin is, as in English, always followed by *u*. There is no *w* in the Roman alphabet.

The consonants *c, g, h, j, s* and *v* are pronounced as follows:

	CLASSICAL	ECCLESIASTICAL	ENGLISH
C before e, i, y	as c in cat	as ch in church	as c in cell
C before a, o, u	as c in cat	as c in cat	as c in cat
G before e, i, y	as g in get	as g in gun	as g in gun
G before a, o, u	as g in get	as g in get	as g in get
H	as h in horse	as h in honour	as h in horse
J	as y in yellow	as y in yellow	as j in judge
S between vowels	as s in soap	as s in rose	as s in rose
S elsewhere	as s in soap	as s in soap	as s in soap
V	as w in wet	as v in verse	as v in verse

N.B. The Romans did not distinguish between *I* and *J* or between *U* and *V* in spelling, but wrote I and V for both consonant and vowel sounds: thus *INJURIA* was actually spelt INIVRIA. For the convenience of the reader I have adopted the traditional practice of spelling the consonantal sounds *J* and *V*, leaving *I* and *U* for the vowels; most editions of the Classics however, now use *I* instead of *J*, and some (e.g. the Oxford Classical texts) also use *U* for *V*.

[xi]

The following combinations of consonants should be noted:

	CLASSICAL	ECCLESIASTICAL	ENGLISH
CH	as ch in chemist	as ch in chemist	as ch in chemist
PH	as ph in physics	as ph in physics	as ph in physics
TH	as th in think	as t in test	as th in think
GN	as gn in ignore	as ny in canyon	as gn in ignore
CC	as kc in bookcase	as tch in match*	as cc in success*
SC	as sk in ask	as sh in shed*	as sc in ascend*

*Only before *e, i* and *y*. Before *a, o* and *u* these are pronounced as in the classical pronunciation.

N.B. The values given to the classical pronunciations of *ch, ph, th, gn* are not precisely those Virgil would have used. They are, however, generally used in schools and Universities.

The ecclesiastical pronunciation has the additional features that *ti* followed by a vowel, except when preceded by *s, x* or *t* is pronounced like *ts* in *rats*: thus *natio* in this pronunciation is like *nah-tsee-oh*; and that *xc* before *e, i,* and *y* sounds like *ksh* or the *cti* in action.

VOWELS. The vowels *a, e, i, o, u* are pronounced as follows:

	CLASSICAL AND ECCLESIASTICAL	ENGLISH
A long	as a in father	as a in mate
short	as a in pat	as a in pat
E long	as ei in reign	as ea in read
short	as e in bet	as e in bet
I long	as i in machine	as i in hide
short	as i in pit	as i in pit
O long	as o in no	as o in no
short	as o in short	as o in pot
U long	as u in rude	as u in tune
short	as u in put	as u in mud

Y, which in Latin is always a vowel, is in the ecclesiastical and English pronunciations the same as I; the classical value is like the French *u* in *tu*, whether long or short.

The following combinations of vowels should be noted:

	CLASSICAL	ECCLESIASTICAL	ENGLISH
AE	as i in ride	as a in mate	as ea in read
OE	as oy in boy	as a in mate	as ea in read
AU	as ow in cow	as ow in cow	as au in haul

N.B. Because the ecclesiastical values of *ae* and *oe* are the same as those of *e*, the consonants *c* and *g* and the groups *cc, sc* and *xc* are pronounced in that style before *ae* and *oe* as before *e, i,* and *y*.

Other combinations of vowels are pronounced as two syllables, except for *eu,* which is one syllable consisting of a short *e* quickly followed by a short *u*. In the English pronunciation, however, it is like *eu* in *neutral*.

STRESS. The syllable of a word that is to be stressed is determined by the following rule:

In words of *two syllables,* the first is stressed.

In words of three or more syllables — if the vowel of the syllable next to the last is long, or a diphthong, or followed by more than one consonant *that syllable is stressed*; if the vowel of the next to last syllable is a short vowel followed by one consonant or none *the syllable before it is stressed.*

Thus in *Última Cumáei vénit jam cármínis áetas* (Virgil) the syllables stressed are those marked with an acute accent. The last syllable of a word is never stressed. It should be noted that the metre of classical latin poetry is based, not on stress-rythm, but on the alternation of long and short syllables, a long syllable being one containing a vowel that is long, a diphthong, or followed by more than one consonant, all other syllables being short. The metre of the quotation cited (called a 'dactylic hexameter') is based on a measure of one long syllable followed by two short ones; the short syllables may be replaced by one long one and at the end of the line must be. In this metre, which is the commonest metre of classical poetry, there are six of these measures, thus:

Ultima/cumae/i/ve/nit jam/carminus/aetas.

The reader may tell which vowels are long and which short, and thereby which syllables are stressed, by referring to the pronunciation guide accompanying each quotation.

PRONUNCIATION GUIDE. A guide to pronunciation is given with each quotation, in which the sounds of the latin are rendered in English spelling. In this guide each syllable is separated from the others by hyphens, and each u to be pronounced as if it were a separate English word. Thus *illae lacrimae* is rendered *ill-lie lack-rim-eye,* which should be pronounced exactly ·as a sequence of the English words *ill, lie, lack,* etc.

If greater accuracy of pronunciation is desired, these pages may be consulted; but the use of the guide alone will secure an accurate enough pronunciation if the following conventions are borne in mind:

A. G is to be pronounced always as in *get*.

B. U is always as in *put* or as the *oo* in *book*; the spelling *oo* is used to represent long *u* as in mood.

C. *ow* is always as in *cow*.

D. EH and IH are used to denote a short E and I, when no other way exists of doing so; conversely AH and DH denote long A and O.

For convenience, *eu* in the guide is treated as the English *eu,* and *y* exactly the same as *i,* even in quotations which are to be pronounced according to the classical system; apart from this, which pronunciation is used will be clear from a comparison of the guide on page XII. Occasionally, a quotation is rendered in two different pronunciations, where either is appropriate. Finally, it is important to remember that the division into syllables in the pronunciation guide does not correspond to the division in latin. The example on page XIII (*illae lacrimae*) is actually divided il-lae la-cri-mae.

Simon Jones.

A cruce salus. *ah croo—cheh sa—loose.*
Salvation from the cross.
Thomas à Kempis (adapted).

A facto ad jus non datur consequentia. *ah fac—toe ad yoose none dat—oor cone—seck—went—ia.*
From fact to law no deduction is allowable.
Law.

A fortiori. *ah forty—oar—eye.*
By a still stronger argument.
Euclid.

A fronte praecipitium, a tergo lupus. *ah fron—teh pry—kip—it—ium, a tare—go loo—pus.*
In front a precipice, behind a wolf.
Pr.

A pereat, quicunque rates et vela paravit primus et invito gurgite fecit iter! *ah peh—reh—at, quee—cun—queh rat—ace et way—la pa—rah—wit pree—muss et in—wee—toe gur—git—eh fay—kit it—ehr.*
O may he perish, whoever it was first designed ships and sails and voyaged over the unwilling deeps!
Propertius. Elegies 1.17.13.

A posse ad esse. *ah poss—seh ad ess—seh.*
From the possible to the actual.
Law.

A posteriori. *ay pos—teer—ee—oar—eye.*
From the latter; from what follows.

A priori. *ay pry—oar—eye.*
From what is before (deduction from cause to effect).

A solis ortu usque ad occasum. *ah sol–is or–too us–kweh ad ock–cah–sum.*
From the rising of the sun even to the setting thereof.
Vulgate. Malachi.I.II.

A vinculo matrimonii. *ah ving–ku–lo mah–trim–oh–ni–ee.*
From the bond of matrimony.
Law.

Ab abusu ad usum non valet consequentia. *ab a–boo–soo ad oo–sum none
val–et cone–seck–went–ia.*
An argument derived from the abuse of a thing does not hold good against
its use.
Law.

Ab honesto virum bonum nihil deterret. *ab hon–ess–toe vi–rum bon–um
ni–hill day–tehr–ret.*
Nothing deters a good man from what is right.
Seneca (adapted).

Ab initio. *ab in–it–i–oh.*
From the beginning.

Abi in malam rem maximam. *ab–ee in mal–am rem max–im–am.*
Go thoroughly to the bad.
Plautus.

Abiit ad plures. *ab–i–it ad ploo–race.*
He has joined the great majority.
Anon.

Abiit, excessit, evasit, erupit. *ab–i–it, ex–kess–sit, ay–wah–sit,
ay–roo–pit.*
He has gone, he has made off, he has escaped, he has broken away.
Cicero. In Catilinam.I.I.

Abite nummi, ego, ego vos mergam, ne mergar a vobis.
*ab–it–eh num–mee, egg–oh, egg–oh, woce mare–gam, nay mar–gar
ah woe–beess.*
Begone money! I will drown you that I be not drowned by you.

Ablata justitia, quid sunt regna nisi magna latrocinia?
*ab–lah–tah, yuss–tit–i–ah, quid sunt rayg–na niss–i mag–na
lat–roe–kin–i–a?*
Abolish justice, and what are kingdoms but great robberies? *St. Augustine.*

[2]

Absentem laedit, cum ebrio qui litigat. *ap—sent—em lie—dit, cum ay—bri—oh quee lee—tig—at.*
He injures the absent who contends with a drunken man.
Publilius Syrus.

Absit invidia verbo. *ap—sit in—wid—i—a ware—boh.*
May there be no illconstruction in the remark; LIT. May ill-will be wanting in the word.
Maxim.

Absit omen. *ap—sit oh—men.*
May the omen be averted.

Absque argento omnia vana. *aps—queh ar—gen—to om—ni—a wah—na.*
Without money all things are vain.
Pr.

Absque hoc. *aps—queh hoke.*
Without this; this being excepted.
Law.

Absque sudore et labore nullum opus perfectum est. *aps—queh soo—door—eh et lab—oor—eh null—lum op—us pear—fect—tum est.*
Without sweat and toil no work is brought to completion.
Pr.

Abstineto a fabis. *aps—tin—ay—toe ah fah—beess.*
Abstain from beans i.e. from elections, decided at Athens by beans.

Abstulit clarum cita mors Achillem;/Longa Tithonum minuit senectus. *aps—tul—it klah—rum kit—a morse a—kill—lem; long—ga tee—thoe—num min—u—it sen—eck—tuss.*
An early death took away the renowned Achilles; a long old age reduced Tithonus to insignificance.
Horace.

Absurdum est ut alios regat, qui seipsum regere nescit. *ap—soor—dum est ut a—li—oce reg—at, quee say—ip—sum reg—eh—reh ness—kit.*
It is absurd that he who does not know how to govern himself should govern others
Pr.

Abuses non tollit usum. *ab—oo—suss none toll—it oo—sum.*
The abuse of a thing does not forbid its use. *Pr.*

[3]

Accedas ad curiam. *ack–kay–dahss ad koo–ri–am.*
You may come to the Court.
Law.

. . . Acceptissima semper/Munera sunt, auctor quae pretiosa facit.
ack–kept–iss–sim–a sem–pear moon–eh–ra sunt, owk–tore quie
pret–i–oh–sa fack–it.
The gifts which the author (by giving) makes precious, are ever the most
acceptable.
Ovid.

Accipe, daque fidem. *ack--kip–eh da–queh fid–em.*
Accept and give the pledge of good faith.
Virgil.

Accipe, sume, cape, sunt verba placentia papae. *ack–kip–eh soo–meh,*
cap–eh, sunt wear–ba plack–en–ti–a pah–pie.
Take, have, and keep are words pleasing to a pope.

Accipere quam facere praestat injuriam. *ack–kip–eh–reh quam fack–eh–*
reh pry–stat in–you–ri–am.
It is better to receive than to do an injury.
Cicero.

Acclinis falsis animus meliora recusat. *ack–cleen–eess fal–cease an–im–us*
mel–i–oh–ra reck–oo–sat.
A mind inclined to what is false rejects better things.
Horace.

Accusare nemo se debet nisi coram Deo. *ack–coo–sah–reh nay–mo*
say day–bet niss–i koh–ram deh–oh.
No one need accuse himself except before God.
Law.

Acerrima proximorum odia. *ack–ehr–rim–a prox–im–oh–rum odd–i–a.*
The feuds of those most akin are the sharpest.
Tacitus.

Acribus, ut ferme talia, initiis, incurioso fine. *ah–crib–us, ut fair–may*
tah–li–a, in–it–i–eece, ing–coo–ri–oh–so fee–nah.
As is usual in such matters, keen in commencing, negligent in concluding.
Tacitus.

Acta exteriora indicant interiora secreta. *ack–ta ex–teh–ri–oh–ra*

in–dict–ant in–teh–ri–oh–ra say–cray–ta.
Outward actions are a clue to hidden secrets.
Law.

Acta senem faciunt. *act–ta sen–em fack–i–unt.*
Deeds make the old man i.e. a man may be called old according to the
extent of what he has done.
Ovid.

Acti labores jucundi. *ack–tea lab–oh–race you–cun–dee.*
Labours accomplished are pleasant.
Pr.

Actio personalis moritur cum persona. *ack–ti–oh pair–soh–nah–liss
mo–rit–oor cum pair–soh–nah.*
A personal action dies with the person.
Law.

Actum, aiunt, ne agas. *ack–tum, ah–yunt, nay ag–ahss.*
They say, "Do not do what is already done." (Cicero also employs this
saying.)
Terence.

Actus legis nulli facit injuriam. *ack–tus lay–giss null–lee fack–it in–you–
ri–am.*
The act of the law does no injury to any one.
Law.

Actus, Dei nemini facit injuriam. *ack–tus, deh–ee nay–nin–ee fack–it
in–you–ri–am.*
The act of God does no injury to any person.
Law.

Actus me invito factus non meus actus. *ack–tus may in–wee–toe fact–tus
none meh–us act–tus.*
An act done against my will is not my act.
Law.

Actus non facit reum, nisi sit rea. *ack–tus none fact–it reh–um, niss–i
sit reh–a.*
The act does not constitute a criminal unless the mind is criminal.
Law.

Acu rem tetigisti. *ack–oo rem tet–ig–iss–tea.*
You have touched the matter with a needle. *Pr.*

[5]

Ad avisandum (or avizandum). *ad ah—vee—sand—um.*
For consideration. (Used when in a case is reserved for consideration.)
Law.

Ad conciliandum auditorem. *ad cone—kill—i—and—um ow—dit—oh—rem.*
For the conciliation of the listener.
Law.

Ad hoc. *ad hoke.*
For this particular matter or purpose.
Pr.

Ad impossibile nemo tenetur. *ad im—poss—sib—ill—eh nay—mo ten—ay—tour.*
No one is held bound to the impossible.
Law.

Ad Kalendas Graecas. *ad kal—end—ahss grie—kahss.*
To the Greek Kalends — i.e. never.
Said to be a saying of Augustus Caesar by Suetonius.

Ad libitum. *ad lib—it—um.*
At pleasure.

Ad majorem Dei gloriam. *ad ma—i—yoh—rem deh—ee glow—ri—am.*
To the greater glory of God.
Motto of the Jesuits.

Ad nauseam. *ad naw—zi—am.*
To a sickening point.

Ad quaestionem juris respondeant judices, ad quaestionem facti
respondeant juratores. *ad kwie—sti—oh—nem you—ris ress—pond—eh—ant
you—dick—ace, ad kwie—sti—oh—nem fact—tea ress—pond—eh—ant you—
rah—toe—race.*
Let the judges answer on the question of law; the jury on the question of fact.
Law.

Ad quod damnum. *ad quod dam—num.*
To what injury.
Law.

Ad referendum. *ad ref—eh—rend—um.*
To be (considered and) brought back again.
Law.

[6]

Ad sanitatem gradus est novisse morbum. *ad—sah—nit—ah—tem grad—us est no—wiss—seh more—bum.*
It is a step towards health to know what the complaint is.
Pr.

Adaequarunt judices. *ad—eye—quah—runt you—dick—ace.*
The judges were equally divided.
Law.

Adde parum parvo, magnus acervus erit. *add—deh pa—rum par—woe, mag—nus ack—air—wus eh—rit.*
Add a little to a little, and there will be a great heap.
Ovid.

Adscriptus glebae. *ad—scrip—tus glay—bye.*
Attached to the soil.
Law.

Adversa virtute repello. *add—wehr—sah wihr—too—teh reh—pel—lo.*
I repulse evil chances by valour.
Motto.

Aedificare in tuo proprio solo non licet quod alteri noceat.
eye—di—fick—ah—reh in tu—oh prop—ri—oh sol—oh none licket quod al—teh—ree nock—eh—at.
It is not allowable to build upon your own land that which may do injury to another.
Law.

Aegis fortissima virtus. *eye—giss for—tiss—sim—a wihr—tus.*
Virtue is a very strong shield.
Motto.

Aequa lege necessitas,/Sortitur insignes et imos,/Omne capax movet urna nomen. *eye—kwah lay—geh neck—ess—sit—ahss, sore—ti—tour in—sig—nace et ee—moce, om—neh cap—ah—x mo—wet urr—na noh—men.*
Necessity has the same law for high and low. The capacious funeral urn shakes up every name.
Horace.

. . . Aequa tellus Pauperi recluditur,/Regumque pueris. *eye—qua tell—lus pow—peh—ree reck—loo—dit—ur, ray—gum—queh pu—eh—reece.*
The equal earth is opened alike to the poor man and the sons of kings.
Horace.

[7]

Aequitas sequitur legem. *eye—quit—ahss seh—quit—ur lay—ghem.*
Equity follows the law.
Law.

Aetas parentum, pejor avis, tulit/Nos nequiores, mox daturos Progeniem vitiosiorem. *eye—tahss pa—rent—um, pay—yore a—weece, tul—it noce nay—qui—oh—race, mox dat—oor—oce proh—ghen—i—em witt—i—oh— si—oh—rem.*
The age of our fathers, worse than our grandfathers, produced us still more vicious, who are soon about to raise a still more iniquitous progeny.
Horace. Odes 3.6.46.

Afflavit Deus et dissipantur. *aff—flah—vit deh—us et diss—sip—ant—ur.*
God has breathed and they are dispersed.
Motto, referring to the defeat of the Spanish Armada.

Agnus Dei. *ah—nyus day—ee*
The Lamb of God.
Vulgate. St. John 1.29.

Alea iacta est. *ah—lee—ah ee—jack—ta est.*
The die is cast.
Juvenal.

Allegans contraria non est audiendus. *al—leg—ahn—ss cone—trah—ri—a none est ow—di—end—us.*
He who alleges things which are contradictory is not to be heard.
Law.

Alii adnutat, alii adnictat, alium amat, alium tenet. *a—li—ee ad—noo—tat, a—li—ee ad—nick—tat, a—lee—um a—mat, a—lee—um teh—net.*
To one she nods, at another she winks; one she caresses, another embraces.
G. Naevius (ca. 270 B.C. ca. 201 B.C.)

Alma mater. *al—ma may—ter.*
A kind mother.
Used to refer to one's old university.

Amantium irae amoris integratio est. *a—man—ti—um ee—rye a—moh—riss in—teg—rah—ti—oh est.*
The quarrels of lovers are the renewal of love.
Terence.

Alpibus Italiam munierat antea natura non sine aliquo divino numine . . .

Quae jam licet considant. *alp—ib—uss eat—al—i—am moon—i—eh—rat ant—eh—ah nah—too—ra none sin—eh al—ick—woe dee—wee—noh noo—min—eh. quie yam lick—et cone—seed—ant.*
The Alps were once raised by nature to protect Italy, not without the favour of the gods . . . Let them now sink in the ground!
Cicero. De provinciis consularibus 14.34. Of Julius Caesar's conquest of Gaul.

Alter ego. *al—tear egg—oh.*
My other self.

Alter remus aquas alter tibi radat harenas, Tutus eris: medio maxima turba mari est. *al—tehr ray—muss ack—wahss al—tehr tib—e rah—dat ha—rain—ahss, too—tuss eh—riss: med—i—oh max—im—a tur—ba ma—ree est.*
Let one ear graze the water, the other the sand; in that way you will be safe: in mid-sea the turmoil is greatest.
Propertius. Elegies 3.3.23f.

Ambiguum pactum contra venditorem interpretandum est. *am—big—u—um pact—um cone—trah wend—it—oh—reh in—tear—pret—and—um est.*
An ambiguous agreement is to be interpreted against the vendor.
Law.

Amici, hodie diem perdidi. *a—mee—kee, hod—i—ay di—em pair—did—ee.*
Friends, to-day I have lost a day.
Titus Vespasianus.

Amicorum esse omnia communia. *a—meek—oh—rum ess—seh om—ni—a com—moon—i—a.*
With friends all things are in common.
Cicero.

Amicus Plato, amicus Socrates, sed magis amica veritas. *a—meek—us plat—oh, a—meek—us soe—crat—ace, sed mag—iss a—meek—a wear—ri—tahss.*
Plato is a friend, Socrates is a friend, but truth is a greater friend than all.
Pr. CF. Aristotle. Nichmachean ethics. 1.6.1.

Amittimus iisdem modis quibus acquirimus. *ah—mit—tim—us i—eess—dem mod—eess quib—us ack—quee—rim—us.*
We lose by the same means whereby we acquire.
Law.

Amor omnia vincit. *am—oar om—n—ia wink—it.*
Love conquers all things.
Pr.

[9]

Amor quaerit juvenes ut ludant cum virginibus; Venus despicit senes, qui impleti sunt doloribus. *am—or quai—rit yu—ven—ace ut lood—ant cum vihr—gin—i—buss; ven—uss day—spick—it sen—ace, quee imp—late—ee sunt doll—oh—rib—uss.*
Love seeks young men to play with maidens; Venus despises the old, who are full of sorrow.
Carmina Burana, 13th cent.

An nescis quantilla prudentia mundus regatur? *an ness—kiss quan—till—lah proo—dent—i—ah mund—us reg—ah—tour?*
Do you not know with how little wisdom the world is governed?
Attributed to Count Axel Oxenstierna.

Amputanda plura sunt illi aetati, siquidem efflorescit ingenii laudibus, quam inserenda. *am—put—anda ploo—ra sunt ill—lee eye—tah—tee, see—quid—em eff—floh—ray—skit ing—ghen—i—ee loud—ib—uss, quam in—seh—rend—a.*
At that age (youth), if it is beginning to show exuberance in its intellectual gifts, more pruning than grafting is needed.
Cicero. Pro Caelio 32/76.

Animula,vagula, blandula!/Hospes, comesque corporis! *an—im—ul—a wag—ul—a, bland—ul—a! hosp—ace, com—ace—queh cor—por—is!*
Soul of mine, fleeting and wandering, guest and companion of my body!
Hadrian.

Animum nunc huc celerem, nunc dividit illuc. *a—nim—um nun—k hoo—k kel—eh—rem, nun—k dee—wid—it ill—loo—k.*
Now hither, now thither, he turns his wavering mind.
Virgil.

Animum rege, qui, nisi paret, Imperat. *a—nim—um reg—eh, quee, niss—i pah—ret, im—peh—rat.*
Rule your mind, which, unless it is your servant, is your master.
Horace.

Animus furandi. *a—nim—us foo—rand—ee.*
The intention of stealing (a felonious design).

Annus mirabilis. *an—nus mi—rah—bill—iss.*
A marvellous year.

Ante victoriam ne canas triumphum. *ann—teh wick—toe—ri—am nay can—ahss tri—um—fum.*

Do not sing your triumph before you have conquered.
Pr.

Apparent rari nantes in gurgite vasto. *ap—pah—rent rah—ree nan—tace in gur—git—eh wass—toe.*
Here and there they are seen swimming in the vast flood.
Virgil.

Aquilam volare doces. *a—quill—am wol—ah—reh dock—ace.*
You are teaching an eagle how to fly.
Pr.

Arbiter bibendi. *ar—bit—ehr bib—end—ee.*
Arbitrator of the drinking (i.e. master of the feast).
Horace.

Arbiter elegantiae. *ar—bit—ehr ay—leg—ant—i—eye.*
A judge of matters of taste.
Tacitus. Annals 16.18.

Arbores serit diligens agricola, quarum aspiciet baccam ipse nunquam. *ar—boh—race seh—rit dee—lig—aynss ag—rick—ol—a, quah—rum ass—pick—i—et back—cam ip—seh nun—quam.*
The diligent husbandman sows trees of which he himself will never see the fruit.
Cicero.

Arcades ambo,/Et cantare pares, et respondere parati. *ar—cad—ess am—boh, et can—tah—reh pa—race, et ray—spond—ay—reh par—rah—tea.*
Arcadians both, equal in the song and ready in the response.
Virgil. Ecologues 7.4.

Argumentum ab auctoritate fortissimum est in lege. *ar—gum—en—tum ab owk—to—rit—ah—te for—tiss—sim—um est in lay—geh.*
An argument derived from authority is of the greatest force in law.
Coke.

Argumentum ad crumenam. *ar—gum—en—tum ad crum—ay—nam.*
An argument to the moneybag i.e. self-interest.

Argumentum ad hominem. *ar—gum—en—tum ad hom—in—em.*
An argument to the man i.e. founded on an opponent's personality or principles; a personal argument.

[11]

Argumentum ad ignorantiam. *ar—gum—en—tum ad ig—noh—rant—i—am.*
An argument to ignorance i.e. devised to take advantage of your adversary's
want of knowledge.

Argumentum ad invidiam. *ar—gum—ent—um ad in—wid—i—am.*
An argument to envy or prejudice (i.e. appealing to those passions).

Argumentum ad judicium. *ar—gum—ent—um ad you—dick—i—um.*
An argument to good judgment.

Argumentum ad verecundiam. *ar—gum—ent—um ad wear—ay—cun—di—am.*
An argument to good feeling i.e. propriety.

Argumentum baculinum. *ar—gum—ent—um back—ul—een—um.*
Argument by club (i.e. force).

Arma amens capio, nec sat rationis in armis. *ar—ma ah—maynss cap—i—oh,*
neck sat rat—i—oh—niss in ar—meess.
Mad I take arms, nor in arms have I reason enough.
Virgil. Æneid 2.314.

Arma pacis fulcra. *ar—ma pah—kiss full—cra.*
Arms are the props of peace.
Motto.

Arma, viri, ferte arma; vocat lux ultima victos;/Reddite me Danais, sinite
instaurata revisam/Proelia: nunquam omnes hodie moriemur inulti.
ar—ma, wi—ree, fair—teh ar—ma; wock—at lux ul—tim—a wick—toce;
red—dit—eh may dan—a—eece, sin—it—eh in—stow—rah—ta reh—wee—sam
proy—li—a: nun—quam om—nace hod—i—ay mo—ri—ay—mur in—ul—tea.
Arms, O men, bring arms; their last day calls the vanquished; let me return
to the Greeks, let me see again my battles renewed; we shall never all
die unavenged this day.
Virgil. Æneid 2.667.

Arma virumque cano. . . *ar—ma wi—rum—queh can—oh.*
Arms and the man I sing.
Virgil. Æneid 1.1.

Ars est celare artem. *arss est kay—lah—reh arr—tem:*
Art consists in concealing art.
Pr.

Ars invendiendi adolescit cum inventis. *arss in—wen—i—end—ee ad—ol—*
ess—kit cum in—wen—teece.

[12]

The art of invention grows young with the things invented.

Ars longa, vita brevis. *arss long—ga, wee—ta breh—wiss.*
Art is long, life is short.
Hippocrates.

Asinus asino, et sus sui pulcher. *ass—in—us ass—in—oh, et sooce su—ee*
pull—kehr.
An ass is beautiful to an ass and a pig to a pig.
Pr.

Assumpsit. *ass—sump—sit.*
He assumed or took upon himself personal responsibility.
Law.

Astraea redux. *ass—try—a red—ux.*
Astraea (goddess of justice) restored as our guide.

At jam non domus accipiet te laeta, neque uxor/Optima, nec dulces occur-
rent oscula nati/Praeripere, et tacita pactus dulcedine tangent.
at yam none dom—us ack—kip—i—et tay lie—ta, neck—weh ux—or op—
tim—a, neck dul—case ock—cur—rent oce—cul—a nah—tea pry—rip—eh—
reh, et tack—it—ah pack—tooce dul—kay—din—eh tang—ghent.
But now your home will never again receive you with joy, nor your best
of wives, nor will your sweet children hasten to snatch your kisses and
thrill your heart with speechless pleasure.
Lucretius. De Rerum Nat. 3.894.

At non ingenio quaesitum nomen ab aevo Excidet: ingenio stat sine morte
decus. *at none in—ghen—i—oh quie—seat—um noh—men ab eye—woe*
ex—kid—et: in—ghen—i—oh stat sin—eh more—teh deck—uss.
But the name won by my genius shall never die: the renown of genius
endures deathless.
Propertius. Elegies 3.2.25f.

At pulchrum est digito monstrari, et dicier,/Hic est!
at pull—crum est dig—it—oh monst—rah—ree, et deek—i—er, Heek est!
But it is a fine thing to be pointed out with the finger, and to be spoken
of, "That is he!"
Persius.

Audacia pro muro habetur. *ow—dahk—i—a pro moo—roh hab—ate—oor.*
Daring serves as a wall.
Sallust.

[13]

Audax omnia perpeti/Gens humana ruit/per vetitum et nefas.
ow—dahx omn—i—a pair—pet—ee gain—ss hoo—mah—na ru—it pair wet—it—um et nef—ahss.
Daring to undergo all things, the human race rushes through that which is forbidden and criminal.
Horace. Odes 1.3.25.

Audendum dextra: nunc ipsa vocat res. *ow—den—dum decks—trah: nunc ip—sa wock—at race.*
Now we must dare to attempt with the help of our right hand: now the event itself calls us to action.
Virgil. Æneid 9.320.

Audi alteram partem. *ow—dee al—teh—ram parr—tem.*
Hear the other side.
St. Augustine. De Duabus Animabus. 14.2.

Audiet pugnas, vitio parentum/Rara juventus. *ow—di—et pug—nahss, wit—i—oh pa—rent—um rah—ra you—went—us.*
Posterity, thinned by the crime of its ancestors, shall hear of those battles.
Horace.

Augurque cum esset, dicere ausus est, optimis auspiciis ea geri, quae pro rei publicae salute gererentur. *ow—gur—queh cum ess—set, dee—keh—reh ow—suss est, op—tim—eece owss—pick—i—eece eh—a gheh—ree, quie proh reh—ee pub—lick—eye sal—oo—teh gheh—reh—rent—ur.*
And when he was augur, he dared to say that things were done under the best auspices which were done for the good of the State.
Cicero. De Senectute.

Aura popularis. *ow—ra pop—ul—ah—riss.*
The popular breeze; the breath of public opinion.
Cicero.

Auream quisquis mediocritatem/Diligit. *ow—reh—am quis—quis med—i—ock—rit—ah—tem dili—git.*
Who so loves the golden mean.
Horace. Odes 2.10.5.

Auribus teneo lupum:/Nam neque quo amittam a me invenio, nique uti retineam scio. *ow—rib—us ten—eh—oh loop—um: nam ne—queh quo ah—mit—tam ah may in—wen—i—oh, nee—queh ut—ee ret—in—eh—am ski—oh.*

I hold a wolf by the ears. Nor do I know by what means I can get rid of him, nor how I am to keep him.
Terence.

Aurora interea miseris mortalibus almam/Extulerat lucem, referens opera atque labores. *ow—roe—ra in—teh—reh—ah miss—eh—reece more—tah—lib—us al—mam ex—tul—eh—rat loo—kem, re—feh—rain—ss op—eh—ra at—queh lab—oh—race.*
Meanwhile the morning had restored to unhappy mortals her gentle light, bringing them back work and toil.
Virgil.

Austria est imperare orbi universo. *ow—stri—a est imp—eh—rah—reh oor—bee oo—niv—air—so.*
Austria is to rule the whole universe.
Pr.

Aut bibat aut abeat. *owt bib—at owt abeh—at.*
Let him either drink or depart.
Cicero.

Aut Caesar aut nihil. *out kie—sar out nih—hill.*
Emperor or nothing.
Motto of Cesare Borgia, 1476-1507.

Aut non tentaris, aut perfice. *owt none ten—tah—riss, out pair—fick—eh.*
Either do not attempt at all, or go through with it.
Ovid.

Aut ridenda omnia aut flenda sunt. *owt reed—end—a om—ni—a owt flen—da sunt.*
All things are cause for either laughter or weeping.
Seneca.

Aut vincere aut mori. *owt wink—eh—ree owt mo—ree.*
Either to conquer or to die. *Pr.*

Ave, Imperator, (USUALLY 'Ave Caesar. ETC'.) morituri te salutant (OR 'te salutamus'). *ah—way, im—peh—rah—tohr, (kye—sar) mo—rit—oo—ree tay sal—oo—tant (tay sal—oot—ah—muss).*
Hail, Caesar, those about to die salute thee.')
Suetonius.

Avia Pieridum peragro loca nullius ante Trita solo. Juvat integros accedere

fontis, Atque haurire, juvatque novos decerpere flores Insignemque meo capiti petere inde coronam Unde prius nulli velarint tempora musae. *ah—wi—a pea—eh—rid—um peh—rag—roe lock—a null—li—uss ant—eh tree—ta sol—oh. yu—wat in—teg—roce ack—kay—deh—reh font—ace, at—queh how—re—reh, yu—wat—queh no—woce day—kehr—peh—reh floh—race in—sig—nem—queh meh—oh cap—it—ee pet—eh—reh in—deh co—roe—nam un—deh pri—uss null—lee way—lah—rint tem—po—ra moo—sye.*
I traverse pathless tracts of the Muses, where no—one's foot has trod before. I delight in coming across untouched springs and drinking from them, I delight in plucking new flowers and in gathering for my head a splendid garland from fields whose flowers the Muses never before wreathed round any man's temples.
Lucretius. De Rerum Natura 1.926-930 & 4.1-5.

Avito viret honore. *a—wit—oh wee—ret hon—oh—reh.*
He flourishes upon ancestral honour.
Motto.

Barbarus hic ego sum, quia non intelligor ulli. *bar—ba—russ heek egg—o sum, qui—a none in—tell—lig—or ull—lee.*
I am a barbarian here, because I am not understood by anyone.
Ovid.

Bastardus nullius est filius, aut filius populi. *bass—tar—duss null—lee—uss est fee—li—uss, owt fee—li—uss pop—ull—ee.*
A bastard is the son of no one, or the son of the public.
Law.

Beati immaculati in via. *beh—ah—tee im—mack—ul—ah—tee in we—ah.*
Blessed are the undefiled in the way.
Vulgate. Ps. 119.1.

Beati misericordes: quoniam ipsis misericordia tribuetur.
beh—ah—tee mi—seh—rick—or—dace: quon—yam ip—seece mi—seh—rick—ordia trib—u—ay—toor.
Blessed are the merciful, for mercy shall be accorded to them.
Vulgate. St. Matthew 5.7.

[16]

Beati monoculi in regione caecorum. *beh–ah–tee mon–ock ul–ee in reg–i–oh–ne kye–co–rum.*
Blessed are the one-eyed in the country of the blind.

Bene dormit qui non sentit quam male dormiat. *beh–neh dor–mit quee none sent–it quam mal–eh dor–mi–at.*
He sleeps well who is not aware that he has slept badly.
Publilius Syrus.

Bene nati, bene vestiti, et mediocriter docti. *beh–neh nah–tee, beh–neh wes–tee–tee et med–i–ock–rit–er doct–tee.*
Well born, well dressed, and moderately learned.

Benedictus benedicat! *beh–neh–dict–tus beh–neh–die–cat.*
May the Blessed One bless! *(A Form of Grace Before Meals.)*

Benedictus qui venit in nomine Domini. *beh–neh–dict–tus, quee vay–nit in noh–min–eh dom–in–ee.*
Blessed is he that cometh in the name of the Lord.
Vulgate. St. Matthew 21.9.

Benignior sententia in verbis generalibus seu dubiis est praeferenda. *ben–ig–ni–or sen–ten–ti–a in wear–beece gen–eh–rah–lib–uss soo du–bi–ees est prae–fer–en–dah.*
The more generous construction is to be preferred in words which are general or doubtful. *Coke.*

Bibere papaliter. *bib–eh–re pah–pal–it–er.*
To drink like a pope.

Bis dat qui cito dat. *biss dat quee kit–oh dat.*
He gives twice who gives quickly.
Pr.

Bona peritura. *bon–a peh–rit–oo–ra.*
Perishable goods.
Law.

Bona prudentiae pars est nosse stultas vulgi cupiditates, et absurdas opiniones. *bon–a proo–den–ti–eye parse est nohss–seh stool–tahss vul–ghee cup–ee–dit–ah–tace, et ap–sur–dahss op–ee–ni–oh–nace.*
It is a good part of sagacity to have known the foolish desires of the crowd and their unreasonable notions.
Erasmus.

[17]

Bona vacantia. *bon—a wack—ant—i—a.*
Goods which are unclaimed or ownerless.
Law.

Boni venatoris est plures feras capere non omnes.
bon—ee way—nah—toe—riss est ploo—race feh—rahss cap—eh—reh,
none om—nace.
It is the characteristic of a good hunter to take much game, not all.
Nonnius.

Boni judicis est ampliare justitiam. *bon—ee you—dick—iss est am—pli—*
ah—reh yuss—ti—ti—am.
It is the part of a good judge to make justice wide.
Law.

Boni pastoris est tondere pecus, non deglubere. *bon—ee past—oh—riss est*
ton—deh—reh peck—us, none day—glub—eh—reh.
It is the duty of a good shepherd to shear the sheep, not to flay them.
Suetonius.

Brevis oratio penetrat caelum. *breh—wiss oh—rah—ti—oh pen—eh—trat*
kye—lum.
A short prayer finds its way to heaven.

Cacoethes scribendi. *cack—o—ay—thess scrib—end—ee.*
An itch for writing.

Caecus amor sui. *kye—cuss a—mor su—ee.*
The blind love of one's self.
Horace.

Caelum crebris imbribus ac nebulis foedum; asperitas frigorum abest.
kye—lum cray—breece im—brib—uss ack neb—ul—eece foy—dum; asp—
eh—rit—ahss free—gor—um ab—est.
The sky (in Britain) is foul through the frequency of rain and fog, but
there are no extremes of cold.
Tacitus. Agricola 12.

Caveant consules ne quid res publica detrimenti caperet.
ca—weh—ant cone—sul—ace nay quid race pub—lick—a date—rim—en—tee cap—eh—ret.
Let the consuls take care that no harm come to the state.
Last decree' of the Roman senate; cited by Cicero, Pro Milone, 70.

Caesarem vehis, Caesarisque fortunam. *kye—sah—rem weh—hiss, key—sah—riss—queh for—too—nam.*
You carry Caesar and Caesar's fortune.
Pr.

Campos ubi Troja fuit. *cam—poce ub—ee troh—ya fu—it.*
The fields where Troy was.
Virgil.

Cara, valeto! Cara, vale, sed non aeternum. *cahra, wal—ay—toe! cah—ra, wal—ay, sed none eye—tear—num.*
Dear one, farewell. Farewell, but not for ever.
Ancient epitaph.

Cari sunt parentes, cari liberi, propinqui, familiares; sed onmes omnium caritates patria una complexa est. *cah—ree sunt pa—ran—tace, cah—ree lee—beh—ree, prop—in—quee, fam—ill—i—ah—race; sed om—nace om—ni—um cah—rit—ah—tace pat—riah do—nah com—plex—a est.*
Dear are our parents, dear are our children, our neighbors, our companions; but all the affections of all men are bound up in one native land.
Cicero.

Cassandrae quia non creditum, ruit Ilium. *cass—sand—ree qui—a none cray—dit—um, ru—it ee—li—um.*
Troy fell because Cassandra was not believed.
Phaedrus.

Castigat ridendo mores. *cass—tee—gat reed—end—oh moh—race*
He (OR it) corrects manners by laughing.

Cato esse quam videri bonus malebat. *cat—oh ess—seh quam wid—ay—ree bon—us mah—lay—bat.*
Cato preferred rather to be, than to seem, good.
Sallust.

Cato mirari se aiebat, quod non rideret Haruspex Haruspicem cum vidisset. *cat—oh mi—rah—ree say ah—yay—bat, quod none ree—deh—reh ha—russ—pecks ha—russ—pick—em cum wid—iss—set.*

[19]

Cato used to say that he wondered that one soothsayer did not laugh when he saw another.
Cicero.

Cautionis est in re plus quam in persona. *kow—teo—niss est in ray plooce quam in pair—sohn—a.*
There is more security in a thing than in a person. (Property is a better security than a personal undertaking.)
Law.
Cave canem. *ca—way can—em.*
Beware of the dog.

Caveat emptor. *ca—wee—at emp—tor.*
Let the buyer beware.

Cedant arma togae, concedat laurea linguae. *kay—dant arr—ma tog—eye, con—kay—dat low—ri—a ling—gwie.*
Let arms yield to the civic gown, let the laurel give place to eloquence.
Cicero.

Cede Deo. *kay—deh deh—oh.*
Yield to God.
Virgil.

Cedite, Romani scriptores; cedite, Graii!/Nescio quid maius nascitur Iliade. *kay—dit—eh, roe—mah—nee scrip—toe—race; kay—dit—eh, grie—yee! ness—ki—o quid mah—yuss nass—kit—ur ee—li—ad—eh.*
Give place, ye Roman writers; give place, ye Greeks! Something is born greater than the Iliad.
Propertius. Elegies 2.34.65f.

Certiorari. *sir—she—o—rare—eye.*
To be made more certain.
Law. Title of a writ.

Certum est quia impossibile est. *care—tum est qui—a im—poss—see—bill—eh est.*
It is certain because it is impossible.
Tertullian. De Carne Christi. 5.

Cessio bonorum. *kess—si—oh bon—oh—rum.*
A surrender of goods.
Law.

Cetera quis nescit? *kay—teh—ra quis ness—kit?*

Who does not know the rest?
Ovid. Amorum 1.5.25.

Ceteris paribus. *kay—teh—reece pah—rib—uss.*
Other things being equal i.e. other things being unaffected.

Ceterum censeo, Karthaginem esse delenda. *kay—teh—rum cane—seh—oh,*
cart—hah—ghin—em ess—seh day—lend—a.
Moreover, I think that Carthage should be destroyed.
Attributed by Plutarch. Life of Cato. to M. Porcius Cato. 234-149 B.C.

Citius quam asparagi conquuntur. *kit—i—uss quam ass—pa—rag—ee co—*
quun—tur.
Quicker than asparagus is cooked.
Proverb.

Cives magistratibus pareant, magistratus legibus. *key—wace mag—iss—trah—*
tib—uss pah—reh—ant, mag—iss—trah—tooce lay—gib—uss.
Let the citizens obey the magistrates and the magistrates the laws.
Pr.

Civis Romanus sum. *key—wiss roe—mah—nus sum.*
I am a Roman citizen.
Cicero.

Civitas ea autem in libertate est posita, quae suis stat viribus, non ex alieno
arbitrio pendet. *key—wit—ahass eh—a ow—tem in lee—bear—tah—teh est*
pos—it—a, quie su—eece stat wee—rib—us, none—ex al—i—ay—noh ar—bit—
ri—oh pen—det.
For that state is in freedom which stands in its own strength, and does not
depend on foreign rule.
Livy.

Coenae fercula nostrae,/Malim convivis quam placuisse cocis.
coy—nye fair—cu—la noss—try, mah—lim con—wee—weece quam plack—u—
iss—seh cock—eece.
I prefer that the courses at our banquet should give pleasure to the guests
rather than to the cook.
Martial.

Coepisti melius quam desinis; ultima primis/Cedunt; dissimiles hic vir, et
ille puer. *coy—pist—ee mel—i—uss quam day—sin—is; ult—im—a pree—meece*
kay—dunt; diss—sim—ill—ace heek wihr, et ill—leh pu—air.
You began better than you end; the last is inferior to the first; the man of

[21]

the present and the boy of the past are very different.
Ovid.

Cogere consilium, cum muros obsidet hostis. *coe—gheh—reh cone—sill—i—*
um, cum moo—roce op—sid—et hoss—tiss.
To call a counsel when the enemy is under the very walls i.e. when too late.
Virgil.

Cogito; ergo sum. *co—git—oh; air—goe sum.*
I think; therefore I am.
Descartes.

Cognovit actionem. *cog—noh—wit act—i—oh—nem.*
He has admitted the action.
Law.

Collige, virgo, rosas, dum flos novus et nova pubes, Et memor esto aevum
sic properare tuum. *coll—lig—eh, wihr—go, ross—ahss, dum floce no—wuss*
et no—wa poo—base, et mem—or ess—toe eye—wum seek prop—eh—rah—
reh tu—um.
Pluck roses, girl, while the flower and your youth are new, and remember
that your life will go as fast (as the rose's).
Ausonius, A.D. 310-395.

Compesce mentem. *com—pess—keh men—tem.*
Restrain your mind.
Pr.

. . . Componitur orbis./Regis ad exemplum; nec sic inflectere sensus/Humanos
edicta valent, quam vita regentis. *com—poe—nit—ur orbis. ray—giss ad ex—*
em—plum; neck seek in—fleck—teh—reh sain—sooce hoo—mah—noce ay—
dict—ta wal—ent, quam wee—ta reg—en—tiss.
The world (or realm) is ordered by the example of the king; nor do royal
edicts appeal to the perceptions of men so much as the life of the ruler.
Claudian.

Concordia discors. *cone—cord—i—ah diss—course.*
A discordant agreement.
Horace. Also Lucan.

Concordia parvae res crescunt, Discordia maximae dilabuntur.
cone—cord—i—ah parr—wye race cray—scunt, diss—cor—di—ah max—im—
eye dee—lab—un—tur.
By the agreement small things grow, by discord the greatest go to pieces.
Sallust.

[22]

Confessus in judicio pro judicato habetur. *cone—fess—suss in you—dee—ki—oh proh you—dick—ah—toe hab—ay—tur.*
One who has confessed in a trial is regarded as having been tried.
Law.

Confirmat usum qui tollit abusum. *cone—fihr—mat oo—sum quee toll—lit ab—oo—sum.*
He confirms the use of a thing who abolishes its abuse.
Law.

Consensus facit legem. *cone—sane—suss fack—it lay—ghem.*
Agreement makes law.
Law.

Consensus facit matrimonium. *cone—sane—suss fack—it mah—tri—moan—i—um.*
Consent makes marriage.
Law.

Consentire non videtur qui errat. *cone—sent—ee—reh none wid—ay—tur quee air—rat.*
He is not deemed to give consent who is under a mistake.
Law.

Consilia qui dant prava cautis hominibus,/Et perdunt operam et deridentur turpiter. *cone—sil—i—a quee dant prah—wa cow—teece hom—in—ib—uss, et pair—dunt op—eh—ram et day—ree—den—tur tur—pit—er.*
Those who give bad advice to the prudent, both lose their pains and are laughed to scorn.
Phaedrus.

Consilium Themistocleum est; existimat enim, qui mari teneat, eum necesse rerum potiri. *cone—sill—i—um them—iss—tock—lay—um est; ex—ist—im—at enim, quee ma—ree ten—eh—at, eh—um neck—ess—seh ray—rum pot—ee—ree.*
It is the opinion of Themistocles; for he considers that who so can hold the sea has command of the situation.
Cicero. Ep. ad Att. Book 10.8.

Consuetudo pro lege servatur. *cone—sway—too—doe proh lay—geh sair—wah—tur.*
Custom is held as law.
Law.

Consule de gemmis, de tincta murice lana,/Consule de facie corporibusque
diem. *cone—sul—eh day ghem—meece, day tink -tah moo—rick—eh lah—
nah, cone—sul—eh day fack—i—ay cor—po—rib—uss—queh di—em.*
Consult daylight as to gems, and as to wool dyed in purple, and consult it
as to the face and the figure as well.
Ovid. Ars Amat. Book 1.250.

Contemporanea expositio est fortissima in lege.
con—tem—po—rah—neh—a ex—poss—it—i—oh est for—tiss—sim—a in la—geh.
An exposition contemporary with the statute or subject at issue, is specially
weighty in law.
Law.

Contempsi gladium Catilinae; non pertimescam tuos.
*cone—temp—see glad—i—um cat—ill—ee—nye; non pair—tim—ess—cam tu—
oce.*
I have despised the sword of Catiline; I shall not dread yours.
Cicero. Phil. 2.46.

Conticuere omnes, intentique ora tenebant. *cone—tick—u—ay—reh om—
nace, in—ten—tee—queh oh—ra ten—ay—bant.*
All were with one accord silent, and deeply attentive held their peace.
Virgil. Æneid 2.1.

Contra bonos mores. *con—trah bon—oce moh—race.*
Contrary to good manners or usage.
Publilius Syrus.

Contra felicem vix deus vires habet. *con—trah fay—lee—kem wicks deh—uss
wee—race habet.*
Against a lucky man even a god scarcely has power.
Publilius Syrus.

Copa Surisca caput Graeca redimita mitella, Crispum sub crotalo docta
movere latus. *cope—a su—risk—a cap—ut grye—kah red—im—ee—ta mit—
ell—lah, crisp—um sub crot—al—oh dock—ta mo—way—reh lat—uss.*
Syrian dancing-girl, her hair bound with a fillet, skilled in swaying her
quivering flanks to the sound of the castanet.
Appendix Vergiliana. prob. 4th cent.

Cras amet qui nunquam amavit, quique amavit cras amet.
*crahss am—et quee nun—quam am—ah—wit, quee—queh am—ah—wit
crahss am—et.*
Tomorrow let him love who has never loved, and he who has loved, let him

love tomorrow.
Pervigilium Veneris. c.3rd cent. A.D.

Credat Judaeus Apella, non ego. *cray—dat you—die—yuss a—pell—la, none egg—oh.*
Let Apella the Jew believe that; I cannot.
Horace. Sat. Book 1.5.100.

Crede quod habes, et habes. *cray—deh quod hab—ace, et hab—ace.*
Believe that you have it, and you have it.
Pr.

Credebant hoc grande nefas et morte piandum,/Si juvenis vetulo non assurrexerat. *cray—day—bant hoke gran—deh nef—ahss et more—teh pi—an—dum, see yu—wen—iss wet—ul—oh none ass—sur—rex—eh—rat.*
They used to regard it as gross impiety and worthy to be expiated by death, if a young man did not rise at the presence of an elder.
Juvenal. Sat. 13.54.

Credite, posteri! *cray—dit—eh, poss—teh—ree!*
Believe it, posterity.
Horace. Odes Book 2.19.2.

Cremutius Cordus postulatur novo ac tunc primum audito crimine, quod editis annalibus laudatoque M. Bruto C. Cassium Romanorum ultimum dixisset. *crem—oo—ti—uss core—duss poss—tul—ah—tur no—woe ack tunc pree—mum ow—dee—toe cree—min—eh, quod aid—it—eece an—nah—lib—uss loud—ah—toe—queh mar—coe brute—oh guy—um cass—si—um roe—mah—noh—rum ull—tim—um dick—siss—set.*
Cremutius Cordus was prosecuted on a new charge, then heard of for the first time, that having praised Marcus Brutus in the history he had published, he called Gaius Cassius the 'Last of the Romans'.
Tacitus. Annals 4.34.

Crescit sub pondere virtus. *cress—kit sub pond—eh—reh wihr—tuss.*
Virtue grows under a burden.
Motto of Earl of Denbigh.

Crudelem medicum intemperans aeger facit. *croo—day—lem med—ick—um in—tem—peh—rahnss eye—ger fack—it.*
An unruly patient makes a harsh physician.
Publilius Syrus.

. . . Crudelis ubique/Luctus, ubique pavor, et plurima mortis imago.
croo—day—liss ub—ee—queh luct—us, ub—ee—queh pa—wore, et ploo—rim—a

[25]

more—tiss im—ah—go.
Everywhere cruel lamentation, everywhere consternation, and death in very numerous shapes.
Virgil. Æneid Book 2.369.

Crimen laesae majestatis. *cree—men lie—sigh mah—yes—tah—tiss.*
The crime of high treason (LIT. injured majesty).
Law.

. . . Crimine ab uno Disce omnes. *cree—min—eh ab oo—noe diss—keh om—nace.*
From one example of their villainy judge them all.
Virgil. Æneid 2.65.

Cruci dum spiro fido. *cru—chee dum spee—roe fee—doh.*
While I breathe I trust in the cross.
Motto.

Cujus est solum, ejus est usque ad coelum. *coo—yuss est sol—um, ay—yuss est uss—queh ad coy—lum.*
He who has the soil owns the property up to the very sky.
Law.

Cui bono? *cu—ee bon—oh?*
For whose advantage?
(Quoted as a maxim of Lucius Cassius, whose expression was "Cui bono fuerit," "who profited by it?") Cicero. Pro Milone 12.

. . . Cui pudor et Justitiae soror, incorrupta fides, nudaque veritas, quando ullum inveniet parum? *cu—ee pud—or et yuss—ti—ti—eye so—roar, in—cor—rup—ta fid—ace, noo—da—queh way—rit—ahss, quan—doe ull—lum in—wen—i—et pa—rum?*
When will modesty, and Justice's sister, uncorrupt faith, and naked truth, ever find another like him?
Horace. Odes. 1.24.6.

Cuicunque aliquis quid concedit, concedere videtur et id, sine quo res ipsa esse non potest. *cu—ee—cun—queh al—i—quiss quid con—kay—dit, con—cay—deh—reh wid—ay—tur et id, sineh quoh race ip—sa ess—seh none pot—est.*
He who grants anything to another person, is supposed also to grant that without which the thing itself cannot exist.
Law.

Cui malus est nemo, quis bonus esse potest? *cu—ee mal—uss est nay—moh,*

quis bon—uss ess—seh pot—est?
To whom no one seems bad, can anyone appear good?
Martial. 12.82.

Culpa sua damnum sentiens, non intelligitur damnum pati.
cul—pah su—ah dam—num sen—ti—aynce, none in—tell—leg—it—ur dam—num pat—ee.
He who sustains a loss by his own fault is not considered to have suffered damage.
Law.

Cum grano salis. *cum grah—noe sal—iss.*
With a grain of salt.
Pr.

Cum multis aliis quae nunc perscribere longum est.
cum mul—teece al—i—eece quie nunc pair—scree—beh—reh long—gum est.
With many other matters which it would now be tedious to write about fully.
Pr. (A hexameter.)

Cum tacent clamant. *cum tack—ent clah—mant.*
When they hold their tongues they cry out (i.e. their silence is eloquent).
Cicero. In Catilinam 1.8.

Cur in theatrum Cato severe venisti?/An ideo tantum veneras, ut exires?
cur in theh—ah—trum cat—oh seh—way—reh way—niss—tee? an id—eh—oh tan—dum way—neh—rahss, ut ex—ee—race?
Why, severe Cato, did you come to the theatre? Did you only come then that you might go away? (On Cato having left the theatre on the occasion of the licentious Floralia.)
Martial Epig. Book 1.1.3.

Cur non, ut plenus vitae conviva, recedis,/Æquo animoque capis securam, stulte, quietem? *cur none, ut play—nuss wee—tie con—wee—wa, reh—kay—diss, eye—quoh an—im—oh—queh cap—iss say—coo—ram stul—teh, qui—ay—tam?*
Fool, why do you not, like a guest satiated with life retire, and with calm mind take your perfect rest?
Lucretius. De Rerum Nat. 3.951.

Curia advisare vult. *coo—ri—a ad—wee—sah—reh woolt.*
The court desires to consider.
Law.

[27]

Cur valle permutem Sabina Divitias operosiores? *cour wal—leh pair—moot—em sab—ee—nah dee—wit—i—ahss op—eh—roe— si—oh—race?*
Why should I exchange my Sabine valley for wealth that will bring me more troubles?
Horace. Odes 3.1. & 7f.

Curiosa felicitas. *coo—ri—oce—a fay—lick—it—ahss.*
Painstaking felicity (of style).
Petronius.

Da veniam culpae. *dah wen—i—am cull—pie.*
Pardon the fault.
Ovid. Heriodes. 7.105.

Damnum absque injuria. *dam—num apse—queh in—you—ri—ah.*
Loss without (illegal) injury.
Law.

Dat Clemens hiemen; dat Petrus ver cathedratus;/Æstuat Urbanus; autumnat Bartholomaeus. *dat clay—mence hi—em—em; dat pet—russ vair cat—ed—rah—tuss; ay—stu—at ur—bah—nuss; ow—tum—nat bar—tol—om—ay—uss.*
Clement (Nov. 23) gives the winter; Peter of the Chair (Feb. 22) gives the spring; Urban (May 25) brings summer; Bartholomew (Aug. 24) the autumn.
W. Lindewood. (d. 1446).

Date et dabitur vobis. *dat—eh et dab—it—ur woe—beece.*
Give, and it shall be given to you.
Vulgate. St. Luke 6.38.

Date obolum Belisario. *dat—eh ob—oll—um bell—iss—ah—ri—oh.*
Give an obolus to Belisarius (a general reduced to beggary).

De facto. *day (dee) fack—toe.*
In point of fact; by right of the fact.

De gustibus non disputandum. *day gust—ib—uss none diss—put—and—um.*

There is no disputing about tastes.
Pr.

De heretico comburendo. *day hay—ray—tick—oh com—boor—end—oh.*
Title of writ against a convicted heretic, who could thereupon be burnt.
Law.

De inimico non loquaris male, sed cogites. *day in—im—ee—coe none lo—*
quah—riss mal—eh, sep cog—it—ace.
Do not speak ill of an enemy, but think it.
Publilius Syrus.

De jure. *day you—reh (dee joor—i).*
By right; by law.

De lana caprina. *day lah—nah cap—ree—nah.*
About goats' wool i.e. a worthless subject.
Pr. Horace Ep. 1.18.15; et al.

De medietate linguae. *day med—i—eh—tah—teh ling—qwie.*
Of a moiety of languages. (Said of a jury or tribunal half composed of
foreigners.)
Law.

De minimis non curat lex. *day min—im—eece none coo—rat lex.*
The law does not concern itself about trifles.
Law.

De mortuis nil nisi bonum. *day more—tu—eece neel niss—i bon—um.*
Of the dead nothing but what is good.
Pr.

De nihilo nihil, in nihilum nil posse reverti. *day ni—hill—oh ni—hill, in ni—*
hill—um neel poss—seh reh—wear—tee.
From nothing nothing can proceed, and nothing can be reduced into
nothing.
Persius. Sat. 3.84.

De profundis. *day proh—fund—eece.*
From the depths.
Vulgate. Ps. 129.1.

De propaganda fide. *day proh—pag—and—ah fid—eh.*
For propagating the faith.
Title of a sacred congregation of the Vatican founded in 1622.

[29]

Decet imperatorem stantem mori. *deck—et im—peh—rah—toe—rem stan—tem mo—ree.*
It becomes an emperor to die standing i.e. "in harness".
Vespasian. (Suetonius: Vesp. Aug. 24.)

Decies repetita placebit. *deck—i—ace rep—et—ee—ta plack—ay—bit.*
Ten times repeated it will please.
Horace. De Arte Poetica 365.

Dediscit animus sero qui didicit diu. *day—diss—kit an—im—uss say—roo quee did—ick—it di—oo.*
The mind is slow in unlearning what it has been long in learning.
Seneca. Troades 631.

Deferar in vicum vendentem thus et odores,/Et piper, et quicquid chartis amicitur ineptis. *day—feh—rar in week—um wen—den—tum thooce et od—oh—race, et pip—er, et quick—quid car—teece a—mick—ee—tur in—ep—teece.*
I (i.e. my writings) shall be consigned to that part of the town where they sell incense, and scents, and pepper, and whatever is wrapped up in worthless paper.
Horace. Epist. Book 2.1.269. He delights and adorns.

Delatores, genus hominum publico exitio repertum. *day—lah—tor—race, gen—uss hom—in—um pub—lick—oh ex—it—i—oh rep—air—tum.*
Informers, a class of men invented to be the public ruin.
Tacitus. Annals Book 4.30.

Delectant etiam castas praeconia formae; Virginibus curae grataque forma sua est. *day—lect—ant et—yam cass—tahss pry—cone—i—a fore—my; wihr—ghin—i—buss coo—rye grah—tack—weh fore—ma su—a est.*
Even chaste girls enjoy hearing their beauty praised; virgins are worried and pleased by their looks.
Ovid. Ars Amatoria 1.

Delectat et ornat. *day—lect—tat et oar—nat.*
He delights and adorns.
Motto of Cree family.

Delegatus non potest delegare. *day—leg—ah—tuss none pot—est day—leg—ah—reh.*
The delegate cannot delegate.
Law. Quoted in this form by Burke: Imp. of Hastings, 1794.

Delenda est Carthago. *day–lend–a est carr–thah–go.*
Carthage must be destroyed.
Cato Major.

Delirant reges, plectuntur Achivi. *day–lee–rant ray–gace, pleck–tun–tur a–kee–wee.*
Kings go mad, the Greeks suffer.
Horace. Epist. Book 1.2.14.

Denique caelesti sumus omnes semine oriundi; Omnibus ille idem pater est. *day–ni–queh kye–less–tee sum–uss om–nace same–in–eh or–i–un–dee; om–nib–uss ill–leh ee–dem pat–ehr est.*
Lastly, we are all sprung from heavenly seed; all of us have that same father.
Lucretius. De Rerum Natura 2.991f.

Desine jam tandem, precibusque inflectere nostris.
day–sin–eh yam tan–dem, preck–ib–uss–queh in–fleck–teh–reh noss–treece.
O give way at length, and yield to our prayers.
Virgil. Æneid 12.800.

Desine, Paulle, meum lacrimis urgere sepulcrum: Panditur ad nullas janua nigra preces. *day–sin–eh, powl–leh, meh–um lack–rim–eece ur–gay–reh sep–ull–crum: pan–dit–ur ad null–lahss yah–nu–a nig–ra preck–ace.*
Cease, Paullus, from pouring tears upon my grave: the gate of darkness opens to no prayers.
Propertius. Elegies 4.11.1f.

Detur pulchriori. *da–tour pull–cri–oh–ree.*
Let it be given to the more beautiful.
Inscription on the apple of discord.

Deo favente. *deh–oh fa–vent–eh.*
God favouring.

Deo gratias. *deh–oh graht–see–ahss.*
Thanks be to God.

Deo ignoto. *deh–oh ig–noe–toe.*
To the unknown God.
"Ignoto Deo" in Vulgate. Acts 17.23.

Deo juvante. *deh–oh yu–van–teh.*
God helping.
Erasmus. (et al).

[31]

Deo optimo maximo. *deh—oh op—tim—oh max—im—oh.*
To God the best and greatest.
Inscription on Monuments.

Deo volente. *deh—oh vol—ent—eh.*
God willing.

Deum cole, regem serva. *de—hum coll—eh, ray—gem sair—vah.*
Reverence God, serve the King.
Motto. Adapted from the Vulgate, I Peter 2.17.

Deus est auctor mali quod est poena, non autem mali quod est culpa.
*deh—uss est owk—tor mal—ee quod est pain—a, none out—em mal—ee
quod est cull—pa.*
God is the author of that evil which is a punishment, but not of that evil
which is wrongdoing.
St. Thomas Aquinas.

Deus det (nobis pacem). *deh—uss det noe—beece pah—chem.*
May God give (us peace).
Ancient form of grace after meat.

Deus ex machina. *deh—uss ex mah—kin—ah.*
A god from some artificial or mechanical contrivance.

Deus nobis haec otia fecit. *deh—uss noe—beece hike oh—ti—a fay—kit.*
A God has made this repose for us.
Virgil. Eclogues 1.6.

Deus propitius esto mihi peccatori. *deh—uss proh—peet—si—uss ess—toe
mi—hee peck—kah—toe—ree.*
God be merciful to me a sinner.
Vulgate. St. Luke 18.13.

Desunt inopiae multa, avaritiae omnia. *day—sunt in—op—i—eye mull—ta,
a—wah—rit—i—eye om—ni—a.*
Poverty wants many things, avarice all things.
Pr.

Deteriores omnes sumus licentia. *day—teh—ri—oh—race om—nace sum—uss
lick—en—ti—ah.*
We are all made the worse by licence.
Terence. Heautontimorumenos iii. 1.74.

Dextrum Scylla latus, laevum implacata Charybdis.

deck–strum skill–la lat–uss, lie–wum im–plah–kah–ta ca–rib–diss.
Scylla is on the right hand side, and inappeasable Charybdis on the left.
Virgil. Æneid 3.420.

Dicite, pontifices, in sacro quid facit aurum? *dee–kit–eh, pon–tiff–ick–
ace, in sack–roe quid fack–it ow–rum?*
Say, ye priests, what does gold do in the sacred place i.e. in the temple?
Persius. Sat. 2.69.

Dicitur, aeternumque tenet per saecula nomen. *dee–kit–ur, eye–tear–
num–queh ten–et pair sie–cull–a noe–men.*
It is called after him, and preserves his name for ever throughout the ages.
Virgil.

Dictum sapienti sat est. *dick–toom sap–ee–en–tee sat est.*
A word to the wise.

Dies irae, dies illa,/Solvet saeclum in favilla. *di–ace ee–ray, di–ace ill–la,
sol–vet say–clum in fa–vill–lah.*
O day of wrath! O that day! The world shall dissolve in ashes.
Sequence from the Roman Mass for the Dead, written by Thomas of Celano c. 1250.

Dies non. *di–ace none.*
A day not reckoned as a day.
Law.

Dies si in obligationbus non ponitur, praesente die debetur.
*di–ace see in ob–lig–ah–ti–on–buss none poe–nit–ur, pry–sen–teh di–
ay day–bay–tur.*
If no day is fixed in obligations, the debt is due on the present day.
Law.

Differtur, numquam tollitur ullus amor. *diff–fehr–tur, num–quam toll–
lit–ur ull–luss am–or.*
Love is put off, but never destroyed.
Propertius. Elegies 2.3.8.

Difficilius est temperare felicitati, qua te non putes diu usurum.
*diff–fick–ill–i–uss est tem–peh–rah–reh fay–lee–kit–ah–tee, quah tay
none put–ace di–oo oo–soo–rum.*
It is more difficult to be moderate in pleasure which you think you will not
enjoy for long.
Tacitus. Hist., Book 2.47.

Dilexi justitiam et odivi iniquitatem: propterea morior in exilio. *dee—lake—sea you—stit—si—am et oh—dee—vee in—ee quit—ah—tem: prop—leh—reh—ah mo—ri—or in ex—ill—i—oh.*
I have loved righteousness and hated iniquity: therefore I die in exile.
Pope Gregory VII, last words: a parady of Psalm 44.9, Vulgate (A.V. Ps. 45).

Doctrina est ingenii naturale quoddam pabulum. *dock—tree—na est in—gen—i—ee nah—too—rah—leh quod—dam pah—bull—um.*
Learning is a kind of natural food of the mind.
Cicero. Adapted from Acad. Quaest. 4.41 and De Sen. 14.

Dolus, an virtus, quis in hoste requirat? *doll—us, an wihr—tus, quis in hoss—teh re—quee—rat?*
Who troubles himself either about valour or fraud in an enemy?
Virgil. Æneid 2.390.

Domine, dirige nos. *dom—in—eh, di—rig—eh noce.*
Lord, direct us.
Motto of City of London.

Dominium a possessione coepisse dicitur. *dom—in—i—um ah poss—sess—si—oh—neh coyp—iss—seh dee—kit—ur.*
Right is said to have commenced in possession.
Law.

Dominus illuminatio mea. *dom—in—uss ill—loom—in—aht—si—oh meh—a.*
The Lord is my light.
Vulgate. Ps. 27.1. Motto Oxford University.

Dominus providebit. *dom—in—uss proh—vid—ay—bit.*
The Lord will provide.
Vulgate. Genesis 22.8.

Dominus vobiscum. *dom—in—uss voe—beece—cum.*
The Lord be with you.
Missal.

Domus procerum. *dom—uss proh—kay—rum.*
The House of Peers.

Domus sua cuique est tutissimum refugium. *dom—uss sue—a cue—eye—que est tew—tiss—im—um ref—ug—i—um.*
Every man's house is his safest refuge.
Coke. Commentary upon Littleton's Tenures 3.73.

[34]

Dona eis requiem sempiternam. *doh—nah eh—eece reh—qui—em sem—pit—air—nam.*
Give them eternal rest.
Mass for the Dead.

Dormit aliquando jus, moritur nunquam. *dor—mit al—i—quan—doe yooce, mo—rit—ur nun—quam.*
A right sleeps sometimes, it never dies.
Law.

Duas tantum res anxius optat,/Panem et Circenses.
du—ahss tan—tum race anx—i—us op—tat, pah—nem et kihr—cane—sace.
Two things only (the people) anxiously desire, bread and the Circus games.
Juvenal. Sat. 10.80.

Dubitando ad veritatem pervenimus. *dub—it—an—doe ad way—rit—ah—tem pair—way—nim—uss.*
By doubting we come at the truth.
Cicero.

Dubitandum non est, quin nunquam possit utilitas cum honestate con-tendere. *dub—it—and—um none est, queen nun—quam poss—sit oo—till—it—ahss cum hon—es—tah—teh cone—ten—reh—reh.*
It is beyond doubt that interest can never be opposed to honour.
Cicero. De Officiis Book 3.3.

Ducunt volentem fata, nolentem trahunt. *dook—unt wol—ent—em fah—ta, noe—lent—em tra—hunt.*
The fates lead the willing, and drag the unwilling.
Seneca. Ep. 107. Quoting Cleanthes.

Dulce bellum inexpertis. *dul—keh bell—lum in—ex—pair—teece.*
War is pleasant to those who have not experienced it.
Erasmus.

Dulce domum. *dull—see do—mum.*
Sweet home.
Winchester College Breaking-up Song.

Dulce est desipere in loco. *dull—keh est day—sip—eh—reh in lock—oh.*
It is sweet to play the fool now and then (LIT. in the place for so doing).
Horace. Odes Book 4.12.

Dulce est miseris socios habuisse doloris. *dull—keh est miss—eh—reece*

sock—i—oce hab—u—iss—seh dol—oh—riss.
It is sweet to the wretched to have had companions in adversity.

Dulce et decorum est pro patria mori. *dull—keh et deck—oh—rum est pro pat—ri—ah mo—ree.*
It is sweet and honourable to die for one's country.
Horace. Odes Book 3.2.14.

Dulcior est fructus post multa pericula ducta. *dull—ki—or est fruc—tuss post mull—ta peh—reek—ul—a duc—ta.*
Fruit is sweeter after many dangers have been undergone for it.
Mediaeval. Quoted by Rabelais, "Pantagruel" 1533.

Dum loquimur, fugerit invida/Ætas: carpe diem. *dum lo—quim—ur, foo—geh—rit in—wid—a eye—tahss: carr—peh di—em.*
While we are speaking envious time will have fled. Seize the present day.
Horace. Odes Book 1.11.7.

Dum se bene gesserit. *dum say ben—eh gess—seh—rit.*
As long as he is of good behaviour.
Law.

Dum spiro, spero. *dum spee—roe, spay—roe.*
While I breathe, I hope.
Motto.

Durante beneplacito. *doo—rant—eh ben—eh—plack—it—oh.*
During our good pleasure; condition of tenancy or service.
Law.

Durante minore aetate. *doo—ran—teh min—oh—reh eye—tah—teh.*
During years of infancy, or period of minority.
Law.

Durate, et vosmet rebus servate secundis. *doo—rah—teh, et woce—met ray—buss sair—wah—teh seck—un—deece.*
Endure, and keep yourselves ready for prosperous fortune.
Virgil. Æneid 1.207.

Dux femina facti. *dux—fay—min—a fack—tee.*
Woman is the leader of the expedition.
Virgil. Æneid.

[36]

E pluribus unum. *ay ploo—rib—uss oo—num.*
From many, one.
Motto of United States.

E tenui casa saepe vir magnus exit. *ay ten—u—ee cas—ah sigh—peh wihr*
mag—nuss ex—it.
Often a great man comes forth from a humble cottage.
Pr.

Ea fama vagatur. *eh—a fah—ma wag—ah—tur.*
That rumour gets around.
Virgil. Æneid 2.

Ecce agnus Dei, ecce qui tollit peccatum mundi. *et—cher ahn—yuss deh—ee,*
et—cheh quee toll—lit peck—kah—tum mun—dee.
Behold the Lamb of God, behold him who taketh away the sin of the world.
Vulgate. St. John 1.29.

Ecce homo! *et—cheh om—oh!*
Behold the man!
Vulgate. St. John 19.5.

Editio princeps. *ed—ish—i—oh prin—seps.*
The original edition.

Edo, ergo sum. *ed—oh, air—goh sum.*
I eat, therefore I exist.
Pr..

Ego et rex meus. *egg—oh et rex meh—uss.*
I and my king.
Attributed to Cardinal Wolsey.

Ego meorum solus sum meus. *egg—oh meh—oh—rum soh—luss sum meh—uss.*

[37]

Of my friends I am the only one I have left.
Terence. Phormio iv.1.21.

Ego sum rex Romanus, et supra grammaticam. *egg—oh sum rex roe—mah—nuss, et sup—rah gram—mat—ic—am.*
I am the King of Rome, and above grammar.
Sigismund. Holy Roman Emperor at the Council of Constance.

Eheu! fugaces, Postume, Postume,/Labuntur anni; nec pietas moram/Rugis et instanti senectae/Afferet, indomitaeque morti. *ay—hue! fug—ah—case, post—um—eh, post—um—eh, lah—bun—tur an—nee; neck pi—eh—tahss moram roo—geese et in—stan—tee seh—neck—tie af—feh—ret, in—dom—it—eye—queh moor—tee.*
Alas! Postumus, Postumus, the flying years glide by; nor can religion give pause to wrinkles, and approaching age, and invincible death.
Horace. Odes Book 2.14.

Epicuri de grege porcum. *ep—ic—oo—ree day greg—eh pore—cum.*
A pig of Epicurus's flock.
Horace. Ep. Book 1.4.16.

Epistula enim non erubescit. *ep—iss—tul—a en—im none ay—rub—ay—skit.*
For a letter does not blush.
Cicero. Epistulae ad Familiares 5.12.

Equi dentes inspicere donati. *eh—quee dent—ace in—spick—eh—reh doe—nah—tee.*
To look a gift horse in the mouth.
St. Jerome. Commentary on Ephesians.

Equo ne credite, Teucri. *eh—quoh nay cray—dit—eh, tew—cree.*
Trust not the horse, Trojans.
Virgil. Æneid 2.48.

Ergo sollicitae tu causa, pecunia, vitae! Per te immaturum mortis adimus iter. *air—goh sol—lick—it—eye too cow—sa, peck—oon—i—a, wee—tie! pair tay im—mah—too—rum more—tiss ad—ee—muss it—ehr.*
You then, money, are the reason why life is full of care! Through you we go on death's journey before our time.
Propertius. Elegies 3.7.1f.

Eripuit caelo fulmen, mox sceptra tyrannis. *ay—rip—u—it kie—loh full—men, mocks scape—tra ti—ran—neece.*
He snatched the lightning from heaven and then the sceptres from tyrants.

Manilius. Astronomica, 1.104 (adapted). Inscription on B. Franklin's bust in allusion to his invention of the lightning rod (1753) and his pro-American services in France.

Errare humanum est. *air—rah—reh hoo—mah—num est.*
It is human to err.
Pr. From St. Jerome: "Errasse humanum est" Epist. 57.12.

Errare malo cum Platone . . . quam cum istis vera sentire.
air—rah—reh mah—loh cum plat—oh—neh . . . quam cum iss—teece way—ra sen—tee—reh.
I would rather err with Plato than perceive the truth with those others.
Cicero. Tusc. Quaest. 1.17.39.

Esse quam videri. *ess—seh quam wid—ay—ree.*
To be rather than to seem.
Latin Version of the Greek maxim, found in Æschylus — "Siege of Thebes" (B.C. 524-456).

Est animus lucis contemptor. *est an—im—uss loo—kiss cone—temp—tor.*
(My) mind is a despiser of the light (i.e. of life).
Virgil. Æneid 9.205.

Est enim malitia versuta, et fallax nocendi ratio. *est en—im mal—it--i—a wear—soo—ta, et fal—lahkss nock—end—ee rat—i—oh.*
For malice is cunning, and men's reason is deceitful in working mischief.
Cicero De Nat. Deorum Book 3.30.

Est genus hominum qui esse primos se omnium rerum volunt,/Nec sunt.
est gen—uss hom—in—um quee ess—seh pree—moce say om—ni—um ray—rum wol—unt, neck sunt.
There is a sort of men who wish to be first in all things, and are not.
Terence. Eunuchus ii.2.17.

Est pater ille quem nuptia demonstrant. *est pat—er ill—leh quam nup—ti—a day—moan—strant.*
He is the father whom marriage indicates as such.
Law.

Est quaedam flere voluptas;/Expletur lacrimis egeriturque dolor.
est quie—dam flay—reh wol—up—tahss; ex—play—tur lack—rim—eece ay—geh—rit—ur—queh dol—ore.
There is a certain pleasure in weeping; grief is appeased and expelled by tears.
Ovid. Tristia Book 4.3.37.

[39]

Estne Dei sedes nisi terra, et pontus, et aer,/Et coelum, et virtus? Superos quid quaerimus ultra?/Juppiter est quodcunque vides, quocunque moveris. *est—neh deh cc say—dace niss—i tair—ra et pon—tuss, et ah—air, et coy—lum, et wihr—tuss? sup—eh—roce quid quie—rim—uss ull—trah? yup—pit—ehr est quod—cun—queh wid—ace, quoh—cun—queh mo—way—riss.*
Has God any habitation except earth, and sea, and air, and heaven and virtue? Why do we seek the highest beyond these? Jupiter is whatsoever you see, wheresoever you move.
Lucan. Pharsalia Book 9.578.

Esto perpetua. *ess—toe pair—pet—u—a.*
Let it last for ever.

Et facere et pati fortiter Romanum est. *et fack—eh—reh et pat—ee fore—ti—tehr roe—mah—num est.*
It is the nature of a Roman to do and suffer bravely.
Livy. Book 2.12.

Et genus et virtus, nisi cum re, vilior alga est. *et gen—uss et wihr—tooce, niss—i cum ray, wee—li—or al—gah est.*
Both rank and valour, without wealth, are more worthless than seaweed.
Horace. Sat. Book 2.5.8.

Et hoc genus omne. *et hoke ghen—uss om—neh.*
And all this sort.
Pr.

Et mala sunt vicina bonis. *et mal—a sunt wee—key—na bon—eece.*
And evil things are neighbours to good.
Ovid. Rem. Am. 3.23.

Et modo quae fuerat semita, facta via est. *et mod—o quie fu—eh—rat say—mit—a, fack—ta wi—a est.*
What was only a path is now made a high road.
Martial. Epig. Book 7.60.

Et quae sibi quisque timebat,/Unius in miseri exitium conversa tulere. *et quie sib—i quiss—queh tim—ay—bat, oo—ni—uss in miss—eh—ree ex—it—i—um con—wear—sa tull—ay—reh.*
And those things which each one dreaded as against himself, they could endure when directed to the destruction of one poor unfortunate wretch.
Virgil. Æneid 2.130.

Et quando uberior vitiorum copia? . . . *et quan—doh oo—beh—ri—or wit—*

i—oh—rum coh—pi—a?
And when was there ever a richer abundance of vices?
Juvenal. Sat. 1.87.

Et rident stolidi verba Latina Getae. *et ree—dent stol—id—ee wear—ba lat—ee—na get—eye.*
And the dull Getan fools laugh at Latin words.
Ovid. Tristia Book 5.10.38.

Et terram rumor transilit et maria. *et tehr—ram room—or trahn—sill—it et ma—ri—a.*
Rumour leaps over both land and sea.
Propertius. Elegies 2.18.38.

Et tu, Brute (fili). *et too, Brute—eh (fee—lee).*
You also, (O son) Brutus.
Caesar's words on being stabbed by Brutus.

Etiam stultis acuit ingenium fames. *et—yam stool—teece ack—u—it in—gen—i—um fam—ace.*
Hunger sharpens the understanding even in fools.
Pr.

Euge, poeta! *eu—geh, po—ay—ta!*
Brave, O poet!
Persius. Sat. 1.75.

Eversis omnibus rebus, cum consilio profici nihil possit, una ratio videtur; quidquid evenerit, ferre moderate. *ay—wear—seece om—nib—uss ray—buss, cum cone—sill—i—oh proh—fick—ee ni—hill poss—sit, oo—na rat—i—oh wid—ay—tur; quid quid ay—way—neh—rit, fer—reh mod—eh—rah—tay.*
When all things have gone wrong, when counsel can avail nothing, one plan seems to remain — whatever shall happen, to endure it with moderation.
Cicero.

Ex abundante cautela. *ex—ab—un—dant—eh cow—tay—lah.*
Out of abundance of caution.
Law.

Ex abusu non arguitur ad usum. *ex ab—oo—soo none ar—gu—it—ur ad oo—sum.*
The abuse of a thing is not an argument for its use.
Law.

[41]

Ex abusu non argumentum ad desuetudinem. *ex ah—oo—suo none ar—gu—men—tum ad day—sway—too—din—em.*
The abuse of a thing is no argument for its discontinuance.
Law.

Ex aequo et bono judicare. *ex eye—quoh et bon—oh you—dick—ah—reh.*
To judge according to what is right and good.
Law.

Ex Africa semper aliquid novi. *ex ah—frick—ah sem—pair al—i—quid no—wee.*
Always something new out of Africa.
Pliny. N. H. 8.6. (Greek proverb).

Ex cathedra. *ex cat—ay—drah (cath—ee—dray).*
From the chair of authority.
Pr.

Ex desuetudine amittuntur privilegia. *ex day—sway—too—dineh ah—mit—tun—tur pree—will—ay—gi—a.*
Rights are lost by disuse.
Law.

Ex diuturnitate temporis omnia praesumuntur esse solemniter acta.
ex di—oo—tur—nit—ah—teh tem—po—riss om—ni—a pry—soo—mun—tur ess—seh sol—em—nit—er ack—ta.
After long duration of time all things are presumed to have been done with due form.
Law.

Ex facto oritur jus. *ex fack—toe o—rit—ur yooss.*
The law arises from fact.
Law. (Blackstone, etc.).

Ex inimico cogita posse fieri amicum. *ex in—im—ee—coe coe—git—ah poss—seh fi—eh—ree am—ee—cum.*
Consider that a friend may be made out of an enemy.
Seneca.

Ex necessitate rei. *ex neck—ess—sit—ah—teh reh—ee.*
From the urgency of the case.
Law.

Ex post facto. *ex post fack—toe.*
After the event.
Law.

Exceptio in non exceptis firmat regulam. *ex—kept—i—oh in none ex—kept—eece fihr—mat ray—gull—am.*
An exception claimed in the case of matters or persons not excepted strengthens the rule.
Law.

Exceptis excipiendis. *ex—kept—eece ex—kip—i—end—eece.*
Those things being excepted which it is requisite should be excepted.
Law.

Exegi monumentum aere perennius. *ex—ay—ghee mon—u—men—tum eye—reh peh—ren—ni—uss.*
I have raised up a memorial more lasting than bronze.
Horace. Odes Book 3.30.1.

Exempli gratia. *ex—em—plea grah—ti—ah.*
By way of example.
Cicero and other authors.

Exercendas leges esse respondit. *ex—ehr—ken—dahss lay—gace ess—seh ress—pond—it.*
He (Tiberius Caesar) answered that the law must be exercised.
Tacitus. Annals 1.72.

Exspectans exspectavi. *ex—speck—tanss ex—peck—tah—vee.*
I waited patiently.
Vulgate. Ps. 40.1.

Exspectata dies aderat. . . . *ex—speck—tah—ta di—ace ad—eh—rat.*
The longed-for day was at hand.
Virgil. Æneid 5.104.

Expedit esse deos: et ut expedit, esse putemus. *ex—ped—it ess—seh deh—oce: et ut ex—ped—it, ess—seh dut—ay—muss.*
It is expedient that there should be gods; and as it is expedient let us believe them to be.
Ovid. Ars Amat. Book 1.1.637.

Experto credite. *ex—pair—toe cray—dit—eh.*
Believe one who knows by experience.
Virgil. Æneid 11.283.

Expressa nocent, non expressa non nocent. *ex—press—a nock—ent, none ex—press—a none noc—ent.*
What is expressed may be prejudicial, what is not expressed cannot be so.
Law.

Expressio unius est exclusio alterius. *ex—press—si—oh oo—nee—uss est ex—clue—si—oh al—teh—ri—uss.*
The naming of one man is the exclusion of the other.
Law.

Extra ecclesiam nulla salus. *ex—trah eck—clay—si—am null—la sal—ooce.*
No salvation outside the Church.
Mediaeval, Adapted from St. Augustine. De baptismo 4.17.24.

Faber quique suae fortunae (or "fortunae propriae").
fab—er quee—queh su—eye for—too—nye (prop—ri—eye).
Every man is the maker of his own fortune.
Sallust. De Republica 1.1. quoted as from Apuleius.

Facilis descensus Averno;/Noctes atque dies patet atri janua Ditis;/Sed revocare gradum, superasque evadere ad auras,/Hoc opus, hic labor est . . . *fack—ill—iss day—scane—suss a—wear—noe; nock—tace at—queh di—ace pat—et ah—tree yah—nu—a dee—tiss; sed reh—wock—ah—reh grad—um, sup—eh—rahss—queh ay—way—deh—reh ad ow—rass, hoke op—russ, heek lab—or est.*
Easy is the descent to Lake Avernus (mouth of Hades); night and day the gate of gloomy Dis (god of Hades) is open; but to retrace one's steps, and escape to the upper air, this indeed is a task; this indeed is a toil
Virgil. Æneid 6.126.

Facinus quos inquinat aequat. *fack—in—uss quoce in—quin—at eye—quat.*
A crime equals those whom it debases.
Lucan. Book 5.287.

Facit indignatio versum. *fack—it in—dig—nat—ti—oh wear—sum.*
Indignation leads to the making of poetry. Often quoted "Facit indignatio versus" - i.e. verses.
Juvenal. Sat. 1.79.

Facta ejus cum dictis discrepant. *fact—a ay—yuss cum dick—teece diss—crep—ant.*

His deeds do not agree with his words.
Cicero. De Fin. Book 2.30.

Facta non verba. *fact—ta none wear—ba.*
Deeds not words.
Pr.

Factum abiit; monumenta manent. *fact—tum ab—i—it; mon—u—men—ta man—ent.*
The deed has gone; the memorial thereof remains.
Ovid. Fast. Book 4.709.

Fallitur, egregio quisquis sub principe credit/Servitium. Nunquam libertas gratior exstat,/Quam sub rege pio. . . . *fal—lit—ur, ay—greg—i—oh quis—quis sub prin—kip—eh cray—dit sair—wit—i—um. nun—quam lee—bear—tahss grah—ti—or ex—stat, quam sub ray—geh pi—oh.*
He who thinks it slavery to be under a distinguished chief, is mistaken. Never does liberty appear more pleasing than under a righteous king.
Claudian. De laudibus Stil. iii.113.

Fallor? An arma sonant? Non fallimur, arma sonabant;/Mars venit, et veniens bellica signa dabat. *fal—lor? an ar—ma son—ant? none fal—lim—ur, ar—ma son—ah—bant; marce wen—it, et wen—i—aynce bell—lick—a sig—na dab—at.*
Am I deceived? Or is it the clash of arms? I am not deceived, it was the clash of arms; Mars approaches, and, approaching, gave the signs of war.
Ovid. Fast. Book 5.549.

. . . Falso damnati crimine mortis. *fal—soe dam—nah—tee cree—min—eh more—tiss.*
Men condemned to death on a false accusation.
Virgil. Æneid 6.430.

Falsum in uno, falsum in omni. *fal—sum in oo—noh, fal—sum in om—nee.*
False in one particular, false in every particular.
Pr.

. . . Fama est obscurior annis. *fah—ma est op—scoo—ri—or an—neece.*
The report thereof has become obscured through age.
Virgil. Æneid 7.205.

Famae numquam pepercit, maritos et adulteros non distinguens; neque adfectui suo aut alieno obnoxia, unde utilitas ostenderetur, illuc libidinem transferebat. *fah—my num—quam pep—ehr—kit, ma—ree—toce et ad—ult—eh—roce none diss—ting—gwaynss; neh—queh ad—feck—tu—ee su—oh out al—i—ay—noh ob—nock—si—a, un—deh oo—till—it—ahss ost—end—eh—ray—*

[45]

tur, ill—luke lib—ee—din—em trahnss—feh—ray—bat.
She never attended to her reputation, and whether her lovers were married or bachelors was indifferent to her; she felt no affection herself and was untouched by others' love, but bestowed her favours on whomever her own advantage indicated. (Of Nero's second wife, Poppaea Sabina.)
(Tacitus. Annals 13.45.)

Famam extendere factis. *fah—nam ex—ten—deh—reh fack—teece.*
To extend fame by deeds.
(Motto of Linnaus, Monckton family, etc.) Virgil. Æn. x.468 (altered).

Felices ter et amplius/Quos irrupta tenet copula, nec malis/Divulsus querimoniis,/Suprema citius solvet amor die. *fay—lee—case tear et am— pli—uss quoce ihr—rup—ta ten—et cope—ul—a, neck mal—eece dee—wool— suss queh—ri—moan—i—eece, sup—ray—mah kit—i—uss sol—wet am—oar di—ay.*
Thrice happy, and more than thrice happy, are those whom an unbroken bond holds, and whom love, unimpaired by evil disputes, will not sunder before their last day.
Horace. Odes Book 1.13.17.

Felicitate corrumpimur. *fay—leek—it—ah—teh cor—rump—im—ur.*
We are corrupted by good fortune.
Tacitus. Hist. Book 1.15.

Felix, heu nimium felix. . . . *fay—leeks, hue nim—i—um fay—leeks.*
Happy, alas! too happy.
Virgil. Æneid 4.656.

Felix qui potuit rerum cognoscere causas;/Atque metus omnes, et inexorabile fatum/Subjecit pedibus, strepitumque Acherontis avari! *fay—leeks quee pot—u—it ray—rum cog—noss—keh—reh cow—sahss; at—queh met— ooce om—nace, et in—ex—oh—rah—bil—eh fah—tum sub—yea—kit ped—ib— uss, strep—it—um—queh ack—eh—ron—tiss a—wear—nee!*
Happy he who has been able to understand the causes of things, and who has put under his feet all fears, and inexorable fate and the roaring of greedy Acheron!
Virgil. Georgics 2.490.

Felo de se. *fay—loe—de say.*
A criminal upon himself (a suicide).
Law.

Feras, non culpes, quod mutari non potest. *feh—rahss, none cull—pace, quod moot—ah—ree none pot—est.*

[46]

Bear, do not blame, what cannot be changed.
Publilius Syrus.

Fere libenter homines id quod volunt credunt. *feh—reh lib—en—ter hom—in—ace id quod wol—unt cray—dunt.*
As a rule men freely believe what they wish.
Caesar. De Bello Gallico. 3.18.

Fertilior seges est alienis semper in agris,/Vicinumque pecus grandius uber habet. *fair—till—i—or seg—ess est al—i—ay—neece sem—per in ag—reece, week—ee—num—queh peck—uss gran—di—uss oo—ber hab—et.*
The crop is more abundant in other people's fields, and our neighbor's herd has more milk than ours.
Ovid. Ars Amat. Book 1.349.

Fervet opus. *fair—wet op—uss.*
The work goes on with a will.
Virgil. Georg. 4.169.

Festina lente. *fess—tee—nah lent—ay.*
Hasten slowly.
Motto attributed to Octavius Caesar. (Suetonius Aug. 25).

Fiat experimentum in corpore vili. *fi—at ex—peh—rim—ent—um in corr—po—reh vee—lee.*
Let the experiment be made on a worthless body.
Pr.

Fiat jus et pereat mundus. *fi—at yooce et peh—reh—at mund—uss.*
Let right be done, and let the world perish.
Attributed by Jeremy Taylor to St. Augustine.

Fiat justitia, ruat coelum. *fi—at yuss—ti—ti—a, ru—at coy—lum.*
Let justice be done, and let the heaven fall.
Pr. Cited by W. Watson, 'Quodlibets of Religion and State' (1602).

Fiat lux. *fi—at looks.*
Let there be light.
Vulgate. Genesis 1.3.

Fidei commissum. *fid—eh—ee com—miss—sum.*
Left to trust; bequeathed in confidence in the heir's integrity.
Law.

Fides Punica. (Also Punica Fides). *fid—ace poon—ic—a.*
Punic (or Phoenician) honour (i.e. faithlessness).
Sallust. Jugurtha 108.3. and in other authors.

Fides sit penes auctorem. *fid—ace set pen—ess owk—toh—rem.*
Let credit be in the possession of the author (i.e. Credit this to the author).
Pr.

Fidus Achates. *fee—duss a—kah—tace.*
Faithful Achates (faithful companion of AEneas).
Virgil. Æneid 6.158. etc.

Fieri curavit. *fi—eh—ree coo—rah—wit.*
He caused this to be made.
On monumental inscriptions: expressed by "F.C."

Fieri facias. *fie—er—ee fa—she—ass.*
Cause it to be done (writ empowering a sheriff to levy).
Law.

Filius nullius. *fee—li—uss null—lee—us.*
The son of no one (an illegitimate son).
Law.

Filius populi. *fee—li—uss pop—ul—ee.*
Son of the people (an illegitimate son).
Law.

Filius terrae. *fee—li—uss tehr—rye.*
Son of the earth (i.e. low, earth-born).
Law.

Filum aquae. *fee—lum a—quie.*
The thread or middle of a stream (parting two lordships or properties).
Law.

Finem respice (or Respice finem). *fee—nem ress—pick—eh.*
Have regard to the end.
Translation of Chilo's saying.

Finge datos currus, quid agas? . . . *fin—geh dat—oce curr—rooce, quid ag—ahss?*
Suppose the chariot of the sun were given you, what would you do?
(Apollo's question to Phaeton.)
Ovid. Metam Book 2.74.

Finis adest rerum. *fee—niss ad—est ray—rum.*
The end of affairs is at hand.
Lucan. Pharsalia Book 3.329.

Finis coronat opus. *fee—niss coh—roh—naht o—puss.*
The end crowns the work.
Ovid.

Firmior quo paratior. *firr—mi—oar quoh pa—rah—ti—oar.*
The stronger being better prepared.
Motto of Earls of Selkirk.

Fistula dulce canit volucres dum decipit auceps;|Impia sub dulci melle
venena latent.
fist—ull—a dool—keh can—it wol—uck—race dum day—kip—it ow—keps;
im—pi—a sub dool—key mell—leh wen—ay—na lat—ent.
The pipe sounds sweetly whilst the fowler is ensnaring the birds; and
villainous poison lies concealed in the sweet honey.
Ovid. (Adapted, the second line being from Book 1.8.104; the other from an un-
known source.

Fit in dominatu servitus, in servitute dominatus. *fit in dom—in—ah—too*
sair—wit—ooce,in sair—wit—oo—teh dom—in—ah—tuss.
In mastery there is bondage, in bondage there is mastery.
Cicero. Pro Rege Dejot 11.

Fit via vi. *fit—wi—a wee.*
A way is made by force.
Virgil. Æneid 2.494.

Fixit in aeternum causas qua cuncta coercet. *fix—it in eye—tear—num*
cow—sahss quah cunc—ta co—air—ket.
He fixed for ever causes whereby he keeps all things in order.
Lucan. Pharsalia Book 2.9.

Flagrante delicto. *flah—gran—teh day—lick—toe.*
Whilst the crime is blazing (in the very act of crime).
Pr.

Flamma recens parva sparsa resedit aqua. *flam—ma reck—aynce parr—wah*
spar—sa rexs—ay—dit a—quah.
The newly kindled fire subsides sprinkled with a little water.
Ovid. Heroides 17.190.

Flectere si nequeo superos, Acheronta movebo. *fleck—teh—reh see neh—*

[49]

queh—oh sup—eh—roce, a—keh—ron—ta mo—way—boe.
If I cannot influence the gods, I will move Acheron (Hades).
Virgil. Æneid 7.312.

Flet victus, victor interiit. *flet wick—tus, wick—tor in—ter—i—it.*
The conquered weeps, the conqueror has perished.
Pr.

Floriferis ut apes in saltibus omnia limant,|Omnia nos itidem depascimur
aurea dicta,|Aurea, perpetua semper dignissima vita. *floh—ri—feh—reece
ut ap—ace in sal—ti—buss om—ni—a lee—mant, om—ni—a noce it—id—em
day—pass—kim—ur ow—reh—a dick—ta, ow—reh—a, pair—pet—u—ah
sem—pair dig—niss—sim—a.wee—tah.*
As the bees in the flower-grown meadows take the sweets from all the
flowers, so we also satiate ourselves with all your golden sayings, golden
indeed, and ever most worthy of endless life (an apostrophe of Epicurus).
Lucretius. De Rer. Nat. Book 3.11.

Foeda est in coetu et brevis voluptas, Et taedet Veneris statim peractae.
*foy—da est in coy—too et breh—wiss wol—up—tahss, et tide—et wen—eh—
riss stat—im peh—rack—tie.*
Pleasure in sex is gross and brief, and desire becomes wearisome as soon as
it is consummated.
Petronius.

Foedum consilium, cum incepto, tum etiam exitu fuit.
foy—dum cone—sill—i—um, cum in—kept—oh, tum et—yam ex—it—oo fu—it.
It was a detestable counsel in its beginning, detestable also in its ending.
Livy. Book 26.38.

. . . Fors et virtus miscentur in unum. *force et wihr—tooce miss—kent—ur
in oo—num.*
Chance and valour are blended in one.
Virgil. Æneid 12.714.

Forsan et haec olim meminisse juvabit. *for—san et hike oh—lim mem—in—
iss—seh yu—wah—bit.*
Perhaps it will be a pleasure to us some day to remember even these things.
Virgil. Æneid 1.203.

Forsitan et nostrum nomen miscebitur istis. *for—sit—an et noss—trum
noe—men miss—kay—bit—ur iss—teece.*
Perchance even our name will be mingled with theirs.
Ovid. Ars Amat. Book 3.339.

[50]

Forte scutum salus ducum. *for–teh skoo–tum sal–ooce doo–cum.*
The safety of leaders is a strong shield.
Motto of Fortescue.

Fortes fortuna adjuvat. *for–tace for–too–na add–yu–wat.*
Fortune gives help to the brave.
Terence. Phormio i.4.26.

Forti et fideli nihil difficile. *fore–tee et fid–ay–lee ni–hill dif–fick–*
ill–eh.
Nothing is difficult to a brave and faithful man.
Motto of Lord Muskerry.

Fortior et potentior est dispositio legis quam hominis.
fore–ti–or et pot–ent–i–or est diss–poss–it–i–oh lay–giss quam hom–
in–iss.
The disposition of the law is more decisive and powerful than that of men.
Law.

Fortis et constantis animi est non perturbari in rebus asperis.
for–tiss et cone–stan–tiss an–im–ee est none pair–tur–bah–ree in ray–
buss ass–peh–reece.
It is the nature of a brave and resolute mind not to be disquieted in difficult
matters.
Cicero.

. . . Fortissimus ille est|Qui promptus metuenda pati, si comminus instent.
for–tiss–sim–uss ill–leh est quee prohmp–tuss met–u–end–a pat–ee,
see com–min–uss in–stent.
He is the bravest man who is swift to encounter horrors even though they
stare him in the face.
Lucan. 7.105.

Fortuito quodam concursu atomorum. *for–tu–it–oh quoh–dam con–*
curr–soo at–om–oh–rum.
By some fortuitous concourse of atoms.
Cicero (adapted from De Nat. Deorum Book 1.24.)

Fortuna arbitriis tempus dispensat iniquis;|Illa rapit juvenes; sustinet illa
senes. *for–too–na ar–bit–ri–eece tem–puss diss–pain–sat in–ec queece;*
ill–la rap–it yu–wen–ace; suss–tin–et ill–la sen–ace.
Chance dispenses life with unequal judgment; she snatches away the young;
and prolongs the life of the old.
Ovid. Ad Livian 371.

[51]

Fortuna multis parcere in poenam solet. *fore—too—na mull—teece park—eh—reh in poy—nam sol—et.*
Fortune is wont to spare many for some future punishment.
Laberius.

Fortuna nimium quem fovet, stultum facit. *fore—too—na nim—ium quem fo—wet, stool—tum fack—it.*
Fortune makes a fool of the man whom she favours over much.
Publilius Syrus.

Fortuna vitrea est; tum cum splendet frangitur. *fore—too—na wit—reh—a est; tum cum splen—det fran—git—ur.*
Fortune is glass; just when it becomes bright it is broken. (Said to be taken from "Senecae Sententiae.")
Publilius Syrus.

Fortunae cetera mando. *for—too—nie kay—teh—ra man—doh.*
I commit the rest to fortune.
Ovid. Metam. Book 2.140.

Fortunae filius. *for—too—nie fee—li—uss.*
A son of fortune.
Horace. Sat. Book 2.6.49.

Fortunatus et ille deos qui novit agrestes. *for—too—nah—tuss et ill—leh deh—oce quee noh—wit ag—rest—ace.*
Happy is he who has known the divinities of the country.
Virgil. Georgics 2.493.

Fragili quaerens illidere dentem,/Offendet solido. *frag—ill—ee quie—raynce ill—lee—deh—reh den—tem, of—fen—det sol—id—oh.*
Striving to fix its teeth in what is easily broken, [envy] dashes them against what is solid.
Horace. Sat. Book 2.1.77.

Frangas non flectas. *fran—gahss none fleck—tahss.*
You may break, you shall not bend.
Motto of Leveson-Gower families.

Frangere dum metuis, frangis crystallina: peccant/Securae nimium, sollicitaeque manus. *fran—geh—reh dum met—u—iss, fran—giss crist—all—lin—a: peck—cant say—coo—rye mim—i—um, sol—lick—it—eye—queh man—ooce.*
When you fear to break vases of crystal, you break them; and the too careful and too anxious hands are apt to do the damage (they are trying

to avoid).
Martial. Epig Book 14.111.

Frangitur ipsa suis Roma superba bonis. *fran—git—ur ip—sa su—eece roh—ma sup—air—ba bon—eece.*
Proud Rome is enervated by her own good fortune.
Propertius 3.13.60.

Fraudare eos qui sciunt et consentiunt nemo videtur. *frow—dah—reh eh—oce quee ski—unt et cone—sent—i—unt nay—moe wid—ay—tur.*
No one is regarded as committing fraud upon those who know and assent to what is done.
Law.

Fraus est celare fraudem. *frowse est kay—lah—reh frow—dem.*
It is fraud to conceal fraud.
Law.

Fraus latet in generalibus. *frowse lat—et in gen—eh—rah—lib—uss.*
Deceit lurks in generalities.
Law.

Frons homini laetitiae et hilaritatis, severitatis et tristitiae index. *frohnss hom—in—ee lite—it—i—eye et hill—a—rit—ah—tiss, seh—way—rit—ah—tiss et trist—it—i—eye in—dex.*
The face of man is the index to joy and mirth, to severity and sadness.
Pliny the Elder 11.37.

Fronti nulla fides. *fron—tee null—a fid—ace.*
There is no trust to be placed in outward looks.
Juvenal. Sat. 2.8.

. . . Frustra vitium vitaveris illud,/Si te alio pravus detorseris. . . . *fruss—trah wit—i—um wee—tah—weh—russ ill—ud, see tay al—i—oh prah—wuss day—tor—seh—riss.*
In vain you avoid that particular fault, if you in your depravity turn aside after another.
Horace. Sat. Book 2.2.54.

. . . Fuge magna; licet sub paupere tecto/Reges et regum vita praecurrere amicos. *fug—eh mag—na; lick—et sub pow—peh—reh tect—oe ray—ges et ray—gum wee—tah pry—curr—reh—reh am—ee—coce.*
Shun great things; it is possible beneath a poor roof to excel, by your life,

kings and the friends of kings.
Horace. Ep. Bk. 1.10.32.

Fugit irreparabile tempus. *fug—it ir—rep—a—rah—bil—eh tem—puss.*
Time flies, never to be recovered.
Virgil. Georgics 3.284.

Fuimus Troes; fuit Ilium, et ingens|Gloria Teucrorum.
fu—im—uss tro—ess; fu—it ee—li—um, et in—gaynce gloh—ri—a tew—croh—rum.
We Trojans have been (i.e. we are things of the past). Troy has been, and
the huge renown of the Trojans.
Virgil. Æneid Book 2.325.

Functus officii. *funk—tuss off—fick—i—ee.*
Having discharged his office.
Law.

Furiosus furore suo punitur. *fu—ri—oh—suss fu—roh—reh su—oh poo—nee—tur.*
A madman is punished by his own madness.
Law.

Furor arma ministrat. *fu—roar ar—ma min—iss—trat.*
Rage supplies arms.
Virgil. Æneid 1.150.

. . . Furor iraque mentem|praecipitant. . . . *fu—roar ee—ra—queh men—tem pry—kip—it—ant.*
Fury and anger carry the mind away.
Virgil. Æneid 2.316.

Furor teutonicus. *fu—ror tew—ton—ick—uss.*
Teuton madness.
Lucan Pharsalia 1.255.

G

Gaudensque viam fecisse ruina. *gow—daynce—queh wi—am fay—kiss—eh ru—ee—nah.*
And rejoicing that he has made his way by ruin.
Lucan. Pharsalia Book 1.150.

Gaudent praenomine molles Auriculae. . . . *gow—dent pry—noh—min—eh moll—ace ow—rick—ul—eye.*
His delicate ears rejoice in a praenomen (or title).
Horace. Sat. 2.5.32.

Genius loci. *ghen—i—uss lock—ee.*
The presiding genius of the place.
Virgil. Æneid 7.136.

Gens superstitioni obnoxia, religionibus adversa. *gaynce sup—air—stit—i—oh—nee ob—nox—i—a, ray—lig—i—oh—nib—uss ad—wear—sa.*
A race prone to superstition, contrary to religion.
Tacitus. Hist. 5.13.

Gens togata. *gaynce tog—ah—ta.*
The race wearing the toga (the Roman race); applied also to civilians generally.
Virgil. Æneid 1.282.

. . . Genus humanum ingenio superavit, et omnes/Praestrinxit, stellas exortus uti aetherius sol. *gen—uss hoo—mah—num in—gen—i—oh sup—eh—rah—wit, et om—nace pry—strink—sit, stell—lahss ex—or—tuss ut—i eye—theh—ri—uss sole.*
He (Epicurus) excelled the human race in genius, and made all other men appear dark, as the glorious sun when risen puts the stars from our sight.
Lucretius. Book 3.1056.

. . . Genus immortale manet, multosque per annos/Stat fortuna domus, et avi numerantur avorum. *gen—uss im—more—tah—leh man—et, mul—toce—*

queh per an—noce stat for—too—na dom—ooce, et a—wee num—eh—rant—ur a—woe—rum.
The race remains immortal, and the fortune of the house endures through many years, and grandsires of grandsires are recorded.
Virgil. Georgics 4.209.

Glebae ascriptus. *glay—bye ass—crip—tuss.*
Attached to the soil.
Law.

Gloria in excelsis. *gloh—ri—a in ex—shell—seece.*
Glory in the highest.
Missal. from Vulgate, St. Luke 2.14.

Gloria virtutem tanquam umbra sequitur. *gloh—ri—a wihr—too—tem tan—quam um—bra seh—quit—ur.*
Glory follows virtue like its shadow.
Cicero. Tusc. Quaest. Book 1.45.

Gloriari non est meum. *gloh—ri—ah—ree none est meh—um.*
It is not mine to glory.
Founded on 1 Cor. 9.16; and Gal. 6.4.

Gradus ad Parnassum. *grad—uss ad parr—nass—sum.*
A step to Parnassus (applied to a dictionary of prosody).

Graecia capta ferum victorem cepit, et artes/Intulit agresti Latio.
grie—ki—a cap—ta feh—rum wick—toe—rem kay—pit, et arr—tace in—tull—it ag—rest—ee lat—i—oh.
Greece, taken captive, captured her savage conqueror, and carried her arts into clownish Latium.
Horace. Ep. Book 2.1.156.

Grammatici certant et adhuc sub judice lis est. *gram—mat—ick—ee care—tant et ad—hook sub you—dick—eh lease est.*
Scholars dispute, and the case is still before the judge.
Horace. Ars Poetica 78.

Gratia Musa tibi. Nam tu solatia praebes;/Tu curae requies, tu medicina mali.
grah—ti—a moo—sa tib—ee. nam too soh—lah—ti—a pry—base; too coo—rye reh—qui—ace, too med—ick—ee—na mal—ee.
Thanks, Muse, to thee. For thou givest me consolation; thou art a respite from care, thou art a medicine for woe.
Ovid. Tristia Book 4.10.117.

[56]

Gratia placendi. *grah—ti—ah plack—end—ee.*
For the sake of giving pleasure.
Cicero etc.

Gratior et pulchro veniens in corpore virtus. *grah—ti—or et pull—croh
wen—i—aynss in core—por—eh wihr—tooce.*
And worth which is the more pleasing when it comes with good looks.
Virgil. Æneid 5.344.

Gravis ira regum est semper. *gra—wiss ee—ra ray—gum est sem—pair.*
The wrath of kings is always heavy.
Seneca. Medea iii. 494.

Gravissimum est imperium consuetudinis. *gra—wiss—sim—um est
im—peh—ri—um cone—sway—too—din—iss.*
Very weighty is the authority of custom.
Publilius Syrus.

Gula paradisum clausit; decollavit Baptistam. *gu—la pa--rad—ee—sum
clow—sit; day—coll—lah—wit bap—tiss—tam.*
Greediness closed Paradise; it beheaded [was the cause of beheading]
John Baptist.
*Pope Innocent III (1160-1216). De Contemptu Mundi, Bk. 2, ch. 18. See Chaucer:
Pardoner's Tale v. 177 and 163.*

Gutta cavat lapidem non vi, sed saepe cadendo. *gut—ta ca—wat
lap—id—em none wee, sed sigh—pee cad—end—oh.*
The drop hollows out the stone not by strength, but by constant falling.
*Said to be found in Gariopontus (of the School of Salerno) in "Passionarius," 1, 17
(c. A.D. 1050). Quoted in the Menagiana, 1713. (See Ovid, Ex Ponto Book 4.10.5.)*

H

Habeas corpus. *hay—be—ass cor—puss.*
You may have the body (*i.e.* let the person be delivered from detention).
Law.

... Habent sua fata libelli. *hab—ent su—a fah—ta lib—ell—lee.*
Books have their fates.
Terentianus Maurus. (2nd Cent. A.D.) Carmen heroicum 258.

Hac sunt in fossa Bedae venerabilis ossa. *hahk sunt in foss—sah bay—day ven—eh—rah—bil—iss oss—sa.*
In this grave are the bones of the venerable Bede.
Bede's epitaph, Durham Cathedral.

Hae tibi erunt artes; pacisque imponere morem,|Parcere subjectis et debellare superbos. *hie—tib—ee eh—runt arr—tace; pah—kiss—queh im—poe—neh—reh moh—rem, par—keh—reh sub—yeck—teece et day—bell—lah—reh sup—air—boce.*
These shall be your arts, to impose the conditions of peace, to spare those who have been subdued and to conquer the proud.
Virgil. Æneid 6.852.

Haec data poena diu viventibus, ut, renovata Semper clade domus, multis in luctibus inque Perpetuo maerore et nigra veste senescant.
hike dat—a poy—na di—oo wee—wen—tib—uss, ut, ren—o—wah—ta sem—per clah—deh dom—ooce, mull—teece in luck—tib—uss in—queh pair—pet—u—oh my—roh—reh et nig—grah west—eh sen—ay—scant.
These penalties are given to those who live long, that family losses recurring continuously, they grow old amongst many woes, in constant grief and in mourning garments.
Juvenal. Sat. 10.243.

Haec dum incipias, gravia sunt,|Dumque ignores ubi cognoris, facilia.
hike dum in—kip—i—ahss, gra—wi—a sunt, dum—queh ig—noh—race ub—i cog—noh—riss, fack—ill—i—a.

These things are serious matters when you begin them and are ignorant concerning them; but when you have become acquainted with them they are easy.
Terence. Heauton. v. 5.14.

Haec igitur lex in amicitia sanciatur ut neque rogemus res turpes, nec faciamus rogati. *hike ig—it—ur lex in am—ic—it—i—ah san—ki—ah—tur ut neh—queh rog—ay—muss race tur—pace, neck fack—i—ah—muss rog—ah—tee.*
Let this then be enrolled as a law in friendship, that we neither ask anything dishonourable nor do anything dishonourable when asked.
Cicero. De Amicitia 12.

Haec mihi videtur ambitio, non eleemosyna. *hike mi—he wid—ay—tur am—bit—i—oh, none ell—eh—ay—moss—in—a.*
This seems to me to be ambition, not charity (of charitable bequests).
Erasmus. Convivium Religiosum.

Haereditas nonquam ascendit. *hie—red—it—ahss nun—quam ass—ken—dit.*
Inheritance never ascends.
Law.

Haeres jure representationis. *hie—ress you—reh re—pray—sen—tah—ti—oh—niss.*
Heir by right of representation.
Law.

Haeres legitimus est quem nuptiae demonstrant. *hie—ress lay—git—im—uss est quem nup—ti—eye day—mone—strant.*
The legitimate heir is he whom the marriage rites indicate as such.
Law.

Hanc cupit, hanc optat; sola suspirat in illa;|Signaque dat nutu, sollicitatque notis. *hanc cup—it, hank op—tat; soh—lah suss—peer—at in ill—lah; sig—na—queh dat noo—too, soll—lick—it—at—queh not—eece.*
For her he longs, her he desires; for her alone he sighs; and he makes signs to her by nods, and entreats her by gestures.
Ovid. Fast. Book 1.417.

Hannibal ad portas. *han—nib al ad pore—tahss.*
Hannibal is at the gates.
Cicero. De Finibus Book 4.9.22.

Has vaticinationes eventus comprobavit. *hahss wah—tick—in—ah—ti—oh—nace ay—wen—tuss com—prob—ah—wit.*

[59]

These prophecies the event verified.
Cicero.

Haud facile emergunt, quorum virtutibus obstat|Res angusta domi. . . .
*howd fack—ill—eh ay—mare—gunt, quoh—rum wihr—too—tib—us op—stat
race an—guss—ta dom—ee.*
They do not easily keep their heads above water, whose straitened circumstances at home stand in the way of their talents.
Juvenal. Sat. 3.164.

Haud igitur redit ad Nihilum res ulla, sed omnes|Discidio redeunt in corpora
materiai. *howd ig—it—ur red—it ad ni—hill—um race ull—la, sed om—nace
dis—kid—i—oh red—eh—unt in core—po—ra mah—teh—ri—ah—ee.*
Therefore there is not anything which returns to nothing, but all things
return dissolved into their elements.
Lucretius. De Rer. Nat. Book 1.250.

Haud minus vitiis, quam armis, vincentur. *howd min—uss wit—i—eece,
quam ar—meece, win—kent—ur.*
They shall be vanquished not less by vices than by force of arms.
Tacitus. Germania 23.

Haud passibus aequis. *howd pass—sib—uss eye—queece.*
With steps not equal; unable to keep pace.
Virgil. Æneid 2.724.

Hectora quis nosset si felix Troja fuisset?|Publica virtuti per mala
facta via est. *heck—to—ra quiss noh—s—set see fay—leeks troh—ya
fu—iss—set? pub—lick—a wihr—too—tee pair mal—a fact—ta wi—a est.*
Who would have known of Hector, if Troy had been fortunate? A highway
is made to valour through disasters.
Ovid. Tristia Book 4.3.75.

Hei mihi! qualis erat; quantum mutatus ab illo|Hectore, qui redit exuvias
indutus Achillis. *hay—ee mi—hee! quah—liss eh—rat! quan—tum moo—
tah—tuss ab ill—loh heck—to—reh, quee red—it ex—u—wi—ahss in—doo—tuss
a—kill—leece.*
Ah me! what a man he used to be! How has he changed from that Hector,
who returned arrayed in the despoiled armour of Achilles!
Virgil. Æneid 2.274.

Heu, miserande puer, si qua fata aspera rumpas, tu Marcellus eris. Manibus
date lilia plenis, purpureos spargam flores animamque nepontis. His saltem
accumulem ponis, et fungar inani munere.
hue, miss—eh—ran—deh pu—er, see quah fah—ta ass—peh—ra rum—pahss,

[60]

*too mar—kel—luss eh—riss man—ib—uss dat—eh lee—li—a play—neece,
pur—pu—reh—oce spar—gam floh—race an—im—am—queh nep—oh—tiss?
heece sal—tem ack—cum—ull—em poe—neece, et fun—gar in—ah—nee
moon—eh—reh.*

Alas, unhappy boy, could you but defeat the cruel fates, you will be
Marcellus. Give me armfuls of lilies, and I shall scatter the shining flowers
and heap up these gifts at least upon the soul of my descendant, and give
him a useless tribute.
Virgil. Æneid 6, 882.

Heu, vatum ignarae mentes! . . . *heu, wat—um ig—nah—rye men—tace!*
Alas for the ignorant minds of the Seers!
Virgil. Æneid 4.65.

Heu Veii veteres! et vos tum regna fuistis, Et vestro posita est aurea sella
foro: Nunc intra muros pastoris bucina lenti Cantat, et in vestris ossibus
arva metunt. *hew way—ee wet—eh—race! et woce tum rayg—na fu—iss—
tiss, et west—roe poss—it—a est ow—reh—a sell—la fo—roe: nunc in—trah
moo—roce pah—stoh—race boo—kin—a lent—ee can—tat et in west—reece
oss—sib—uss are—wa met—unt.*

Alas for ancient Veii! You too were a kingdom then, and in your market-
place the golden throne was set: now within your walls sounds the horn of
the idle shepherd, and among your bones they mow the fields.
Propertius. Elegies 4.10.25-30.

Hic erat! hic jurata manet! rumpantur iniqui! Vicimus: assiduas non tulit
illa preces. *heek eh—rat! heek you—rah—ta man—et! rum—pant—ur
in—ee—quee! week—im—uss: ass—sid—u—ahss none tul—it ill—la preck—ace.*
She was here! She swore it, and she remains! Let my enemies burst! I have
conquered: she could not resist my continual entreaties.
Propertius. Elegies 1.8.27f.

Hic coquus scite ac munditer condit cibos. *heek co—quuss skit—ayhack
mun—dit—er con—dit kib—oce.*
This cook seasons his dishes cunningly and elegantly.
Plautus.

Hic est mucro defensionis tuae. *heek est moo—croe day—fen—si—oh—niss,
tu—eye.*
Here is the point of your defence.
Cicero. Pro Caecina 29.84.

Hic locus est partes ubi se via findit in ambas. *heek lock—uss est parr—tace
ub—ee say wi—a fin—dit in am—bahss.*

[61]

Here is the place where the way divides itself into two parts.
Virgil. Æneid 6.540.

Hic Rhodos, hic salta. *hic rod—oss, hic sal—tah.*
Here is Rhodes, leap here.
Latinized from Æsop, Fab. 203, "The Boaster." An athlete boasts of a victory obtained by him in Rhodes with a prodigious leap, to which Rhodians can testify. A bystander says: "When a thing is a fact, there is no need to appeal to testimony. Here is Rhodes; leap here!" Erasmus *(Adagia, par. 1572, 641, 28)* gives the expression as: "Hic Rhodus, hic saltus." — Here is Rhodes, here the leap" [can be performed].

Hic situs est Phaeton currus auriga paterni;|Quem si non tenuit, magnis tamen excidit ausis. *heek sit—uss est pha—et—one curr—rooce ow—ree—ga pat—air—nee; quem see none ten—u—it, mag—neece tam—en ex—kid—it ow—seece.*
Here is Phaeton buried, charioteer of his father's car; who, if he did not manage it, nevertheless fell in a greatly daring attempt.
Ovid. Metam. Book 2.327.

Hi motus animorum atque haec certamina tanta Pulveris exigui jactu compressa quiescent *hee mote—ooce an—im—oh—rum at—queh hike care—tah—min—a tan—ta pull—weh—riss ex—ig—oo—ee yak—too com—press—sa qui—ace—kent.*
These turbulent spirits and mighty conflicts will die down and be calmed by throwing a little dust.
Virgil. Georgics 4.86f.: of fighting bees.

Hinc illae lacrimae. . . . *hinc ill—lie lack—rim—eye.*
Hence those tears.
Terence. Andria, i.1.99. Horace. Ep. Book 1.19, 41.

Hinc lucem et pocula sacra. *hinc loo—kem et poe—kul—a sack—ra.*
Hence light and the sacred vessels.
Motto of Cambridge University. (origin unknown)

Hinc quam sit calamus saevior ense patet. *hink quam sit cal—am—uss sie—we—or en—seh pat—et.*
From this it is clear how much the pen is crueller than the sword.
Robert Burton 1577-1640.

His amor unus erat, pariterque in bella ruebant. *heece am—or oo—nuss eh—rat, par—it—air—queh in bell—la ru—ay—bant.*
Between them was mutual love, and together they were wont to rush into the battle.
Virgil. Æneid 9.182.

[62]

Hoc genus omne. *hoke gen—uss om—neh.*
All this sort of people.
Horace. Sat. Book 1.2.2.

Hoc opus, hic labor est. . . . *hoke op—uss, heek lab—or est.*
This is the work, this is the labour.
Ovid. Ars Amat. Book 1.453. (cf. 'Facilis Descensus Averno' of which this is a parody.)

Hoc tamen infelix miseram solabere mortem:|Æneae magni dextra cadis. . . .
hoke tam—en in—fay—leeks miss—eh—ram soh—lah—beh—reh more—tem:
eye—nay—eye mag—nee dex—trah cad—iss.
This, unhappy man, shall comfort you in your sad death—you fall by the
right hand of the great Æneas.
Virgil. Æneid 10.829.

Hoc volo, sic jubeo; sit pro ratione voluntas. *hoke wol—oh, seek yub—eh—*
oh; sit proh rat—i—oh—neh wol—un—tahss.
I desire this, and so I command this; let my will stand for a reason.
Juvenal. Sat. 6.223.

Hominis est errare, insipientis perseverare. *hom—in—iss est err—rah—reh,*
in—sip—i—ent—iss pair—seh—wah—reh.
It is the nature of man to err, of a fool to persevere in error.
Pr.

Hominum sententia fallax. *hom—in—um sen—ten—ti—a fal—lahkss.*
The judgment of men is fallible.
Ovid. Fast. Book 5.191.

Homo antiqua virtute et fide. *hom—oh an—tee—quah wihr—too—teh*
et fid—ay.
A man of old-fashioned virtue and good faith.
Terence. Adelphi iii.3.86.

Homo coronatus. *hom—oh co—roan—ah—tuss.*
A man who has received the first tonsure preparatory to superior orders.
Law.

Homo delirus, qui verborum minutiis rerum frangit pondera.
hom oh day—lee—russ, quee wear—boh—rum min—oot—i—eece ray—rum
fran—git pon—deh—ra.
A crazy man, who detracts from the weight of his subject by splitting words.
Aulus Gellius.

Homo novus. *hom—oh no—wuss.*

A new man; an upstart.
Cicero. De Off. 1.39.138; et passim.

Homo proponit, sed Deus disponit. *hom—oh proh—pon—it, sed deh—uss diss—pon—it.*
Man proposes, but God disposes.
Thomas à Kempis. De Imit. Christi, Book 1.19.2. (See Prov. 16.9.)

Homo sum; humani nihil a me alienum puto. *hom—oh sum; hoo—mah—nee ni—hill ah may al—i—ay—num put—oh.*
I am a man; and I think nothing appertaining to mankind foreign to me.
Terence. Heaut. i.1.25.

Homo unius libri. *hom—oh oo—nee—uss lib—ree.*
A man of one book.
Thomas Aquinas. Definition of a learned man.

Honesta quam splendida. *hon—ess—ta quam splen—did—a.*
Honourable things rather than splendid.
Pr.

Honestum non est semper quod licet. *hon—ess—tum none est sem—per quod lick—et.*
What is lawful is not always honourable.
Law.

Honor est praemium virtutis. *hon—or est pry—mi—um wihr—too—tiss.*
Honour is the reward of virtue.
Cicero. Brutus, 82 (adapted).

Honorantes me honorabo. *hon—oh—ran—tace may hon—oh—rah—boh.*
I will honour those who honour me.
Motto of Hastings, Earl of Huntingdon.

Honorum caeca cupido. *hon—oh—rum kie—ca cup—ee—doh.*
The blind longing for honours.
Lucretius. De Rer. Nat. 3m 59.

Honos alit artes . . . jacentque ea semper, quae apud quosque inprobantur. *hon—oce al—it are—tace . . . yak—ent—queh eh—a sem—pehr, quie ap—ud quoce—queh in—prob—ant—ur.*
Honour fosters the arts . . . and those arts are always neglected, which everyone disapproves of.
Cicero. Tusculan Disputations 1.2.

Horresco referens. *horr—resk—oh ref—eh—raynce.*
I shudder as I tell it.
Virgil. Æneid 2.204.

Horror ubique animos, simul ipsa silentia terrent. *horr—ror ub—e—queh*
an—im—oce, sim—ul ip—sa sil—en—ti—a terr—rent.
Horror everywhere alarms the soul, and the very stillness also is terrifying.
Virgil. Æneid 2.755.

Hortus siccus. *hoar—tuss sick—cuss.*
A dry garden (a collection of dried plants).

Hospes nullus tam in amici hospitium devorti potest,|Quin ubi triduum
continuum fuerit, jam odiosus siet;|Verum, ubi dies decem continuos
immorabitur,|Tametsi dominus non invitus patitur, servi murmurant.
hoss—pace null—luss tam in am—ee—key hoss—pit—i—um day—wore—tee
pot—est, queen ub—i trid—u—um con—tin—u—um fu--eh—rit, yam
od -i—oh—suss si—et; way—rum, ub—i di—ace deck—em con—tin—u—oce
im—mo—rah—bit—ur, tam—et—see dom—in—uss none in—wee—tuss
pat—it—ur, sair—wee mur—mu—rant.
No guest can be so welcome to the hospitality of a friend, but when he has
stayed three continuous days he becomes unwelcome; and indeed if when
he has stayed ten days the master of the house does not endure him un-
willingly, the servants grumble.
Plautus. Miles Gloriosus iii. 1.146.

Hostem qui feriet mihi erit Karthaginiensis Quisquis erit, quoiatis siet.
hoss—tem quee feh—ri—et mi—he eh—rit cart—hah—ghin—i—ain—siss,
quiss—quiss eh—rit, quoh—yah—tiss si—et
He that will smite the enemy shall be a Carthaginian to me, whoever he
may be, whatever his country.
Ennius Annals cited in Cicero Pro Balbo 22/51.

Hostis si quis erit nobis, amet ille puellas: Gaudeat in puero, si quis amicus
erit. Tranquillo tuta descendis flumine cumba: Quid tibi tam parvi litoris
unda nocet? *hoss—tiss see quiss eh—rit noh—beece, am—et ill—leh pu—ell—*
lahss: gow—deh—at in pu—eh—roe, see quiss am—ee—cuss eh—rit. trang—
quill—loh too—tah day—sken—diss flue—min—eh cum—bah: quid tib—e
tam par—wee lee—to—riss un—da nock—et?
Whoever will be my enemy, let him love women: let him take pleasure in a
boy, whoever will be my friend. For then you sail your boat safely down a
calm stream: what harm can the waves of so slight a shore do you?
Propertius. Elegies 2.4.17-20.

I

Ibis redibis non morieris in bello. *ee—bis red—ee—biss none mo—ri—ay—riss in bell—oh.*
Thou shalt go, thou shalt return, never in battle shalt thou perish.
Utterance of the Oracle, doubtful in meaning through the absence of punctuation and the uncertainty of the position of the word "non."

Ibit eo quo vis, qui zonam perdidit, inquit. *ee—bit eh—oh quoh wees, quee zoh—nam pair—did—it, in—quit*
He who has lost his purse, said he, will go wherever you wish.
Horace. Ep. Book 2.2.40.

Id arbitror|Adprime in vita esse utile, Ut ne quid nimis.
id ar—bit—ror ad—pree—may in wee—tah ess—seh oo—till—eh, ut nay quid nim—iss.
Excess in nothing, — this I regard as a principle of the highest value in life.
Terence. Andria i. 1.33.

Idem atti quod titi. *ee—dem ah—tee quod tih—tee.*
Sauce for the goose is sauce for the gander.
M. Terentius Varro. (116-27 B.C.)

Idem velle et idem nolle, ea demum firma amicitia est.
ee—dem well—leh et ee—dem nole—leh, eh—a day—mum fihr—ma am—ee—kit—i—a est.
To desire the same thing and to dislike the same thing, that alone makes firm friendship.
Sallust. Catil 20. From Catiline's Oration to his Associates.

Ignis fatuus. *ig—niss fat—u—uss.*
A foolish fire (a Will-o'-the-wisp).

Ignobile vulgus. *ig—noh—bill—eh wool—guss.*
The low-born crowd.
Virgil. Æneid 1.149.

[66]

Ignorant populi, si non in morte probaris,|An scieris adversa pati. . . .
*ig—noh—rant pop—ul—ee, see none in more—teh prob—ah—riss, an
ski—eh—riss ad—wear—sa pat—ee.*
The peoples of the world would not know, if you had not proved it in your
death, whether you knew how to suffer adverse fate.
Lucan. Pharsalia Book 8.626. Of Pompey.

Ignorantia facti excusat. *ig—noh—ran—ti—a fack—tee ex—coo—sat.*
Ignorance of fact is an excuse.
Law.

Ignorantia legis excusat neminem. *ig—no—ran—ti—a lay—giss ex—co—sat
nem—in—em.*
Ignorance of the law excuses no one.
Law.

Ignoratio elenchi. *ig—no—ray—shi—o ell—eng—kie.*
A proof ignoring what ought to be proved.
Pr.

Ignoto Deo. *ig—noh—toh deh—oh.*
To the unknown God.
Vulgate. Acts 17.23.

Ignotum per ignotius. *ig—noh—tum pair ig—noh—ti—uss.*
That which is unknown by that which is still more unknown (to attempt to
prove a doubtful matter by a still more doubtful argument).
*Pr. Quoted by Chaucer Canon Yeoman's Tale, 904 in reference to the "secree of secrees"
in alchemy.*

Iliacos intra muros peccatur et extra. *ee—li—ack—oce in—trah moo—roce
peck—kah—tur et ex—trah*
Fault is committed both within the walls of Troy and without.
Horace. Ep. Book 1.2.16.

Ille mi par esse deo videtur, Ille, si fas est, superare divos, Qui sedens
adversus identidem te Spectat et audit Dulce ridentem.
*ill—leh mee par ess—seh deh—oh wid—ate—ur, ill—leh, see fahss est, sup—eh—
rah—reh dee—woce, quee sed—aynce ad—wehr—suss iden—tid—em tay
speck—tat et ow—dit dull—keh reed—en—tem.*
That man seems to me to be like a god,—if it is lawful, to surpass the gods
—who so often sits opposite you, and sees and hears you sweetly laughing.
Catullus. Poem 51.1-5: an imitation of a poem by Sappho.

. . . Ille potens sui/Laetusque deget, cui licet in diem/Dixisse, Vixi; cras

[67]

vel atra|Nube polum pater occupato, Vel sole puro.

ill—leh pot—aynce su—ee lie—tuss -queh day—get, cu—ee lick—et in di—em dix—iss—seh, wick—see; crahss well ah—trah noo—beh pol—um pat—er ock—cup—ah—toe, well sol—eh poo—roh.

He will live a joyful man and his own master, who can say at the end of the day "I have lived; whether the Father of all chooses on the morrow to fill the sky with black cloud, or whether with pure sunlight."
Horace. Odes. Book 3.29.41.

Ille unum se civium et consensui imparem respondit.

ill—leh oo—num say key—wi—um et cone—sane—su—ee im—par—em ress—pond—it

He (the Emperor Claudius) replied that he was himself one of the citizens and no match to their unanimity.
Tacitus. Annals 12.5.

Illi dies per somnum, nox officiis et oblectamentis vitae transigebatur; utque alios industria, ita hunc ignavia ad famam protulerat.

ill—lee de—ace pehr som—num, nox off—fick—i—eece et ob—leck—tah—men —teece wee—tie trahn—sig—ay—bah—tur; ut—queh al—i—oce in—dust—ri—a, it—a hunk ig—nah—we—a ad fah—mam proh—tull—eh—rat.

He (Petronius) spent his days asleep, his nights in work and in life's amusements; while others are famous through hard work, his laziness had made him famous.
Tacitus. Annals 16.18.

Illi mors gravis incubat Qui notus nimis omnibus Ignotus moritur sibi.

ill—lee morse gra—wiss in—cub—at quee noh—tuss nim—iss om—nib—uss ig—noh—tuss mo—rit—ur sib—ee

On him does death lie heavily who, only too well known to everyone, dies to himself unknown.
Seneca. Thyestes 2, chorus.

Illi robur et aes triplex|Circa pectus erat, qui fragilem truci|Commisit pelago ratem Primus.

ill—lee robe—ur et ice trip—lex kier—kah pect—tuss eh—rat, quee frag—ill—em truck—ee com—mee—sit pel—ag—oh rat—em pree—muss.

Oak and triple brass were round his breast who first entrusted his frail bark to the savage sea.
Horace. Odes Book 1.3.9.

Imberbis juvenis, tandem custode remoto, Gaudet equis canibusque, et aprici gramine campi. *im—bear—biss yu—wen—iss, tan—dem cuss—toh—deh re—moh—toh, gow—det eh—queece can—ib—uss—queh, et ap—reek—ee*

[68]

grah—min—eh cam—pea.
The beardless youth, his tutor being at length dismissed, delights in horses, and dogs, and the sunny expanse of the turf.
Horace. De Arte Poetica 162.

Immedicabile vulnus Ense recidendum est. *im—med—ick—ah—bill—eh wool—nuss ain—seh reck—ee—den—dum est.*
A wound that cannot be healed must be cut back with the sword.
Ovid. Metamorphoses 1.190.

Immortales mortales si foret fas flere Flerent divae Camenae Naevium Poetam. *im—more—tah—lace more—tah—lace see for—et fahss flay—reh flay—rent dee—wye cam—ay—nye nye—we—um po—ate—am.*
If it were right for the immortals to weep for mortal men, the heavenly Muses would weep for Naevius the poet.
Epitaph of Naevius ob. 201 B.C. composed by himself.

Imponere Pelio Ossam. *im—poh—neh—reh pay—li—oh oss—sam.*
To pile Ossa upon Pelion.
Virgil. Georgics 1.281.

Imprimatur. *im—pry—mate—ur.*
Let it be printed.

Improbis aliena virtus semper formidolosa est. *im—prob—eece al—i—ay—na wihr—tooce sep—pair fore—mid—ull—oh—sa est.*
To the wicked the virtue of others is always fearful.
Sallust, adapted. See "Regibus boni."

Imum nolo; summum nequeo; quiesco. *ee—mum noh—low; sum—mum neh—queh—oh; qui—ay—scoh.*
I desire not the lowest; I am not capable of the highest; I keep quiet.
Joseph Hall, D.D. (Bishop of Exeter and Norwich (1574-1656). Motto on his vicarage, Hawsted, Suffolk c. 1601.

In aequali jure melior est conditio possidentis. *in eye—quah—lee you—reh mell—i—or est con—dit—i—oh poss—sid—en—tiss.*
In a case of equal right, the position of the person in possession is the better.

In audiendi officio perit gratia si reposcatur. *in ow—di—en—dee off—fick—i—oh peh—rit grah—ti—a see rep—oh—scah—tur.*
In the function of listening the grace is lost if the listener's attention is demanded, not as a favour, but as a due.
Pliny the Younger. Ep. Book 1.13.

In Anglia non est interregnum. *in ang—gli—ah none est in—ter—ray—gnum.*
In England there is no interregnum recognised.
Law.

In cruce salus. *in croo—cheh sal—ooce*
In the cross there is safety.
Thomas à Kempis. Imit. Christi Book 2. ch. 12.

In dubiis benigniora sunt semper praeferenda. *in dub—i—eece ben—eeg—ni—*
—oh—ra sunt sem—per pry—feh—ren—da.
In doubtful matters the more merciful view is always to be preferred.
Law.

In loco parentis. *in lock—oh pa—rent—iss.*
In the place of a parent.
Law.

In memoria aeterna erit justus: ab auditione mala non timebit.
in mem—oh—ri—ah ate—air—nah eh—rit yuss—tuss: ab ow—dit—si—oh—neh
mal—ah none tim—ay—bit.
The righteous shall be had in everlasting remembrance: he will not be afraid
of any evil tidings.
(Vulgate, Psalm III.6 (A.V. Ps. 112): used in Gradual of Mass for the Dead.)

In nova fert animus mutatas dicere formas Corpora. *in no—wa fairt an—im*
—us moot—ah—tahss dee—keh—reh fore—mahss corr—po—ra.
My mind leads me to speak of forms changed into new bodies.
Ovid. Metam. Book 1.1.

In omni adversitate fortunae, infelicissimum est genus infortunii, fuisse
felicem. *in om—nee ad—wear—sit—ah—teh fore—too—nie, in—fay—lee—*
kiss—sim—um est gen—uss in—fore—too—ni—ee, fu—iss—seh fay—leek—em
In every time of ill-fortune, the grimmest kind of misery is to have been
happy.
Boethius. De consolatione philosophiae 2. Prose 4.

In omnibus fere minori aetati succurritur. *in om—nib—uss feh—reh min—*
oh—ree eye—tah—tee suc—cur—rit—ur.
In almost everything a person not of age is protected by the law.
Law.

In omnibus quidem, maxime tamen in jure aequitas est.
in om—nib—uss quid—em, max—im—ay tam—en in you—reh eye—quit—
ahss est.
In all things indeed there is equity, but most of all in law.
Law.

In paradisum deducant te Angeli: in tuo adventu suscipiant te Martyres, et perducant te in civitatem sanctam Jerusalem. Chorus Angelorum te suscipiat, et cum Lazaro quondam paupere aeternam habeas requiem.
in pa—rad—ee—sum day—doo—cant tay an—gel—ee: in tu—oh ad—ven—too su—ship—i—ant tay mar—tyr—ace, et pair—doo—cant tay in chee—vit—ah—tem sank—tam yeh—roo—sal—em. corr—uss an—gel—oh—rum tay su—ship—i—at, et cum laz—a—roe quon—dam pow—peh—reh ay—tare—nam ab—eh—ahss reh—qui—em.
Into Paradise may the Angles lead thee: at thy coming may the Martyrs receive thee, and take thee into the holy city, Jerusalem. The choir of Angels receive thee, and with Lazarus, once a poor man, do thou have eternal rest.
Anthem from the Roman Catholic Burial Service.

In partibus infidelium. *in parr—ti—buss in—fid—ay—li—um.*
In parts of the world occupied by unbelievers.
Mediaeval.

. . . In perpetuum, frater, ave, atque vale. *in pair—pet—u—um, frah—tare, a—way, at—queh wal—ay.*
For ever, brother, hail and farewell.
Catullus. 101.10.

In posse. *in poss—seh.*
In possibility; a condition which may be regarded as possible.
Law.

In propria persona. *in prop—ri—ay per—soh—nay.*
In his own person.

In proverbium cessit, sapientiam vino obumbrari. *in proh—wear—bi—um kess—sit, sap—i—en—ti—am wee—noh ob—um—brah—ree.*
It has passed into a proverb that wisdom is clouded by wine.
Pliny the Elder. 23.1.23.

In puris naturalibus. *in poo—reece nah—tur—ah—lib—uss.*
In an absolute state of nature (*i.e.* naked).

In rebus asperis et tenui spe fortissima quaeque consilia tutissima sunt.
in ray—buss ass—peh—reece et ten—u—ee spay for—tiss- sim—a quie—queh cone—sil—i—a too—tiss—sim—a sunt.
In great straits and when hope is small, the boldest counsels are the safest.
Livy.

[71]

In se magna ruunt. *in say mag—na ru—unt.*
Great interests collide (*lit.,* great things rush upon themselves).
Lucan.

In solo Deo salus. *in soh—loe deh—oh sal—ooce.*
Salvation in God alone.
Motto of Lascelles.

In statu pupillari. *in stat—you pew—pill—lair—eye.*
In the state of a pupil (or ward).

In statu quo. *in stat—yew quoh.*
In the condition in which it was.

In te, Domine, speravi. *in tay, dom—in—eh, speh—rah—wee.*
In thee, O Lord, have I put my trust.
Vulgate. Ps. 31.1. (Motto of Earls of Strathmore and of other families.)

. . . In utrumque paratus. *in ut—rum—queh pa—rah—tuss.*
Prepared for either alternative.
Virgil. Æneid 2.61.

In vacuo. *in vac—you—oh.*
In empty space.

In vino veritas. *in wee—noh way—rit—ahss.*
In wine there is truth.
Pr.

Incenditque animum famae venientis amore. *in—ken—dit—queh*
an—im—um fah—my wen—i—ent—iss a—more—eh.
And fires his soul with the love of approaching fame.
Virgil. Æneid 6.889.

Inceptis gravibus plerumque et magna professis,|Purpureus, late qui
splendeat, unus et alter Adsuitur pannus. *in—kept—eece gra—wib—uss*
play—rum—queh et mag—na pro—fess—seece, poor—pu—reh—uss, lah—tay
q̇uee splen—deh—at, oo—nuss et alt—air ad—su—it—ur pan—nuss.
Often to weighty enterprises, and such as profess great objects, one or two
purple patches are sewed on to make a fine display in the distance.
Horace. De Arte Poetica 14.

Incerta pro nullis habentur. *in—care—ta proh null—leece hab—en—tur.*
What is uncertain is counted as nothing.

. . . Incessu patuit Dea. . . . *in—kess—soo pat—u—it deh—a.*
By her gait the goddess was known.
Virgil. Æneid 1.405.

Incipe; dimidium facti est coepisse. Supersit|dimidium: rursum hoc incipe,
et efficies. *in—kip—eh; dee—mid—i—um fact—tee est coy—pis—seh.*
sup—air—sit dee—mid—i—um: roor—sum hoc in—kip—eh, et eff—fick—i—ace.
Begin; to begin is half the work. Let half still remain; again begin this, and
thou wilt have finished.
Ausonius.

Incipe, parve puer, risu cognoscere matrem. *in—kip—eh, par—weh pu—air,*
ree—soo cog—noh—skeh—reh mah—trem.
Begin, little boy, to recognize your mother by a smile.
Virgil. Ecologues 4.60.

Incipere multo est quam impetrare facilius. *in—kip—eh—reh mull—toe—est*
quam im—pet—rah—reh fact—ill—i—uss.
It is much easier to begin than to finish.
Plautus. Poenulus v. 2.14.

Inclusio unius est exclusio alterius. *in—clue—si—oh oo—nee—uss est*
ex—clue—si—oh al—teh—ri—uss.
The inclusion of the one means the exclusion of the other.
Law.

Index expurgatorius. *in—decks ex—purr—gat—ore—i—us.*
Expurgatory index (catalogue of forbidden writings).

Indica tigris agit rabida cum tigride pacem|Perpetuam: saevis inter se
convenit ursis.|Ast homini ferrum letale incude nefanda|Produxisse
parum est. . . . *in—dick—a tig—riss a—git rab—id—ah cum tig—rid—eh*
pah—kem pair—pet—u—am: sigh—weece in—ter say con—wen—it ur—seece
ast hom—in—ee fair—rum lay—tah—leh in—coo—deh ne—fan—dah proh—
duck—tiss—seh par—um est.
The Indian tiger keeps a perpetual peace with the savage tiger; there is agreement among themselves with cruel bears. But man makes small account of
beating out the deadly sword on the accursed anvil.
Juvenal. Sat. 15.163.

Indignatio principis mors est. *in—dig—nay—she—oh prin—sip—iss morse est.*
The displeasure of the ruler is death.
Said of Henry VIII of England in 1529.

[73]

Infandum, regina, jubes renovare dolorem. *in—fahn—dum, ray—ghee—na, yub—ace ren—o—wah—reh dol—oh—rem.*
You bid me, O queen, to reopen unspeakable grief.
Virgil. Æneid 2.3.

Infra dig. — Infra dignitatem. *in—fra dig—nit—ate—em.*
Beneath one's dignity.
Pr.

. . . Ingenio stat sine morte decus. *in—gen—i—oh stat sin—eh more—teh peck—uss.*
Deathless honour waits upon genius.
Propertius. Book 3 El. 2.26.

Ingentes animos augusto in corpore versant. *in—gen—tace an—im—oce ow—guss—toh in cor—po—reh wear—sant.*
They have mighty minds labouring within a stunted body.
Virgil. Georgics 4.83.

Ingrata patria, ne ossa quidem habebis. *in—grah—ta pat—ri—a, nay oss—sa quid—em hab—ay—biss.*
Ungrateful country, you shall not even have my bones.
Attributed to Scipio Africanus.

Ingrediturque solo, et caput inter nubila condit. *in—gred—it—ur—queh sol—oh, et cap—ut in—taire noo—bil—a con—dit.*
She (Fame) walks on the earth, and her head is concealed in the clouds.
Virgil. Æneid 4.177.

Iniqua nunquam regna perpetuo morant. *in—ee—qua non—quam ray—gna pair—pet—u—oh mo—rant.*
Unjust rule never endures perpetually.
Seneca. Medea 196.

Iniquissima haec bellorum condicio est: prospera omnes sibi vindicant, adversa uni imputantur. *in—eke—wiss—sim—a hike bell—loh—rum con—dick—i—oh est: pross—peh—ra om—nace sib—e win—dick—ant, ad—wear—sa oo—nee im—put—ant—ur.*
This is the unfairest feature of wars: everyone claims successes for himself; reverses are blamed on one man.
Tacitus. Agricola 27.

Initium sapientiae timor Domini. *in—eet—si—um sap—i—ent—si—ay tee—mor dom—in—ee.*
The fear of the Lord is the beginning of wisdom.
Vulgate. Ps. 110.10.

Injuria absque damno. *in—you—ri—a aps—queh dam—noh.*
Injury without loss.
Law.

Injuria injuriam cohibere licet. *in—you—ri—a in—you—ri—am*
coe—hib—eh—reh lick—et.
We may hinder one injury by means of another.
Law.

Insanis et tu, stultique prope omnes. *in—sah—niss et too, stul—tee—quah*
prop—eh om—nace.
You yourself are mad, and almost all men are fools.
Horace. Sat. Book 2.3.32.

Insipientis est dicere, Non putaram. *in—sip—i—ent—iss est dee—keh—reh,*
none put—ah—ram.
It is the part of a fool to say, I should not have thought it.
Scipio Africanus.

Integer vitae, scelerisque purus,/Non eget Mauris jaculis neque arcu.
in—teg—air wee—tie, skel—eh—riss—queh poo—russ, none egg—et mow—reece
yack—ul—eece ne—queh ar—coo.
The man upright in his life, and free from crime, does not need Moorish
javelins or bow.
Horace. Odes Book 1.22.1.

Inter quadrupedes gloria prima lepus. *in—ter quad—rup—ed—ace gloh—ri—a*
pree—ma lepp—uss.
Among four-footed creatures the hare has the first rank (as food).
Martial. Epig. Book 13.92.

. . . Inter silvas Academi/quaerere verum. . . . / *in—tare sill—wahss acad—ay—*
mee guie—reh—reh way—rum.
To seek for truth among the woods of Academus.
Horace. Ep. 2.2.45.

Inter spem curamque, timores inter et iras,/Omnem crede diem tibi
diluxisse supremum:/Grata superveniet, quae non sperabitur, hora.
in—ter spem coo—ram—queh, tim—oh—race in—ter et ee—rhass, om—nem
cray—deh di—em tib—ee dee—lux—iss—seh sup—ray—mum: grah—ta sup
—er—wen—i—et, quie none spay—rah—bit—ur, hoe—ra.
In the midst of hope and anxiety, in the midst of fear and anger, believe
every day that has dawned to be your last: you will be thankful for the
hour which comes unlooked-for.

[75]

Interdum lacrimae pondera vocis habent. *in—tear—dum lack—rim—eye pond—eh—ra woe—kiss hab—ent.*
Sometimes tears have the weight of words.
Ovid. Ep. ex Pont. Book 3.1.158.

Interea dulces pendent circum oscula nati:|Casta pudicitiam servat domus.
. . . in—teh—reh—ah dull—case pen—dent keer—cum oce—cull—a nah—tee: cass—ta pud—ee—kit—i—am sair—wat do—muss.
Meantime his sweet children hang about his lips: his pure home preserves that which is decent.
Virgil. Georgics 2.523.

Intolerabilius nihil est quam femina dives. *in—toll—eh—rah—bill—i—uss ni—hill est quam fay—min—a dee—wace.*
Nothing is more unbearable than a woman of wealth.
Juvenal. Sat. 6.460.

Intonuere poli, et crebris micat ignibus aether;|Praesentemque viris intentant omnia mortem. *in—ton—u—ay—reh poll—ee, et cray—breece mick—at ig—nib—uss eye—thair; pry—sent—em—queh wi—reece in—tent—ant om—ni—a more—tem*
The heavens thundered and the air shone with frequent fire; and all things threatened men with instant death.
Virgil. Æneid 1.90.

Introite, nam et hic dii sunt. *in—tro—it—eh, nam et heek di—ee sunt.*
Enter, for here too are gods.
Tr. of Heraclitus (quoting Aristotle).

Inventas aut qui vitam excoluere per artes,|Quique sui memores alios fecere merendo. *in—went—ahss owt quee wee—tem ex—col—u—ay—reh per arr—tace, quee—queh su—ee mem—o—race al—i—oce fay—kay—reh meh—rend—oh.*
Men who have ennobled life by their discoveries in the arts, and who have earned by desert the remembrance of others.
Virgil. Æneid 6.663.

Inveterascet hoc quoque, et quod hodie exemplis tuemur, inter exampla erit. *in—wet—eh—rah—sket hoke quock—weh, et quod hod—i—ay ex—em—pleece tu—aim—ur, in—tehr ex—em—pla eh—rit.*
This too will become an old established custom, and what we are justifying by precedents will become a precedent.
Tacitus. Annals 11.24: attributed to the Emperor Claudius.

Invidia Siculi non invenere tyranni|Majus tormentum. *in—wid—i—ah sick—ul—ee none in—way—nay—reh ti—ran—nee mah—yuss tore—men—tum.* The Sicilian tyrants have not invented a worse torment than envy. *Horace. Ep. Book 1.2.58.*

Invita Minerva. *in—wee—tah min—air—wah.* Minerva being unwilling (*i.e.* unwilling to bestow genius or inspiration). *Horace. De Arte Poetica 385.*

Io triumphe! *i—oh tri—um—feh!* Hail, conqueror! (*lit.* Ho! triumph!)

Ipsa dissimulatione famae famam auxit. *ip—sa diss—sim—ul—ah—ti—oh—neh fah—my fah—mam owk—sit.* By his very concealment he added fame to fame. *Tacitus. Agricola 18.*

Ipsa mihi dixi: Si valet ille venit. *ip—sa mi—hee dick—see: see walet ee—lay wen—it.* I said to myself, "If he is well he will come." *Ovid. Heroides 2.20.*

Ipse dixit. *ip—seh dick—sit.* He himself has said it. *Cicero, De Nat. Deorum, 1.5.10.*

Ira furor brevis est; animum rege, qui, nisi paret|Imperat: hunc frenis, hunc tu compesce catena. *ee—ra fu—ror breh—wiss est; an—im—um reg—eh, quee, niss—ee pah—ret im—peh—rat: hunc fray—neece, hunc too com—pace— keh cat—ay—nah.* Anger is short madness; rule your mind, which if it does not obey will command; restrain it with a bit, restrain it with a chain. *Horace. Ep. Book 1.2.62.*

Ire tamen restat Numa quo devenit et Ancus. *ee—reh tam—en rest—at num—a quoh day—way—nit et an—cuss.* It yet remains for you to go where Numa and Ancus have gone (to death). *Horace. Ep. Book 1.6.27.*

Is ordo vitio careto, ceteris specimen esto. *iss ore—doh wit—i—oh ca—ray—toe, kay—teh—reece speck—im—en ess—toe.* Let this rank (the nobility) be free from vice, and an example to others. *Twelve Tables at Rome.*

Isque habitus animorum fuit, ut pessimum facinus auderent pauci, plures

vellent, omnes paterentur. *iss—queh hab—it—uss an—im—oh—rum fu—it,*
ut pess—sim—um fack—in—uss ow—day—rent pow—key, ploo—race well—ent,
om—nace pa—teh—rent—ur.
Such was the condition of their minds that some few dared to commit
the vilest crime, many were inclined to, and all permitted it.
Tacitus. Hist. Book 1.28.

. . . Istam|Oro (si quis adhuc precibus locus), exue mentem.
iss—tam oh—roe (see quis ad—hook preck—ib—uss lock—uss) ex—u—eh
men—tem.
I pray of you, if my entreaties as yet avail anything, put aside that intention.
Virgil. Æneid 4.318.

Is non inritato hoste neque lacessitus honestum pacis nomen segni otio
imposuit. *iss none in—ree—tah—toe hoss—teh neh—queh lack—ess—seat—*
uss hon—ess—tum pah—kiss noh—men sayg—nee oat—i—oh im—poss—u—it.
He (Turpilianus, governor of Britain from A.D. 61) neither provoked the
enemy nor was provoked by them, and gave the honourable name of peace
to this sluggish inactivity.
Tacitus. Annals 14.39.

Ita amicum habeas, posse ut facile fieri hunc inimicum putes.
it—a a—meek—um hab—eh—ahss, poss—seh ut fack—ill—eh fi—eh—ree hunc
in—im—ee—cum put—ace.
So possess your friend as though you thought that he might easily be trans-
formed into an enemy.
Publilius Syrus.

Ita oportuit intrare in gloriam suam. *it—a op—ore—tu—it in—trah—reh in*
gloh—ri—am su—am.
So he ought to enter into his glory.
Adapted from Vulgate. St. Luke 24.26.

Ite nunc fortes ubi celsa magni Ducit exampli via. Cur inertes Terga nudatis?
Superata tellus Sidera donat. *ee—teh nunc fore—tace ub—i kell—sa mag—nee*
doo—kit ex—em—plea we—a. coor in—air—tace tare—ga noo—dah—tiss?
sup—eh—rah—ta tell—loose seed—eh—ra doh—nat.
Go now bravely where the high road or glorious precedent leads. Why do
you timidly expose your backs? Earth conquered gives the stars.
Boethius.

Jacta alea esto. *yack–ta ah–leh–a est–oh.*
Let the die be cast.
Suetonius. Caes. 32. (Caesar, on crossing the Rubicon.)

. . . Jam desuetudine longa|Vix subeunt ipsi verba Latina mihi.
yam day–sway–too–din–eh long–gah wix sub–eh–unt ip–see wear–ba
lat–ee–na mi–hee.
From long disuse the Latin words scarcely recur to me.
Ovid. Tristia Book 5.7.57.

Jam Fides, et Pax, et Honos, Pudorque|Priscus, et neglecta redire Virtus|
Audet; apparetque beata pleno Copia cornu. *yam fid–ace, et pahk–ss,*
et hon–oce, pud–ore–queh priss–cuss, et neg–lect–ta red–ee–reh wihr–
tuss ow–det; ap–pah–ret–queh beh–ah–ta play–noe coe–pi–a core–noo.
Now Faith and Peace and Honour, and ancient Modesty and neglected
Virtue venture to return; and blessed Plenty appears with full horn.
Horace. Carmen Saeculare 57.

Jejunus raro stomachus vulgaria temnit. *yay–you–nuss rah–roe*
stom–ack–us wool–gah–ri–a tem–nit.
The hungry stomach rarely despises common food.
Horace. Sat. Book 2.2.38.

Jove enim tonante cum populo agi non esse fas.
yo–weh en–im ton–ant–eh com pop–ul–oh ag–ee none ess–seh fahss.
When Jove is thundering it is not right to be treating with the people.
Cicero. Philippics 5.3.

Judex damnatur ubi nocens absolvitur. *yoo–decks dam–nah–tur ub–i*
nock–aynce ab–sol–wit–ur.
The judge is condemned when a guilty person is acquitted.
Publilius Syrus.

Judex non potest esse testis in propria causa. *yoo—decks none pot—est ess—seh test—is in prop—ri—ah cow—sah.*
A judge cannot be a witness in one of his own cases.
Coke.

Judicis officium est, ut res, ita tempora rerum/quaerere.
you—dick—iss off—fick—i—um est, ut race, it—a—temp—or—a ray—rum quie—reh—reh.
It is the duty of a judge to enquire not only into the matter but into the circumstances of the matter.
Ovid. Tristia Book 1.1.37.

Judicium a non suo judice datum nullius est momenti.
you—dick—i—um ah none su—oh you—dick—eh da—tum null—lee—uss est moe—men—tee.
Judgment given not by the properly appointed judge, is of no consequence.
Law.

Judicium parium aut leges terrae. *you—dee—ki—um pah—ri—um out lay—gace ter—rye.*
The judgment of our equals or the laws of the land.
Magna Charta Clause 39.

Juppiter omnipotens, audacibus annue coeptis. *yup—pit—er om—nip—ot—aynce, ow—dah—kib—uss ann—nu—eh coyp—teece.*
All powerful Jupiter, be favourable to our daring attempt.
Virgil. Æneid 9.625.

Jurare in verba magistri. *yoo—rah—reh in wear—ba mag—iss—tree.*
To swear by the words of a master; to argue in favour of a thing because "the master said so."
Said of the Pupils of Pythagoras. See "Ipse dixit."

Jus cevile. *yooce key—wee—leh.*
The law of civil or private rights; the civil or common law.
Cicero. De Officiis 3.17.

Jus gentium. *yooce gent—i—um.*
The law of nations.
Cicero. De Officiis 3.17.

Jus postliminii. *yooce post—lim—in—i—ee.*
The right or law of recovery of forfeited rights.
Digesta 29.15.15. See also Cicero Pro Balbo 11.28.

Justae causae facilis est defensio. *yuss—tie cow—sigh fack—ill—iss est day—fane—si—oh.*
The defence of a just cause is easy.
Cicero.

Justissimus unus|Qui fuit in Teucris, et servantissimus aequi.
yuss—tiss—sim—uss oo—nuss quee fu—it in tew—crease, et sair—want—iss—sim—us eye—quee.
Amongst the Trojans the one most upright of all, and most observant of what is just.
Virgil. Æneid 2.427.

Justitia erga Deum religio dicitur; erga parentes pietas.
yous—ti—ti—a air—gah deh—um ray—lig—i—oh dee—kit—ur; air—gah pa—rent—ace pi—et—ahss.
Justice to God is called religion; to our parents, piety.
Cicero. De Partitione Orat. 22.78 (adapted).

Justitia est constans et perpetua voluntas suum cuique tribuens.
you—stit—i—a est cone—stahnss et pehr—pet— u—a wol—un—tahss su—um cu—ee—queh trib—u—aynce.
Justice is a constant and continual will apportioning to each man his own.
Roman Jurists after Plato's Republic 1.6. p. 331 E.

Justitia non novit patrem nec matrem; solum veritatem spectat.
yous—ti—ti—a none noe—wit pat—rem neck mah—trem; soh—lum way—rit—ah—tem speck—tat.
Justice knows neither father nor mother, but has regard only to truth.
Law.

Justitia tanta vis est, ut ne illi quidem qui maleficio et scelere pascuntur, possint sine ulla particula justitiae vivere. *you—stit—i—a tan—ta weece est, ut nay ill—lee quid—em quee mal—eff—ick—i—oh et skel—eh—reh pah—scun—tur, poss—sint sin—eh ull—lah part—ick—ull—ah you—stit—i—eye wee—weh—reh.*
So great a force is justice that not even those who live by ill-doing and crime can manage to exist without some small share of justice.
Cicero. De Off. 2.11.40.

Justitiae partes sunt non violare homines; verecundiae non offendere.
yous—ti—ti—eye parr—tace sunt none wi—ol—ah—reh hom—in—ace; weh—ray—cund—i—eye none off—fend—eh—reh.
It is the part of justice not to injure men, of propriety not to give them offence.
Cicero. De Off. 1.28.99.

Justum et tenacem propositi virum,/non civium ardor prava jubentium,/
non vultus instantis tyranni,/mente quatit solida. *yuss—tum et ten -ah—kem
proh—po—sit—ee wi rum, none key—wi—um arr—door prah—wa yub—ent—
i—um, none wool—tuss in—stan—tiss ti—ran—nee, men—teh quat—it
sol—id—ah.*
Neither the rage of the citizens commanding what is base, nor the angry
look of the threatening tyrant, can shake the upright and determined man
from his firm purpose.
Horace. Odes Book 3.3.1.

Justum judicium judicate. *yuss—tum you—ditch—i—um you—dick—ah—teh.*
Judge just judgment.
Vulgate. St. John 7.24.

Justus ut palma florebit. *yuss—tuss ut pal—ma flo—ray—bit.*
The just shall flourish as a palm-tree.
Vulgate. Ps. 92.12.

Jamque opus exegi, quod nec Jovis ira, nec ignes,/Nec poterit ferrum, nec
edax abolere vetustas. *yam—queh op—uss ik—ay—ghee, quod neck yo—wiss
ee—ra, neck ig—nace, nec pot—eh—rit fair—rum, neck ed—ahx ab—ol—ay—reh
wet—uss—tahss.*
And now I have completed a work which neither the wrath of Jove, nor
flame, nor sword, nor devouring age, can have power to destroy.
Ovid. Metam. Book 15.827.

Jam seges est ubi Troja fuit, resecandaque falce/Luxuriat Phrygio sanguine
pinguis humus. *yam seg—ess est ub—i troh—ya fu—it, reh—seck—and—a—
queh fal—keh lux—u—ri—at frig—i—oh sang—gwyn—eh pin—gwiss hum—uss.*
Fields are now where Troy was, and the ground ready for sickle and fat
with Phrygian blood, brings forth abundantly.
Ovid. Heroides 1.42.

Jam ver egelidos refert tepores,/Jam caeli furor aequinoctialis Jucundis
Zephyri silescit auris./Linquantur Phrygii, Catulle, campi Nicaeaeque ager
uber aestuosae: Ad claras Asiae volemus urbes./Jam mens praetrepidans
avet vagari,/Jam laeti studio pedes vigescunt. *yam wear ay—ghel—id—oce
reff—ehrt tep—oh—race, yam key—lee fu—ror eye—quin—ock—ti—ah—liss
you—cun—deece zeff—i—ree sill—ay—skit ow—reece. ling—quan—tur
fri—ghi—ee, cat—ull—leh, camp—ee nee—kye—eye—queh ag—ehr oo—ber
ice—tu—oh—sye: ad clah—rahss ass—i—eye wol—ay—muss ur—base. yam
maynce pry—trep—id—ahnss a—wet wag—ah—ree, yam lie—tee stud—i—oh
ped—ace wig—aysk—unt.*
Now spring brings back mild warmth, now the frenzy of the equinoctial
skies is stilled by the pleasant westerly breezes. Let the plains of Phrygia,

Catullus, be left behind, and the rich lands of hot Nicaea: let us fly to the famous cities of Asia! Now my spirit in agitation is eager to wander, now, merry with enthusiasm, my feet grow lively.
Catullus. Poem 46.1-8.

. . . Labor omnia vincit/Improbus, et duris urgens in rebus egestas. *lab—or om—ni—a wink—it im—prob—uss, et doo—reece ur—gaynce in ray—buss egg—ess—tahss.*
Persistent labour overcomes all things, and poverty spurring us on through hard surroundings.
Virgil. Georgics 1.145.

Laborare est orare. *lab—or—ah—reh est oh—rah—reh.*
To work is to pray.
Pr. Mediaeval. See "Qui orat."

Laetus in praesens animus, quod ultra est/oderit curare, et amara lento/ temperet risu. Nihil est ab omni/Parte beatum. *lie—tuss in pry—saynce an—im—us, quod ool—trah est oh—deh—rit coo—rah—reh, et am—ah—ra lent—oh tem—peh—ret ree—soo. Ni—hill est ab om—nee parr—teh beh—ah—tum.*
The mind, happy in the present, will hate to care for what is beyond, and will temper bitter things with an indifferent smile. There is nothing blessed in every particular.
Horace. Odes Book 2.16.24.

Lapsus calami. *lap—suss cal—am—eye.*
A slip of the pen.

Lapsus linguae. *lap—suss ling—gwee.*
A slip of the tongue.

Lasciva est nobis pagina, vita proba est. *lass—key—wa est noh—beece pag—ee—na, wee—ta prob—a est.*
My pages are full of licence, but my life is right.
Martial. Epig. Book 1.5.8.

... Latet anguis in herba. *lat—et an—gwiss in hair—bah.*
A snake lies hidden in the grass.
Virgil. Eclogues 3.93. (See also 'Qui Legitis'.)

Laudamus veteres, sed nostris utimur annis. *lowd—ah—muss wet—eh—race,
sed noss—treece oo—tim—ur ann—neece.*
We praise the years of old, but make the most of our own.
Ovid. Fast. 1.225.

... Laudant illa sed ista legunt. *lowd—ant ill—la sed iss—ta leg—unt.*
They praise those, but they read these books all the same.
Martial. Epig. Book 4.49.10.

Laudibus arguitur vini vinosus Homerus. *lowd—ib—uss arr—gu—it—ur
wee—nee wee—noce—uss ho—may—russ.*
By his praises of wine Homer is proved a wine-bibber.
Horace. Ep. 1.19.6.

Lector intende: laetaberis. *leck—tor in—ten—deh: lie—tah—beh—riss.*
Reader, carry on: you will enjoy yourself.
Apuleius. Metamorphoses 1.1.

Legatus est vir bonus peregrare missus ad mentiendum rei publicae causa.
*lay—gah—tuss est wihr bon—uss peh—regg—rah—reh miss—suss ad ment—i—
end—um reh—ee pub—lick—eye cow—sah.*
An ambassador is an honest man sent to tell lies abroad for the sake of his
country.
Sir Henry Wotton 1604.

Legeant prius, et postea despiciant. *ledge—eeh—ant pri—uss, et
post—eh—ah dess—pitch—i—ant.*
Let them read first and despise afterwards.
Lope de Vega.

Legem brevem esse oportet quo facilius ab imperitis teneatur.
*la—gem breh—wem ess—seh op—or—tet quoh fack—ill—i—uss ab
im—peh—rit—eece ten—eh—ah—tur.*
It is right that a law should be short in order that it may be the more easily
grasped by the unlearned.
Seneca. Ep. 94.

Leges posteriores priores contrarias abrogant. *lay—gace post—eh—ri—oh—
race pri—oh—race con—trah—ri—ahss ab—rog—ant.*
Later laws repeal former ones which are inconsistent.
Law

Legis constructio non facit injuriam. *lay–giss con–struck–ti–oh none fack–it in–you–ri–am.*
The construction (or interpretation) of the law is not to do an injury to anyone (*i.e.* the law must be interpreted so as not to do obvious injury by strict literal interpretation.)
Law.

Lesbia mi dicit semper male nec tacet umquam De me: Lesbia me dispeream nisi amat. Quo signo? quia sunt totidem mea: deprecor illam. Assidue, verum dispeream nisi amo. *lez–bi–a mee dee–kit sem–pehr mal–eh neck tack–et um–quam day may: lez–bi–a may diss–peh–reh–am niss–ee am–at. quoh sig–noh? qui–a sunt tot–id–em mah–a: day–preck–or ill–lam ass–sid–u–ay, way–rum diss–peh–reh–am niss–ee am–oh.*
Lesbia always speaks ill of me and never stops talking about me: I'll be damned, if Lesbia does not love me. How can I tell? Because with me it is just the same: I curse her continually, and yet I'll be damned, if I do not love her.
Catullus. Poem 92.

. . . Letum non omnia finit. *lay–tum none om–ni–a fee–nit.*
Death does not end all things.
Propertius 4.7.1.

Levis sit tibi terra. *leh–wiss sit tib–ee ter–ra.*
May the earth be light upon thee.
Inscription frequent on tombstones of ancient Rome. Abbreviated "S.T.T.L."

Lex aliquando sequitur aequitatem. *lakes al–i–quan–doe seh–quit–ur eye–quit–ah–tem.*
Law sometimes follows equity.
Law.

Lex appetit perfectum. *lakes ap–pet–it pair–feck–tum.*
The law aims at perfection.
Law.

Lex neminem cogit ad impossibile. *lakes nay–min–em coe–git ad im–poss–see–bill–eh.*
The law forces no one to do what is impossible.
Law.

Lex nemini operatur iniquum; nemini facit injuriam.
lakes nay–min–ee op–eh–rah–tur in–ee–quum; nay–min–ee fack–it in–you–ri–am.
The law effects injustice to no one; and does injury to no one.
Law.

[85]

Lex prospicit non respicit. *lex proh—spick—it none ress—pick—it.*
The law is prospective not retrospective.
Law.

Lex sumptuaria. *lex sump—tu—ah—ri—a.*
A sumptuary law.
Tacitus. Annals, Book 3.52. etc; also Cicero. Ep. ad Att. 13.47.1.

Lex talionis. *lex tah—li—oh—niss.*
The law of retaliation.
Pr.

Libenter homines id quod volunt credunt. *li—bent—er hom—in—ace id quod wol—unt cray—dunt.*
Men freely believe that which they desire.
Caesar. De Bello Gallico 3.18.

Libera me ab homine malo, a meipso. *lee—beh—rah may ab hom—in—eh mal—oh, ah may—ip—soh.*
Deliver me from the evil man, even from myself.
St. Augustine.

Libera me, Domine, de morte aeterna, in die illa tremenda, quando caeli movendi sunt et terra, dum veneris judicare saeculum per ignem.
lee—beh—rah may, dom—in—eh, day more—teh ay—tehr—nah, in de—ay ill—lah trem—end—ah, quan—doh chay—lee mo—ven—dee sunt et tehr—ra, dum vane—eh—riss you—dick—ah—reh sake—ull—um pehr in—yem.
Deliver me, Lord, from everlasting death, in that dreadful day, when the heavens and the earth shall be shaken, when Thou shalt come to judge the world by fire.
Responsory for the Absolution after Masses for the Dead.

Libertas est potestas faciendi id quod jure licet. *lee—bear—tahss est pot—ess—tahss fack—i—en—dee id quod you—reh lick—et.*
Liberty is the power of doing what is allowed by law.
Law.

Ligna ferre in silvam. *lig—na fehr—reh in sill—wam.*
To carry logs to the wood.
Proverbial of a pointless action.

. . . Linguae centum sunt, oraque centum|Ferrea vox. *ling—gwie kent—um sunt, oh—ra—queh kent—um fer—reh—a wohks.*
It (rumour) has a hundred tongues, a hundred mouths, a voice of iron.
Virgil. Georgics 2.44 (adapted).

[86]

Lite pendente. *lee–teh pen–dent–eh.*
Whilst the lawsuit is pending.
Law.

Litem parit lis, noxaitem noxam parit. *lee–tem pa–rit lease, nox–ait–em*
nox–am pa–rit.
Strife produces strife, and injury produces injury.
Law.

Littera enim occidit, Spiritus autem vivificat. *lit–teh–ra en–im ock–chid–*
it, spee–rit–uss ow–tem vee–vi–fick–at.
The letter kills, but the spirit makes alive.
Vulgate. 2 Cor. 3.6.

Litteratum esse, quos odisse divites solent. *lit–teh–rah–tum ess–seh,*
quoce oh–diss–seh dee–wit–ace sol–ent.
A man of letters, of the kind that rich men hate.
Petronius.

Literae humaniores. *lit–eh–ree hume–an–i–oar–ease.*
Polite literature (The title of the classical honour school at Oxford).

Lividi limis oculis semper aspiciunt aliorum commoda. *lee–wid–ee lee–*
meece ock–ul–eece sem–per ass–pick–ie–unt al–i–oh–rum com–mode–a.
Envious men always look askance upon the good fortune of others.
Cicero.

Locum tenens. *lock–um ten–enze.*
Holding the place of.

Locus classicus. *lock–uss class–sick–uss.*
The classical place.

Locus standi. *lock–uss stand–eye.*
Place of standing; position assumed in arguing.

Lucus a non lucendo. *loo–kuss ah none loo–ken–doh.*
Lucus (a grove), so called from non lucendo (not admitting light). (This
supposed derivation is referred to by Quintilian, 1, 16, and by numerous
ancient authors and commentators.)
Pr.

Lugete, O Veneres, Cupidinesque! *lug–ay–teh, oh wen–eh–race,*
cup–ee–din–ace–queh!
Mourn, O ye Venuses and Cupids!
Catullus. Carmen 3.1.

[87]

Lumina sis oculis etiam bonus ancu' reliquit. *loom—in—a seece ock—ul—eece et—yam bon—uss an—cu re—lee—quit.*
Even the good Ancus's eyes were darkened in death.
Lucretius, De Rerum Nat. 3, 1025.

Lupum auribus teneo. *lup—um ow—rib—uss ten—eh—oh.*
I hold a wolf by the ears.
Proverbial, of inextricable danger.

Lupus in fabula. *loo—puss in fah—bull—eh.*
The wolf in the story (who appeared when spoken of).
Terence. Adelphi iv. 1.21.

Lusus naturae. *luce—uss nay—ture—ee.*
A freak of nature.
Pr.

Lux in tenebris. *looks in ten—eb—reece.*
Light in darkness.
Vulgate. St. John 1.5.

Lux, etsi per immunda transeat, non inquinatur. *looks, et—see per im—mun—da trahn—seh—at, none in—quin—ah—tur.*
The light, even though it passes through pollution, is not polluted.
St. Augustine. In Joann. 4.

Lux mundi. *looks mun—dee.*
The light of the world.
Vulgate. St. John 8.12.

M

. . . Magna comitante caterva. *mag—nah com—it—ant—eh cat—air—wah.*
A great crowd accompanying.
Virgil. Æneid 2.40.

Magna dii curant, parva neglegunt. *mag—na diee coo—rant, parr—wa neg—leg—unt.*

The gods are careful about great things, and neglect small ones.
Cicero. De Nat. Deorum 2.66.

Magna est veritas, et praevalet. *mag—na est weh—rit—ahss, et prie—wal—et.*
Great is truth, and it prevails.
Vulgate. 3 Esdras. 4.41.

Magna feres tacitas solatia mortis ad umbras,/A tanto cecidisse viro.
mag—na feh—race tack—it—ahss soh—lah—ti—a more—tiss ad um—brass,
ah tan—toh keh—kid—iss—seh wi—roh.
You will carry with you the great solace to the silent shades of death, that
you were vanquished by so great a man.
Ovid. Metam. Book 5.191.

Magna movet stomacho fastidia, seu puer unctis./Tractavit calicem manibus.
mag—na mo—wet stom—ack—oh fass—tee—di—a, sue pu—er unc—teese
track—tah—wit cal—ick—em man—ib—uss.
An intense disgust turns the stomach, should the servant touch the cup
with his greasy hands.
Horace. Sat. Book 2.4.78.

Magnanimi heroes, nati melioribus annis. *mag—nan—im—ee hay—roe—ess,*
nah—tee mel—i—oh—rib—uss ann—neece.
Great-souled heroes, born in happier years.
Virgil. Æneid 6.64.

Magnas inter opes inops. *mag—nahss in—ter op—ace in—ops.*
A pauper in the midst of wealth.
Horace. Odes. Book 3.16.28.

Magni animi est proprium placidum esse, tranquillumque, et injurias atque
offensiones semper despicere. *mag—nee an—im—ee est prop—ri—um*
plack—id—um ess—seh, tran—quill—lum—queh, et in—you—ri—ahss at—queh
off—fence—i—oh—nace sem—per day—spick—eh—reh.
It is the nature of a great mind to be calm and undisturbed, and ever to
despite injuries and misfortunes.
Seneca. De Clementia 1.5.

. . . Magni nominis umbra. *mag—nee noe—min—iss um—bra.*
The shadow of a great name.
Lucan. Pharsalia Bk. 1.135.

Magno jam conatu magnas nugas dixerit. *mag—noe yam coe—nah—too*
mag—nahss noog—ahss dix—eh—rit.
She will set forth great trifles with great effort.
Terence. Heautontimorumenos 4.1.8.

. . . Magnorum haud unquam indignus avorum. *mag—noe—rum howd un—quam in—dig—nuss a—woh—rum.*
Never at any time unworthy of his great ancestors.
Virgil. Æneid. 12.649.

Magnum in parvo. *mag—num in parr—woe.*
A great deal in a small space.
Pr.

Magnum iter ascendo, sed dat mihi gloria vires. *mag—num it—ehr ass—ken—doh, sed dat mih—he gloh—ri—a wee—race.*
Great are the heights I must climb, but glory gives me strength.
Propertius. Elegies 4.10.3.

Magnum narras vix credibile. *mag—num nahr—rahss wicks cray–dee—bill—eh.*
You relate a great thing hardly to be believed.
Horace. Sat., Book 1.9.52.

Magnus ab integro saeclorum nascitur ordo. *mag—nuss ab in—teg—roe sigh—kloh—rum na—skit—ur ore—doh.*
The great course of the ages is born anew.
Virgil. Eclogues, 4.5. (See also 'Ultima Cumaei').

Magnus animus remissius loquitur et securius. *mag—nuss an—im—us rem—iss—si—uss lo—quit—ur et say—coo—ri—uss.*
A great mind speaks with more ease and more composure.
Seneca.

Major et apud posteros futurus, si minor esse voluisset. *mah—yor et ap—ud poss—teh—ros fut—oo—russ, see min—or ess—seh wol—u—iss—set.*
He would be greater to posterity if he had been willing to be less great.
Aubrotus Miraeus. Elogia Belgica. Of Erasmus.

Major privato visus, dum privatus fuit, et omnium consensu capax imperii, nisi imperasset. *mah—your pree—wah—toe wee—suss, dum pree—wah—tuss fu—it, et om—ni—um cone—sane—soo cap—ahks im—peh—ri—ee, niss—ee im—peh—rahss—set.*
He seemed greater than a private citizen while he was one, and by the consent of all would have been considered capable of government, if he had not governed.
Tacitus. Hist., 1.49.

... Major rerum mihi nascitur ordo, Majus opus moveo.
*mah—your ray—rum mi—hee nah—skit—ur orr—doh, mah—yuss op—uss
mo—weh—oh.*
A greater train of events springs up before me; I undertake a more difficult
task.
Virgil. Æneid 7.44.

Majora credi de absentibus. *mah—your—a cray—dee day ap—sent—ib—uss.*
Greater things are believed of those who are absent.
Tacitus. Hist. Book 2.83.

Majorum gloria posteris lumen est. *mah—your—em gloh—ri—a post—eh—reece
loo—men est.*
Ancestral glory is a lamp to posterity.
Sallust. Jugurtha 85.

Mala mali malo mala contulit omnia mundo,/Causa mali tanti femina
sola fuit. *mah—la mal—ee mah—loh mal—a con—tul—it om—ni—a
mun—doh, cow—sa mal—ee tan—tee fay—min—a soh—la fu—it.*
The jawbone of the evil one brought all evil to the world by means of an
apple; the cause of so much evil was woman alone.
Mediaeval.

Mala ultro adsunt. *mal—a ult—roe ad—sunt.*
Evil things come spontaneously.
Pr.

Malam rem cum velis honestare, improbes. *mal—am rem cum wellis
hon—ess—tah—reh, im—prob—ace.*
When you wish to dignify a thing which is bad, disapprove it.
Publilius Syrus.

Male narrando fabula depravatur. *mal—eh narr—ran—doh fah—bull—a
day—prah—wah—tur.*
A story is ruined through being badly told.
Pr.

... Malignum spernere vulgus. *ma—lig—num spare—neh—reh wool—guss.*
To scorn the ill-conditioned rabble.
Horace. Odes Book 2.16.39.

Malivolus semper sua natura vescitur. *mal—i—wol—uss sem—per su—ah
nah—too—rah wess—kit—ur.*
An evil-disposed person feeds always upon his own disposition.
Publilius Syrus.

[91]

Malo in consilio feminae vincunt viros. *mal—oh in cone—sill—i—oh fay—min—eye wink—unt wi—roce.*
Women beat men in evil counsel.
Publilius Syrus.

Malorus immensa vorago et gurges. *mal—oh—rus im—main—sa wo—rah—goe et gur—gace.*
An immense gulf and whirlpool of evils.
Adapted from Cicero.

Malum est consilium quod mutari non potest. *mal—um est cone—sill—i—um quod moo—tah—ree none pot—est.*
It is bad counsel which cannot be altered.
Publilius Syrus.

Malus, bonum ubi se simulat, tunc est pessimus. *mal—uss, bon—um ub—i say sim—ull—at, tunc est pess—sim—uss.*
A bad man is worst of all when he pretends to be good.
Publilius Syrus.

Mandare suspendium alicui. *man—dah—re suss—pend—i—um al—ick—u—ee.*
To order anyone to be hanged.
Apuleius

Manibus pedibusque. *man—ib—uss ped—ib—uss—queh.*
With hands and feet; with all one's power.
Pr.

Mantua me genuit; Calabri rapuere; tenet nunc/Parthenope. Cecini pascua, rura, duces. *man—tu—a may gen—u—it; cal—ab—ree rap—u—ay—re; ten—et nunc par—then—op—ay. ceck—in—ee pass—cu—a, roo—ra, duc—ace.*
Mantua bore me; the people of Calabria carried me off; Parthenope (Naples) holds me now. I have sung of pastures, of fields, of chieftains.
Virgil's Epitaph, said to be by himself.

Manum de tabula! *man—um day tab—ull—ah!*
Take your hand from the picture; desist from touching it up further.
Cicero. Ep. 7.25.1.

Mare clausum. *ma—reh clow—sum.*
A sea closed (to commerce).

Margarita e stercore. *mar—gar—ita ay ster—corr.*
A pearl from the dunghill.
Pr.

Maria montesque polliceri coepit. *ma—ri—a mon—tace—queh poll—lick—ay—ree coy—pit.*
He began to promise seas and mountains.
Sallust. Catilina 23.3 (Pr.)

Maxima bella ex levissimis causis. *max—im—a bell—la ex leh—wiss—sim—eece cow—seece.*
The greatest feuds have had the smallest causes.
Pr.

Maxima debetur puero reverentia. . . . *max—im—a day—bay—tur pu—eh—roh reh—weh—rent—i—a.*
The greatest regard is due to a child.
Juvenal. Sat. 14.47.

Maximum remedium est irae mora. *max—im—um ray—med—i—um est ee—rye mo—ra.*
Delay is the greatest remedy for anger.
Seneca. De Ira 2.28.

Me laudent doctae solum placuisse puellae, Pontice, et injustas saepe tulisse minas. *may loud—ent dock—tie soh—lum plack—u—iss—seh pu—ell—lie, pon—tick—eh, et in—you—stahss sye—peh tul—iss—seh min—ahss.*
Let my praise be only that I pleased a learned girl, Ponticus, and often bore her unfair threats.
Propertius. Elegies 1.7.11f.

Me, me; adsum qui feci; in me convertite ferrum. *may, may; ad—sum quee fay—key; in may con—wear—u teh ferr—rum.*
Seize me, seize me; I am here who have done it; turn your sword against me.
Virgil. Æneid 9.427.

. . . Me nemo ministro/fur erit. . . . *may, nay—mo min—ist—roh foor eh—rit.*
No one shall be a thief with me as his helper.
Juvenal. Sat. 3.46.

Me raris juvat auribus placere. *may rah—reece yu—wat ow—rib—uss plack—ay—reh.*
It is my delight to give pleasure to a select few.
Martial. Epig. Book 2.86.12.

Mea culpa, mea culpa, mea maxima culpa. *meh—ah cul—pah, meh—a cul—pah, mea max—im—ah cul—pah.*
My sin, my sin, my grievous sin.
Missal.

[93]

. . . Mea fraus omnis: nihil iste, nec ausus,/Nec potuit; coelum hoc, et conscia sidera testor. *mah—a frowse om—niss: ni—hill iss—teh, neck ow—suss, neck pot—u—it; coy—lum hoke, et cone—ski—a see—deh—ra test—or.* Mine is all the deceit: he neither dared nor was capable of, any part of it; this I call heaven to witness and the stars which know the truth. *Virgil. Æneid 9.428.*

. . . Mea/Virtute me involvo. *meh—ah wihr—too—teh may in—wol—woe.* I wrap myself up in my virtue. *Horace. Odes Book 3.29.54.*

Medice, cura teipsum. *med—ic—eh, coo—rah tay—ip—sum.* Physician, heal thyself. *Vulgate. St. Luke 4.23.*

Medicina calamitatis est aequanimitas. *med—ick—ee—na cal—am—it—ah—tiss est eye—quan—im—it—ahss.* The medicine for disaster is even-mindedness. *Publilius Syrus.*

Medio tutissimus ibis. *med—i—oh too—tiss—sim—uss ee—biss.* You will go safest by the middle course. *Ovid. Metam. 2.137.*

Me juvet in gremio doctae legisse puellae, Auribus et puris scripta probasse mea. *may yu—wet in grem—i—oh dock—tie lay—ghiss—seh pu—ell—lie, ow—rib—uss et poo—reece scrip—ta prob—ahss—seh meh—a.* I enjoy having read my verse as I lay on the breast of a learned girl, and having pleased her pure ears with my writings. *Propertius. Elegies 2.13.11f.*

Meliora sunt ea quae natura, quam quae arte perfecta sunt. *mel—i—oh—ra sunt eh—a quie nah—too—rah, quam quie arr—teh pair—fect—a sunt.* Better are those things which are finished by nature, than those finished by art. *Cicero.*

Mellitum venenum blanda oratio. *mel—lit—um wen—ay—num blan—da oh—rah—ti—oh.* A flattering speech is a honeyed poison. *Pr.*

Memento Mori. *mem—en—toe more—eye.* Remember that you must die. *Pr.*

Memento semper finis, et quia perditum non redit tempus.
men—en—toe sem—pair fee—niss, et qui—a pair—dit—um none red—it tem—puss.
Remember always your end, and that lost time does not return.
Thomas 'a Kempis, Imit. Christi, Book 1. ch. 25.11.

Mendacium in damnum potens. *men—dah—ki—um in dam—num pot—aynce.*
A falsehood powerful in working injury.
Petronius. Capture of Troy.

Mendico ne parentes quidem amici sunt. *men—dee—coe nay pa—ren—tace quid—em am—ee—key sunt.*
Not even his own parents are friends to a beggar.
Pr.

Mens cujusque is est quisque. *maince coo—yuss—queh iss est quiss—queh.*
Each man's mind is the man himself.
Cicero. De Republica.

Mens immota manet; lacrimae volvuntur inanes. *maynce im—mote—a man—et; lack—rim—eye wol—wunt—ur in—ah—nace.*
His mind remains unshaken; the tears flow in vain.
Virgil. Æneid 4.449.

Mensa et toro. *main—sah et to—roe.*
From bed and board.
Law.

. . . Mens omnibus una sequendi. *maynce om—nib—uss oo—na seh—quen—dee.*
All have the same inclination to follow.
Virgil. Æneid 10.182.

Mens sana in corpore sano. *maynce sah—nah in cor—por—is sah—noh.*
A sound mind in a sound body.
Juvenal.

Mens sibi conscia recti. *maince sib—e cone—ski—a reck—tee.*
A mind knowing what is right.
Virgil. Æneid 1.604.

. . . Meorum/finis amorum. *meh—oh—rum fee—niss a—moh—rum.*
End (*i.e.* last and final) of my loves.
Horace. Odes Book 4.11.31.

[95]

Meum est propositum in taberna mori;/vinum sit appositum morientis ori,/
ut dicant cum venerint angelorum chori,/"Deus sit propitius huic potatori!"
*meh–um est proh–pos–it–um in tab–air–nah moh–ree; vee–num sit
ap–pos–it–um more–i–ent–iss oh–ree, ut dee–cant cum vain–eh–rint
an–gel–oh–rum coh–ree, "deh–uss sit proh–peet–si–uss hoo–ic poe–
tah–toe–ree!"*
It is my intention to die in a tavern; let the wine be placed near to my
mouth as I expire, so that when the choirs of angels come, they may say,
"God be merciful to this drinker!"
Carmina Burana. (A collection of medieval songs).

Mi neque amare aliam neque ab hac desciscere fas est: Cynthia prima fuit,
Cynthia finis erit. *mee neh–queh am–ah–reh al–i–am neh–queh ab hahk
day–skee–skeh–reh fahss est: kint–he–a pree–ma fu–it, kint–he–a
fee–niss eh–rit.*
For me it is lawful neither to love another nor to desert this one: Cynthia
was the first, Cynthia shall be the end.
Propertius. Elegies 1.12.19f.

. . . Micat inter omnes/Julium sidus, velut inter ignes/Luna minores.
*mick–at in–ter om–nace you–li–um see–duss, well–ut in–ter ig–nace
loo–na min–oh–race.*
The Julian star (the fame of Marcellus married to Julia) shines out among
them all, even as the moon among the lesser lights of heaven.
Horace. Odes Book 1.12.46.

Mihi forsan, tibi quod negarit,/porriget hora. *mi–he fore–san, tib–i quod
neg–ah–rit, por–rig–it hoe–ra.*
To me, perhaps, the hour will reach out what it denied to you.
Horace. Odes, Book 2.16.31.

Mihi quanto plura recentium seu veterum revolvo tanto magis ludibria
rerum mortalium cunctis in negotiis obversantur. Quippe fama spe
veneratione potius omnes destinabantur imperio quam quem futurum
principem fortuna in occulto tenebat. *mi–he quan–toe ploo–ra reck–en–
ti–um sue wet–eh–rum reh–wol–woe tan–toe mag–iss lood–ib–ri–a
ray–rum more–tah–li–um cunk–teece in neg–oh–ti–eece ob–wehr–
san–tur. quip–peh fah–mah spay wen–eh–rah–ti–oh–neh pot–i–uss
om–nace day–stin–ah–ban–tur im–peh–ri–oh quam quem fut–oo–rum
prin–kip–em for–too–na in ock–cull–toe ten–ay–bat.*
The more I consider events recent or long past, the more laughable in every
aspect do human affairs seem to me. For in renown, expectation, and esteem
everyone was more likely to become emperor than the man whom Fortune
was secretly keeping for that purpose. Claudius.
Tacitus. Annals 3.18.

[96]

Miles gloriosus. *mil—ace gloh—ri—oh—suss.*
A vain glorious soldier.
Plautus. Title of Comedy.

Militiae species amor est. . . . *mil—it—i—eye speck—i—ace am—or est.*
Love is a kind of warfare.
Ovid. Ars Amat. Book 2.233.

Mille modi veneris. *mil—leh mod—ee wen—eh—riss.*
There are a thousand ways of making love.
Ovid. Ars Amat. Book 3.787.

Ministri sceleribus. *min—iss—tree skeh—leh—rib—uss.*
Ministers to his crimes.
Tacitus. Annais, Book 6.36.

. . . Minuentur atrae/carmine curae. *min—u—en—tur ah—try carr—min—eh
coo—rye.*
Gloomy cares will be made less by song.
Horace. Odes, Book 4.11.

. . . Minus aptus acutis/naribus horum hominum. . . . *min—uss ap—tuss
a—coo—teece nah—rib—uss hoe—rum hom—in—um.*
Less ready against the sharp sneers of these men.
Horace. Sat. Book 1.3.29.

Minus hercule calles pravissimis opinionibus ea putari mendacia quae vel
auditu nova vel visu rudia vel certe supra captum cogitationis ardua videan-
tur; quae si paulo accuratius exploraris, non modo compertu evidentia
verum etiam factu facilia senties. *min—uss hehr—cull—eh cal—lace prah—
wiss—sim—eece op—ee—ni—oh—nib—uss eh—a put—ah—ree men—dah—ki—a
quie well ow—dee—too no—wah well wee—soo rud—i—a well care—tay sup—
rah cap—tum cog—it—ah—ti—oh—niss are—du—a wid—eh—ant—ur; quie see
pow—loh ack—coo—rah—ti—uss ex—ploh—rah—riss, none mod—oh com—
pair—too ay—wid—en—ti—a way—rum et—yam fack—too fack—ill—i—a
sen—ti—ace.*
You certainly have little knowledge of how the stupid foolishly believe that
those things are lies which seem new to their ears, or awkward to their eyes,
or indeed too difficult for their intelligence to reach; but if you look at them
more carefully, you will find them not only obviously true but even easily
done.
Apuleius. Metamorphoses 1.3.

Minus saepe pecces si scias quid nescias. *min—uss sigh—peh peck—case see*

ski—ahss quid ness—ki—ahss.
Often you sin less if you know what you are ignorant of.
Publilius Syrus.

Mirabile dictu. *mee—rah—bil—eh dick—too.*
Wonderful to say.
Cicero, Virgil etc.

Mirum est lolio victitare te, tam vili tritico. *mee—rum est lol—i—oh wick—it—tah—reh tay, tam wee—lee trit—ick—oh.*
It is strange that you should live on tares when wheat is so cheap.
Plautus. Miles Gloriosus i.

. . . Misera est magni custodia census. *miss—eh—ra est nag—nee cuss—toe—di—a cane—sooce.*
The care of a great fortune is wretchedness.
Juvenal. Sat. 14.304.

Miserere mei. *miss—eh—ray—re meh—ee.*
Have mercy on me.
Vulgate. Ps. 51. 1.

Miserum credo, cui placet nemo. *miss—eh—rum cray—doh, cu—ee plack—et nay—moe.*
I consider him an unhappy man whom no one pleases.
Martial. Epig. Book 5.29.9.

. . . Mitte hanc de pectore curam. *mitt—teh hanc day peck—to—reh coo—ram.*
Dismiss this anxiety from your breast.
Virgil. Æneid 6.85.

. . . Mobilium turba quiritium. *moe—bill—i—um tour—ba qui—rit—i—um.*
The crowd of changeable citizens.
Horace. Odes Book 1.1.7.

Modicae fidei, quare dubitasti? *mod—itch—ay fid—eh—ee, quah—ay dub—it—ah—stee?*
O thou of little faith, wherefore didst thou doubt?
Vulgate. St. Matthew 14.31.

Modo liceat vivere est spes. *moo—doh lick—ee—at wee—weh—reh est space.*
While there's life there's hope.

Modus operandi. *mo—duss op—er—an—die.*
Method of doing anything.

Modus vivendi. *mo—dus viv—en—die.*
A means of existing; said of a compromise effected.

Molle meum levibus cor est violabile telis. *moll—leh meh—um leh—wib—uss core est wi—ol—ah—bill—eh tay—lease.*
My tender heart is subject to injury from the light arrows (of Cupid).
Ovid. Heroides, 15.79.

Mollissima tempora fandi. *moll—liss—sim—a tem—po—ra fahn—dee.*
The most impressionable time for speaking.
Virgil. Æneid 4.293.

Mone sale. *mon—ay sal—eh.*
Advise with wit.
Pr.

Moniti, meliora sequamur. *mon—it—te, mel—i—oh—ra seh—quah—mur.*
Admonished, let us follow better things.
Virgil. Æneid 3.188.

Monstrum horrendum, informe, ingens, cui lumen ademptum.
moan—strum horr—rend—um, in—form—eh, in—gaynce, cu—ee loom—en ad—emp—tum.
A monster frightful, formless, immense, with sight removed.
Virgil. Æneid 3.658.

More majorum. *moh-reh mah—yoh—rum.*
After the fashion of our ancestors.
Pr.

Mores deteriores increbescunt. *moh—race day—teh—ri—oh—race in—creb—ay—scunt.*
Degenerate manners grow apace.
Plautus. Mercator v. 1.9.

Moribus antiquis res stat Romana virisque. *moh—rib—uss an—teak—weece race stat Roe—mah—na wi—reece—queh.*
The Roman state stands by its customs and men of ancient times.
Ennius.

. . . Mors ipsa refugit/saepe virum. . . . *morse ip—sa re—foo—git sigh—peh wi—rum.*

[99]

Death itself has often run away from a man.
Lucan. Pharsalia Book 2.74.

Mors laborum ac miseriarum quies est. *morse lab—oh—rum ac miss—eh—ri—ah—rum qui—ace est.*
Death is rest from labours and miseries.
Cicero (adapted). Catil. 4.4.7.

Mortales inimicitias, sempiternas amicitias. *more—tah—lace in—im—ee—kit—i—ahss, sem—pit—air—nahss am—ee—kit—i—ahss.*
Our enmities mortal, our friendships eternal.
Cicero. Pro Rab. Postumo. 12.32.

Mortalium rerum misera beatitudo. *more—tah—li—um ray—rum miss—eh—ra beh—ah—ti—too—doh.*
Wretched is the bliss of mortal affairs.
Boethius.

Mortuum flagellas. *more—tu—um flag—ell—lahss.*
You are beating the dead.
Pr.

. . . Motos praestat componere fluctus. *moh—toce pry—stat com—poe—neh—reh fluck—tooce.*
It is better to allay the troubled waters.
Virgil. Æneid 1.135.

. . . Mulier cupido quod dicit amanti/In vento et rapida scribere oportet aqua. *mul—i—air cup—id—oh quod dee—kit am—an—tee in went—oh et rap—id—ah scree—beh—reh op—or—tet a—quah.*
What a woman tells her lover should be written in the wind or in the running water.
Catullus. Carmen 70.

Mulier est hominis confusio. *mul—i—air est hom—in—is cone—foo—si—oh.*
Woman is man's confusion (*i.e.* confounding).
Vincent of Beauvais. Spec. 346.

Mulieres duas pejores esse quam unam. *mul—i—eh—race du—ahss pay—yoh—race ess—seh quam oo—nam.*
Two women are worse than one.
Plautus. Curculio v. 1.2.

Multa fidem promissa levant. . . . *mul—ta fid—em proh—miss—sa leh—want.*

[100]

Many promises impair confidence.
Horace. Ep. Book 2.2.10.

Multa novit vulpis, sed felis unum magnum. *mul—ta noh—wit wool—pis, sed fail—iss oo—num mag—num.*
The fox knows many devices, but the cat one great one only (*i.e.* climbing a tree).
Pr.

Multa senem circumveniunt incommoda. . . . *mul—ta sen—em kihr—cum—wen—i—unt in—com—mod—a.*
Many disadvantages attend an old man.
Horace. De Arte Poetica 169.

Multi multa, nemo omnia novit. *mull—tee mull—ta, nay—moh om—ni—a noe—wit.*
Many have known many things, no one all things.
Coke.

Multis minatur, qui uni facit injuriam. *mul—teece min—ah—tur, quee oo—nee fack—it in—you—ri—am.*
He who does an injury to one, threatens many.
Publilius Syrus.

Multis terribilis, caveto multos. *mul—teece ter—rib—il—iss, ca—way—toe mul—toos.*
Being a cause of fear to many, beware of many.
Ausonius.

. . . Multum est demissus homo. . . . *mul—tum est day—miss—suss hom—oh.*
He is a very unassuming man.
Horace. Sat. Book 1.3.57.

. . . Multum ille et terris jactatus et alto. *mul—tum ill—leh et teh—reece yak—tah—tuss et al—toe.*
Much was he cast about both by land and by sea.
Virgil. Æneid 1.3.

Multum legendum esse non multa. *mul—tum leg—end—um ess—seh none mul—ta.*
Read much, not many (things, *or* books).
Pliny the Younger. Ep. Book 7.9.

Mundus universus exercet histrionem. *mun—duss oo—ni—wear—suss*

ex—air—ket hiss—tri—oh—nem.
The whole world cultivates (the art of) the actor.
Petronius Arbiter.

Munit haec et altera vincit. *moon—it hike et al—teh—ra wing—kit.*
This defends and that conquers.
Pr.

Murum ligneum. *moo—rum lig—neh—um.*
A wooden wall (the Delphic Oracle's expression, meaning a ship.)
Cornelius Nepos.

Mutatis mutandis. *mute—ate—ize mut—and—ize.*
Those things being exchanged which the sense requires should be changed.
Law.

Mutum est pictura poema. *moo—tum est pic—too—ra po—ay—ma.*
A picture is a dumb poem.
Pr.

. . . Nam dives qui fieri vult,/Et cito vult fieri. . . . *nam dee—wace quee fi—eh—ree wult, et kit—o wult fi—eh—ree.*
For he who desires to become rich desires also to become rich quickly.
Juvenal. Sat. 14.176.

Nam et ipsa scientia potestas est. *nam et ip—sa ski—en—ti—a pot—est—ahss est.*
For knowledge itself is power.
Francis Bacon, 1561-1626. Religious Meditations of Heresies.

Nam multum loquaces merito omnes habemur. *nam mull—tum lo—quah—case meh—rit—oh om—nace hab—ay—mur.*
For we (women) are all rightly considered very talkative.
Plautus. Aulularia ii.2.5.

Nam neque Pyramidum sumptus ad sidera ducti, Nec Jovis Elei caelum imitata domus, Nec Mausolei dives fortuna sepulcri, Mortis ab extrema

condicione vacant. *nam neh—queh pea—ram—id—um sump—tooce ad see—deh—ra duck—tee, neck yo—wiss ay—lay—ee kye—lum im—it—ah—ta dom—uss, neck mouse—oh—lay—ee dee—wace fore—too—na sep—ull—cree, more—tiss ab ex—tray—mah con—dick—i—oh—neh wack—ant.*
For neither the Pyramids raised to the stars at such cost, nor the temple of Jupiter at Elis that matches the skies, nor the great wealth of Mausolus' tomb, are free from the end imposed by death.
Propertius. Elegies 3.2.19-22.

Nam tua res agitur, paries cum proximus ardet;/Et neglecta solent incendia sumere vires. *nam tu—a race ag—it—ur, pa—ri—ace cum prox—im—us arr—det; et neg—lect—a sol—ent in—ken—di—a soo—meh—reh wee—race.*
For it is your concern surely when the wall of your neighbour's house is burning; and fire neglected is apt to gain in power.
Horace. Ep. Book 1.18.84.

Namque erit ille mihi semper Deus. *nam—queh er—it ill—leh mi—hee sem—pair deh—uss.*
For he shall always be to me as a God.
Virgil. Eclogues 1.7.

Nascimur poetae, fimus oratores. *nah—skim—ur po—ay—tie, fee—muss oh—rah—toe—race.*
We are born poets, we are made orators.
Attributed to Cicero.

Natio comoeda est. *nat—ti—oh coe—moy—da est.*
The nation is like a comedy.
Juvenal. Sat. 3.100.

Natura abhorret vacuum. *nah—too—ra ab—horr—ret wack—u—um.*
Nature abhors a vacuum.
Pr.

Natura naturans. *nah—too—ra nah—too—rahnss.*
Nature causing nature.
Pr.

Natura, quam te colimus inviti quoque! *nah—too—ra, quam tay coll—im—uss in—wee—tee quo—queh!*
O Nature, how we worship thee even against our wills!
Seneca. Hippolytus Act iv. 1116.

Naturam expellas furca, tamen usque recurret. *nah—too—ram ex—pell—lahass foor—kah, tam—en uss—queh re—curr—ret.*

You may drive out nature with a fork, but she will ever return again.
Horace. Ep. Book 1.10.24.

Naturam quidem mutare difficile est. *nah—too—ram quid—em moot—ah—reh diff—fick—il—eh est.*
It is difficult indeed to change nature.
Seneca. De Ira Bk. 2.20.

Naufragium sibi quisque facit. . . . *now—frag—i—um sib—ee quis—queh fack—it.*
Each man makes his own shipwreck.
Lucan. Pharsalia 1.499.

Ne credas laudatoribus tuis. *nay cray—dahss low—dah—toe—rib—uss tu—eece.*
Do not believe those who praise you.
Pr.

Ne cuivis dextram injeceris. *nay cu—ee—wiss dayk—stram in—yay—keh—riss.*
Do not effusively offer your right hand to everyone.
Pr.

Ne feminae quidem exsortes periculi: quia occupandi rei publicae argui non poterant, ob lacrimas incusabantur. *nay fame—in—eye quid—em ex—sore—tace peh—ree—cull—ee: qui—a ock—cup—an—dee reh—ee pub—lick—eye are—gu—ee none pot—eh—rant, ob lack—rim—ahce ink—oo—sah—ban—tur.*
Not even women were immune from the danger: because they could not be charged with taking control of the State, they were accused of weeping.
Tacitus. Annals 6.10.

Ne plus ultra. *nee plus ul—tra.*
No more beyond (*i.e.* There is nothing which surpasses this).

Ne prius antidotum quam venenum. *nay pri—uss ant—tid—ot—um quam wen—ay—num.*
So not take the antidote before the poison.
Pr.

Ne puero gladium. *nay pu—eh—roh glad—i—um.*
Do not give a child a sword.
Pr.

Ne quid respublica detrimenti accipiat. *nay quid race—pub—lick—a day—trim—ent—ee ack—kip—i—at.*

Let not the commonwealth suffer any injury.
Caesar. Bellum Civile 1.5.3. and Cicero. Pro Milone, 26.70; etc.

Ne sutor supra crepidam. *nay soo—tor soo—prah cray—pee—dam.*
Let not the cobbler go above his last.
Pliny. N.H. 35.36.

Ne sutor ultra crepidam. *nay soo—tor ul—trah cray—pee—dam.*
Let not the cobbler go beyond his last.
Erasmus. Quoted as a proverb.

. . . Ne tempora perde precando. *nay tem—po—ra pair—deh preck—and—oh.*
Do not lose the time in praying.
Ovid. Metam. 11.286.

Ne vile fano. *nay wee—leh fah—noe.*
Bring nothing vile to the temple.
Pr.

Nec cui de te plusquam tibi credas. *neck cu—ee day tay plooce—quam tib—ee cray—dahss.*
Do not believe anyone about yourself more than yourself.
Pr.

. . . Nec divis homines componier aequum est. *neck dee—weece hom—in—ace com—poe—ni—er eye—quum est.*
Nor is it fair to compare men with gods.
Catullus. Carm. 68.141.

Nec in negotiis erit negotii causa. *neck in neg—oh—ti—eece eh—rit neg—oh—ti—ee cow—sa.*
Nor will he be in business for the mere sake of being busy.
Seneca. Epist. 22.

Nec magis incepto vultum sermone movetur,/quam si dura silex aut stet Marpesia cautes. *neck mag—iss in—kept—oh wool—tum sair—moe—neh mo—way—tur, quam see doo—ra sil—ex owt stet mar—pay—si—a cow—tace.*
Nor was she more moved in her expression by his words, than if she had stood there a piece of hard stone, or the rugged rock Marpesia.
Virgil. Æneid 6.470.

. . . Nec me meminisse pigebit Elissae:/dum memor ipse mei, dum spiritus hos reget artus. *neck may mem—in—iss—seh pig—ay—bit eh—liss—sie: dum memor ip—seh meh—ee, dum spee—rit—uss hoce reg—et ar—tooce.*

Nor shall it ever vex me to remember Elissa whilst I shall remember myself, or whilst the life rules these limbs of mine.
Virgil. Æneid 4.335.

Nec mihi jam patriam antiquam spes ulla videndi,/Nec dulces natos.
neck mi—hee yam pat—ri—am an—tee—quam space ull—la wid—end—ee, neck dull—case nah—toce.
Nor have I now any hope of seeing my ancient country or my sweet children.
Virgil. Æneid 2.137.

Nec misere quisquam, qui bene vixit, obit. *neck miss—eh—ray quiss—quam, quee ben—eh week—sit, ob—it.*
No one has died miserably who has lived well.

Nec molles opu' sunt motus uxoribus hilum. *neck moll—lace op—uss—unt moe—tooce ux—oh—rib—uss hee—lum.*
Wives have no need to use lascivious movements.
Lucretius. De rerum natura 4.1268.

Nec obolum habet unde restim emat. *neck ob—oll—um hab—et un—deh ress—tim eh—mat.*
Nor has he a penny left to buy a rope with.
Pr.

Nec pietas ullast velatum saepe videri Vertier ad lapidem atque omnis accedere ad aras . . . Sed mage pacata posse omnia mente tueri.
neck pi—et—ahss ull—last way—lah—tum sye—peh wid—ay—ree wear—ti—ehr ad lap—id—em at—queh om—neece ack—kay—deh—reh ad ah—rahss . . . sed mag—eh pah—kah—tah poss—seh om—ni—a men—teh tu—ay—ree.
Nor is there any piety in being often seen bowing one's veiled head before a stone or going up to every altar . . . but rather in being able to observe the universe with a quiet mind.
Lucretius. De reum natura 5.1198f. & 1203.

. . . Nec placidam membris dat cura quietem. *neck plack—id—am mem—breece dat coo—ra qui—ay—tem.*
Nor does care grant quiet rest to the limbs.
Virgil. Æneid 4.5.

Nec quaerere nec spernere honorem. *neck quie—reh—reh neck spare—neh—reh hon—oh—rem.*
Neither to seek nor to despise honour.
Pr.

Nec scire fas est omnia. *neck skee—reh fahss est om—ni—a.*

It is not allowed us to know everything.
Horace. Odes Book 4.4.22.

Nec servum meliorem ullum, nec deteriorem dominum fuisse.
neck sair—wum mel—i—oh—rem ull—lum, nec day—teh—ri—oh—rem dom—in—um fu—iss—seh.
There was never any better servant, nor any worse master.
Suetonius.

Nec sibi, sed toti genitum se credere mundo. *neck sib—i, sed toe—tee gen—it—um say cray—deh—reh mun—doh.*
To believe himself born, not for himself, but for the whole world.
Lucan. Pharsalia 2.383.

Nec sit terris ultima/Thule. *neck sit ter—reece ul—tim—a thoo—leh.*
Nor shall Thule be the extremity of the world.
Seneca. Medea iii. 375.

Nec sumit aut ponit secures/arbitrio popularis aurae. *neck soo—mit owt po—nit say—coo—race ar—bit—ri—oh pop—ul—ah—ris ow—rye.*
Nor does he assume or resign the supreme power at the bidding of popular favour.
Horace. Odes Book 3.2.19.

Nec te quaesiveris extra. *neck tay quie—see—weh—riss ex—trah.*
And ask no opinion but your own.
Persius. Satires 1.7.

Necesse est facere sumptum, qui quaerit lucrum. *neck—ess—seh est fack—eh—reh sump—tum, quee quee—rit luck—rum.*
It is necessary that he who seeks gain should first have to incur expense.
Plautus.

Necessitas non habet legem. *neck—ess—it—ahss none hab—et lay—gem.*
Necessity has no law.
Pr. Attr. to Publilius Syrus.

Necessitati quod libet telum utile est. *neck—ess—sit—ah—tee quod lib—et tay—lum oo—till—eh est.*
Any sort of weapon is useful to necessity.
Publilius Syrus.

Nemine contradicente (*or* nemine dissentiente). *nem—in—i con—tra—die—sent—i (nem—in—i diss—sent—i—ent—i).*
No one speaking to the contrary; or, no one differing in opinion.

[107]

Nemini credo qui large blandus est. *nay—min—ee cray—do quee larr—gay bland—uss est.*
I believe no one who is profuse with flattery.
Plautus. Aulularia ii. 2.19.

Nemo allegans suam turpitudinem audiendus. *nay—moe al—leg—ah—nss su—am tur—pit—oo—din—em ow—di—end—uss.*
No one testifying to his own baseness should be listened to.
Law.

Nemo contra Deum nisi deus ipse. *nay—moh con—trah deh—um niss—ee deh—uss ip—seh.*
No one against God, except God himself.
Pr. Quoted by Goethe in his Autobiography.

Nemo debet esse judex in propria causa. *nay—moh day—bet ess—seh you—decks in prop—ri—ah cow—sah.*
No one ought to be judge in his own case.
Law.

Nemo enim fere saltat sobrius, nisi forte insanit. *nay—moh en—im feh—reh sal—tat soh—bri—uss, niss—ee fore—teh in—sah—nit.*
For almost no—one dances when sober, unless perhaps he is mad.
Cicero. Pro Murena 6.13.

Nemo impetrare potest a papa bullam nunquam moriendi.
nay—moh im—pet—rah—reh pot—est ah pah—pah bull—lam nun—quam mo—ri—end—ee.
No one can obtain from the pope a dispensation for never dying.
Thomas á Kempis.

Nemo me impune lacessit. *nay—mo may im—poo—neh lack—ess—sit.*
No one provokes *or* injures me with impunity.
Motto of the Scottish Order of the Thistle.

Nemo nascitur artifex. *nay—mo nahss—kit—ur art—if—ex.*
No one is born an artificer.
Quoted by Erasmus.

Nemo potest esse felix sine virtute. *nay—moe pot—est ess—seh fay—leeks sin—eh wihr—too—teh.*
No one can be happy without virtue.
Cicero.

Nemo potest nudo vestimenta detrahere. *nay—moe pot—est noo—doh*

west–im–ent–a day–tra–heh–reh.
No one can strip a naked person.
Law.

Nemo repente venit turpissimus. *nay–moe re–pen–teh wen–it*
tur–pis–sim–uss.
No one ever became thoroughly bad all at once.
Juvenal. Sat. 2.83.

Nemo tam pauper vivit quam natus est. *nay–mo tam pow–pehr wee–wit*
quam nah–tuss est.
No one lives so poor as he is born.
Seneca. Quare bonis viris, etc. fin.

Nemo vir magnus sine aliquo afflatu divino unquam fuit.
nay–mo wirr mag–nus sin–eh al–i–quoh aff–flah–too dee–wee–noh
un–quam fu–it.
No one has become a great man without some degree of divine inspiration.
Cicero. De Nat. Deorum 2.66.

Nequaquam satis in re una consumere curam. *nay–quah–quam sat–iss in*
ray oo–na cone–soo–meh–reh coo–ram.
It is by no means enough to spend all our pains upon one object.
Horace. Sat. Book 2.4.48.

Neque culpa neque lauda teipsum. *nah–queh cul–pah neh–queh lowd–ah*
tay–ip–sum.
Neither blame yourself nor praise yourself.
Pr.

Neque enim potest quisquam nostrum subito fingi neque cujusquam
repente vita mutari aut natura converti. *neh–queh en–im pot–est quiss–*
quam noss–trum sub–it–oh fing–ghee neh–queh coo–yuss–quam
rep–en–tay wee–ta moot–ah–ree out nah–too–ra con–wear–tee.
For none of us can be formed in a moment, neither can anyone's life be
suddenly altered or his character changed.
Cicero. Pro Sulla 25/69.

Neque femina, amissa pudicitia, alia abnuerit. *ne–queh fay–min–a, ah–*
miss–sah pud–ee–kit–i–ah, al–i–a ab–nu–eh–rit.
Nor will a woman, her modesty being gone, refuse anything else.
Tacitus. Annals Book 4.3.

Neque frustra praestantissimus sapientiae firmare solitus est, si recludantur
tyrannorum mentes, posse aspici laniatus et ictus, quando et corpora
verberibus, ita saevitia, libidine, malis consultis animus dilaceretur.
nah—queh froo—strah price—tan—tiss—sim—uss sap—i—en—ti—eye fihr—mah—
reh sol—it—uss est, see reck—lood—ant—ur tih—ran—noh—rum men—tace,
poss—seh asp—ick—ee lan—i—ah—tooce et ick—tooce, quan—doe et core—
por—a wehr—beh—rib—uss, it—a sye—wit—i—ah, lib—ee—din—eh, mal—eece
cone—sull—teece an—im—uss dee—lack—eh—ray—tur.
The wisest of all men was not vain in his assertion that if one were to open
up the souls of tyrants, one might see cuts and wounds, where as with the
lash on the body, so the spirit was torn apart by cruelty, lust, and wickedness.
Tacitus. Annals 6.6: probably referring to Plato, Republic 9.6, p. 579.

Neque lac lacti magis est simile. *nah—que lack lack—tee mag—iss est*
sim—ill—eh.
Nor is milk more like to milk.
Plautus. Amphitruo ii. 1.54.

Neque mala, vel bona, quae vulgus putet. *neh—queh mal—a, well bon—a,*
quie wool—guss put—et.
The views of the multitude are neither bad nor good.
Tacitus. Annals Book 6.22.

Neque meliorem umquam servum neque deteriorem dominum fuisse.
neh—queh mel—i—oh—rem um—quam sehr—wum neh—queh day—teh—ri—
oh—rem dom—in—um fu—iss—seh.
There had never been a better servant or a worse master. (Said by Passi-
enus of the Emperor Gaius 'Caligula'.)
Tacitus. Annals 6.20.

. . . Nequeo monstrare, et sentio tantum. *neh—queh—oh mone—strah—reh,*
et sen—ti—oh tan—tum.
I cannot describe it, I only feel it.
Juvenal. Sat. 7.56.

Nequitiam vinosa tuam convivia narrant. *nay—quit—i—am wee—noe—sa*
tu—am con—wee—wi—a narr—rant.
Your drunken banquets tell your vileness.
Ovid. Amorum Book 3.1.17.

Nihil enim facilius quam amor recrudescit. *ni—hill en—im fack—ill—i—uss*
quam am—or ray—croo—day—skit.
For nothing grows again more easily than love.
Seneca. Epist. 69.

Nihil est annis velocius. *ni–hill est ann–niece way–loke–i–uss.*
Nothing is swifter than the years.
Ovid. Metam. 10.520.

. . . Nihil est ab omni/Parte beatum. *ni–hill est ab om–nee parr–teh beh–ah–tum.*
There is nothing blessed in every respect.
Horace. Odes Book 2.16.

Nihil est in intellectu quin prius fuerit in sensu. *ni–hill est in in–tell–lect–oo quin pri–uss fu–eh–rit in sayn–soo.*
There is nothing in the comprehension which has not previously existed in the senses.
Tr. of Aristotle, De Anima. Quoted in this form by Navizanus, "Sylva Nuptialis," Book 5, sec. 77.

Nihil est miserius quam animus hominis conscius. *ni–hill est miss–eh–ri–uss quam an–im–uss hom–in–uss cone–ski–uss.*
Nothing is more wretched than the mind of a man conscious of guilt.
Plautus. Mostellaria iii. 1.13.

Nihil est miserum nisi cum putes; contraque beata sors omnis est aequanimitate tolerantis. *nih–hill est miss–eh–rum niss–ee cum put–ace; con–trah–queh beh–ah–ta sorss om–niss est eye–quan–im–it–ah–teh toll–eh–ran–tiss.*
Nothing is miserable unless because you think it is; conversely, every fortune is happy of a man who endures it calmly.
Boethius. De consolatione philosophiae.

Nihil est quod Deus efficere non possit. *ni–hill est quod deh–uss eff–fick–eh–ray none poss–sit.*
There is nothing which God cannot effect.
Cicero. De Nat. Deorum Book 3.39.92.

Nihil est sanitati multo vino nocentius. *ni–hill est sah–nit–ah–tee mull–toe wee–noe nock–en–ti–uss.*
Nothing is more hurtful to health than much wine.
Pr.

Nihil est tam populare quam bonitas. *ni–hill est tam pop–ul–ah–reh quam bon–it–ahss.*
Nothing is so popular as kindness.
Cicero. Pro. Ligar. 12.

Nihil hic nisi carmina desunt. *ni–hill heek niss–ee car–min–a day–sunt.*

[111]

Nothing but songs is wanting here.
Virgil. Eclogues 3.67.

. . . Nihil me, sicut antea, juvat/scribere versiculos. . . . *ni—hill may, see—cut an—teh—ah, yu—wat scree—beh—reh wair—sick—ul—oce.*
Writing verses does not at all please me as it formerly did.
Horace. Epodon 11.1.

Nihil morosius hominum judiciis. *ni—hill moe—roh—si—uss hom—in—um you—dick—i—eece.*
Nothing is more captious than man's judgments.
Erasmus.

Nihil prodest improbam mercem emere. *ni—hill proh—dest im—prob—am mare—kem em—eh—reh.*
There is no profit in buying bad merchandise.
Pr.

Nihil scire est vita jucundissima. *ni—hill skee—reh est wee—ta you—cun—diss—sim—a.*
The happiest life is to know nothing.
Pr.

Nihil simul inventum est et perfectum. *ni—hill sim—ul in—wen—tum est et pair—fect—tum.*
Nothing is invented and perfected at the same time.
Pr.

Nihil tam absurdum dici potest ut non dicatur ab aliquo philosophorum. *ni—hill tam ap—soor—dum dee—key pot—est ut none dee—kah—tur ab al—i—quoh fil—oss—o—foh—rum.*
There is nothing which can be spoken so absurd that it might not be spoken by some one of the philosophers.
Cicero. De Divinat. 2.58.

Nihil tam firmum est, cui periculum non sit etiam ab invalido. *ni—hill tam fihr—mum est, cu—ee peh—reek—ull—um none sit et—yam ab in—wal—id—oh.*
Nothing is so sure that it may not be in danger, even from a feeble person.
Quintus Curtius.

Nil actum credens, dum quid superesset agendum. *neel ac—tum cray—daynce, dum quid sup—er—ess—set a—gen—dum.*
Believing nothing done whilst there remained anything else to be done.
Lucan. Phars. Book 2.657.

Nil adeo magnum neque tam mirabile quicquam Quod non paulatim minuant mirarier omnes. *neel ad—eh—oh mag—num neh—queh tam mee—rah—bill—eh quick—quam quod none pow—lah—tim min—u—ant mee—rah—ri—ehr om—nace.*
There is nothing so great or so marvelous that gradually everyone's wonder at it does not grow less.
Lucretius. De rerum natura 2.1028f.

Nil ait esse prius, melius nil caelibe vita. *neel a—it ess—seh pri—uss, mel—i—uss neel kye—lib—eh wee—tah.*
He declares that there is nothing to be preferred to, nothing better than, a bachelor life.
Horace. Ep. Book 1.1.88.

Nil aliud, quam bene ausus vana contemnere. *neel al—i—ud, quam ben—eh ow—suss wah—na con—tem—ne—reh.*
Nothing else than that he dared well to despise vain things.
Livy. Book 9.17. of Alexander.

Nil desperandum Teucro duce et auspice Teucro. *neel day—spay—ran—dum tew—croh duck—eh et ow—spick—eh tew—croh.*
There is no need for despair when Teucer is your leader and guide.
Horace. Odes 1.7.27.

Nil ego contulerim jucundo sanus amico. *neel egg—oh con—tul—eh—rim you—cun—doh sah—nuss a—mee—coe.*
Whilst in my senses I shall prefer nothing to a pleasant friend.
Horace. Sat. Book 1.5.44.

Nil feret ad manes divitis umbra suos. *neel feh—ret ad mah—nace dee—wit—iss um—bra su—oce.*
The shade of the rich man will carry nothing to his abode in the other world.
Ovid. Tristia Book 5.14.12.

Nil habet infelix paupertas durius in se,/quam quod ridiculos homines facit. . . . *neel hab—et in—fay—leeks pow—pair—tahss doo—ri—uss in say, quam quod ree—dick—ul—oce hom—in—ace fack—it.*
Unhappy poverty has in it nothing harder than the fact that it makes men a laughing stock.
Juvenal. Sat. 3.152.

Nil igitur mars est ad nos neque pertinet hilum. *neel ig—it—ur morse est ad noce neh—queh pair—tin—et hee—lum.*
Therefore death is nothing to us and of no importance.
Lucretius. De Rerum Nat. 3.830.

[113]

Nil metuunt jurare, nihil promittere parcunt. *neel met—u—unt you—rah—reh, ni—hill proh—mitt—teh—reh parr—kunt.*
They fear not to swear anything, they spare not to promise anything.
Catullus. Carm. 64.145.

Nil mortalibus arduum est:/coelum ipsum petimus stultitia. . . .
neel more—tah—lib—uss arr—du—um est: coy—lum ip—sum pet—im—uss stoll—ti—ti—ah.
Nothing is difficult to mortals; we strive to reach heaven itself in our folly.
Horace. Odes Book 1.3.37.

Nil nimium studeo, Caesar, tibi velle placere Nec scire utrum sis albus an ater homo. *neel nim—i—um stud—eh—oh, kye—sar, tib—e well—leh plack—ay—reh neck skee—reh oot—rum seece al—buss an ah—tehr hom—oh.*
I am not too eager, Caesar, to wish to please you, nor to know whether you are a white or black man.
Catullus. Poem 93.

Nil oriturum alias, nil ortum tale fatentes. *neel o—rit—oh—rum al—i—ahss, neel or—tum tah—leh fat—en—tace.*
Confessing that nothing equal to you will arise or has at any time arisen.
Horace. Ep. Book 2.1.17.

. . . Nil sine magno/Vita labore dedit mortalibus. . . . *neel sin—eh mag—noe wee—ta lab—oh—reh ded—it more—tah—lib—uss.*
Life gives nothing to mortals except with great labour.
Horace. Sat. Book 1.9.59.

Nil tam difficile est quin quaerendo investigari possiet. *neel tam diff—fick—il—eh est queen quie—ren—dah in—west—ee—gah—ree poss—si—et.*
Nothing is so difficult that it may not be found out by research.
Terence. Heautontimorumenos iv. 2.8.

Nimia est miseria pulchrum esse hominem nimis. *nim—i—a est miss—eh—ri—a pull—crum ess—seh hom—in—em nim—is.*
It is an extremely wretched thing to be an over-handsome man.
Plautus. Miles Gloriosus i. 1.68.

. . . Nimia illaec licentia/profecto evadet in aliquod magnum malum.
nim—i—a ill—uke lick—en—ti—a proh—fect—toe ay—wah—det in al—i—quod mag—num mal—um.
That outrageous license will assuredly develop into some great disaster.
Terence. Adelphi iii. 4.63.

Nimium altercando veritas amittitur. *nim—i—um al—tear—can—doe way—*

rit—ahss ah—mitt—ti—tur.
In too much disputation the truth is lost.
Publilius Syrus.

Nisi Dominus frustra. *niss—i dom—in—uss fruss—trah.*
Unless the Lord keep the city the watchman waketh in vain (*lit.* unless the Lord in vain).
Motto of City of Edinburgh (adapted from Ps. 127, 1, Vulgate).

Nisi forte rebus cunctis inest quidam velut orbis, ut quem ad modum temporum vices ita morum vertantur. *niss—ee fore—teh ray—buss cunk—teece in—est quee—dam well—ut ore—biss, ut quem ad mod—um tem—po—rum wick—ace it—a moe—rum wear—tan—tur.*
Or else perhaps there is a kind of cycle in everything, so that just like the seasons, so social customs change and return.
Tacitus. Annals 3.55.

Nisi prius. *niss—i pry—us.*
Unless previously
Law.

Nitimur in vetitum semper, cupimusque negata. *neat—im—ur in wet—it—um sem—pair, cup—im—uss—queh neg—ah—ta.*
We strive ever after what is forbidden, and desire the things which are denied us.
Ovid. Amorum Book 3.4.17.

Nobis non licet esse tam disertis,/qui musas colimus severiores.
noh—beece none lick—et ess—seh tam diss—air—teece, quee moo—sahss coll—im—us seh—way—ri—oh—race.
To us who cultivate the stricter muses, it is not allowed to be so eloquent.
Martial. Epig. 9.12.16.

Nocentem qui defendit sibi crimen parat. *nock—en—tem quee day—fen—dit sib—ee cree—men pa—rat.*
He who protects a guilty person is preparing a crime against himself.
Publilius Syrus.

Noctis erat medium; quid non amor improbus audet? *nock—tiss eh—rat med—i—um; quid non am—or im—prob—uss ow—det?*
It was midnight; what does not shameless love dare?
Ovid. Fast. 2.331.

Nocturna versate manu, versate diurna. *nock—tur—nah wear—sah—teh*

[115]

man—oo, wear—sah—teh di—ur—nah.
Read (*lit.* turn over) with nightly and daily labour (the Greek authors).
Horace. De Arte Poetica 269.

Nolens volens. *noh—laynce woll—aynce.*
Willing or unwilling.
Pr.

Noli me tangere. *noh—lee may tan—geh—reh.*
Touch me not.
Vulgate. St. John 20.17.

Nolite putare quemquam hominem aliquid discere ab homine. Admonere
possumus per strepitum vocis nostrae. *noh—lee—teh put—ah—reh quem—
quam hom—in—em al—ick—wid dee—skeh—reh ab hom—in—eh. ad—mon—
ay—reh poss—sum—uss pehr strep—it—um woe—kiss noss—try.*
Do not suppose that any man learns anything from another man. We can
only bring things to others' minds through the noise of our voice.
St. Augustine.

Nolite timere. *noh—lee—teh ti—may—reh.*
Fear not.
Vulgate. Genesis 43.23. Also Seneca Ep. 12.

Nolle prosequi. *noh—li proh—seh—quie.*
To be unwilling to prosecute.
Law.

Nolo episcopari. *noh—loe ep—iss—cop—ah—ree.*
I am unwilling to be made a bishop.
Pr.

Nomen atque omen. *noh—men at—queh oh—men.*
A name and also an omen.
Plautus. Persa iv. 4.73.

. . . Nomen toto sparget in orbe suum. *noh—men toe—toe spar—get in
or—beh su—um.*
He spreads his name throughout the whole world.
Martial. Epig. Book 6.60.2.

Non amo te, Sabidi, nec possum dicere quare;/hoc tantum possum
dicere, non amo te. *none am—o tay, sab—id—ee, neck poss—sum dee—keh—
reh quah—ray; hoke tan—tum poss—sum dee—keh—reh, none am—o—tay.*
I do not love thee, Sabidius, nor can I tell why; this only I can tell, I do

not love thee.
Martial. Epig. Book 1.33.

Non Angli, sed Angeli. *none an—glee, sed an—gell—ee.*
Not Angles, but Angels.

Non auriga piger. *none ow—rig—a pig—er.*
No fat charioteer (no lazy person as manager).
Pr.

Non bene conveniunt, nec in una sede morantur,/Majestas et amor. . . .
none ben—eh con—wen—i—unt, neck in oo—nah say—deh mo—ran—tur,
mah—yes—tahss et a—more.
Majesty and love do not agree, nor abide in one place.
Anon.

Non bene olet, qui bene semper olet. *none ben—eh o—let, quee ben—eh*
sem—per o—let.
He does not smell well who always has a nice scent upon him.
Martial. Epig. Book 2.12.4.

Non bonus somnus est de prandio. *non bon—oos som—oos est de pran—*
dee—oh.
Sleep after luncheon is not good.
Plautus. Mostell. iii. 2.8.

Non compos mentis. *none com—poss men—tiss.*
Not in full possession of the mind.
See Cicero. In L. Pisonem. 20, 48.

Non cuivis homini contingit adire Corinthum. *none cu—ee—weece*
hom—in—ee con—tin—git ad—ee—reh co—rin—thum.
It is not given to every man to reach Corinth.
Horace. Ep. Book 1.17.36.

Non decipitur qui scit se decipi. *none day—kip—it—ur quee skit say day—*
kip—ee.
He is not cheated who knows that he is being cheated.
Coke.

Non ego hoc ferrem, calidus juventa,/Consule Planco. *none eg—oh hoke*
fer—rem, cal—id—uss yu—wen—tah, cone—sul—eh plan—coe.
Nor would I have borne this, hot with youth, when Plancus was consul.
Horace. Odes Book 3.14.27.

[117]

Non ego illam mihi dotem duco esse, quae dos dicitur,/Sed pudicitiam, et pudorem, et sedatum cupidinem. *none eg–oh ill–lam mi–hee dote–em doo–koh ess–seh, quie dose dee–kit–ur, sed pud–ee–kit–i–am, et pud–oh–rem, et say–dah–tum cup–ee–din–em.*
I do not consider that a dowry to me which is called a dowry, but purity and modesty and quiet desire.
Plautus. Amph. 2.210.

Non ego mendosos ausim defendere mores. *none egg–oh men–dose–oce ow–sim day–fen–deh–reh moh–race.*
I may not dare to defend habits blemished by immorality.
Ovid. Amorum Bk. 2.4.1.

Non enim ignavia magna imperia contineri. *none en–um ig–nah–wi–ah mag–na im–peh–ri–a con–tin–ay–ree.*
For great empires are not maintained by cowardice (*or*, laziness).
Tacitus. Annals Book 15.1.

Non enim gazae, neque consultaris/summovet lictor miseros tumultus/ mentis, et curas laqueata circum/Tecta volantes. *none en–im gah–zye, neh–queh cone–sul–ah–riss sum–mo–wet lick–tor miss–eh–roce tu–mul–tooce men–tiss, et coo–rahss la–queh–ah–ta kihr–cum teck–ta wol–ant–ace.*
For neither wealth nor the consular lictor expels the wretched tumults of the mind, and the cares hovering round the roofs with the panelled ceilings.
Horace. Odes Bk. 2.16.9.

Non equidem invideo; miror magis. . . . *none e–quid–em in–wid–eh–oh; mee–roar mag–iss.*
Truly I do not envy, but I rather wonder.
Virgil. Eclogues 1.11.

Non est ad astra mollis e terris via. *none est ad ass–tra moll–lis ay tear–reece wi–ah.*
There is no easy way to the stars from the earth.
Seneca. Hercules Furens ii. 437.

Non est, crede mihi, sapientis dicere, Vivam./Sera nimis vita est crastina; vive hodie. *none est, cray–deh mi–hee, sap–i–ent–iss dee–keh–re, wee–wam. say–rah nim–iss wee–ta est crahss–tin–a; wee–weh hod–i–ay.*
It is not, believe me, the sign of a wise man to say, "I will live." Life put off till the morrow is too late; live to-day.
Martial. Epig. Book 1.16.16.

Non est de pastu omnium quaestio, sed de lana. *none est day pah–stoo om–ni–um quay–sti–oh, sed day lah–nah.*
It is not a question of the feeding of all the sheep, but of their wool (*i.e.* of their fleeces).
Pius II.

Non est factum. *none est fact–tum.*
It is not my deed.
Law.

Non est in medico semper relevetur ut aeger. *none est in med–ick–oh sem–pair reh–leh–way–tur ut eye–gair.*
It is not always in the physician's power to cure the sick person.
Ovid. Ep. ex Pont. Book 1.3.17.

Non est princeps super leges, sed leges supra principem. *none est prin–keps sup–air lay–gayce, sed lay–gace sup–rer prin–kip–em.*
The prince is not above the laws, but the laws above the prince.
Pliny the Younger. Paneg. Traj. 65.

Non est remedium adversus sycophantae morsum. *non est rem–ed–i–um ad–wear–suss see–co–fan–tie more–sum.*
There is no remedy against the bite of a flatterer (*or,* slanderer).
Pr.

Non est ulla studiorum satietas. *none est ull–la stud–i–oh–rum sat–i–eh–tahss.*
There is no satiety in study.
Erasmus. Colloquia.

Non ex jure manum consertum sed magi' ferro Rem repetunt regnumque petunt, vadunt solida vi. *none ex you–reh man–um cone–sehr–tum sed mag–i–fehr–roe rem rep–et–unt rayg–num–queh pet–unt, wa–dunt sol–id–ah wee.*
Not by joining issue according to law but rather by the sword do they seek reparation and aim at supreme power, and make their way with full force.
Ennius. Annals 8, fr. 275, cited by Cicero, Epistulae ad Familiares 7.13.

Non habet commercium cum virtute voluptas. *none hab–et com–mare–ki–um cum wihr–too–teh wol–up–tahss.*
Pleasure has no commerce with virtue.
Cicero (adapted). De Senectute 12.42.

Non haec jocosae conveniunt lyrae. *none hike yoh–coe–sigh con–wen–i–unt li–rye.*

These things do not accord with humorous poetry.
Horace. Odes 3.3.69.

Non hominis culpa sed ista loci. *none hom—in—uss cul—pa—sed iss—ta lock—ee.*
The fault is not of the man but of the place.
Ovid. Tristium 5.7.60.

Non ille pro caris amicis,/Aut patria timidus perire. *none ill—leh proh cah—reece a—mee—keese, owt pat—ri—ah tim—id—uss peh—ree—reh.*
He was not afraid to die for friends whom he loved, or for his native land.
Horace. Odes Book 4.9.51.

Non injussa cano. *none in—yuss—sa can—oh.*
I do not sing unbidden.
Virgil. Eclogues 6.9.

Non invisa feres pueris munuscula parvis. *none in—wee—sa feh—race pu—air—ris moon—uss—cul—a par—weece.*
You will bear no unwelcome presents to the little children.
Horace. Ep. Book 1.7.17.

Non liquet. *none li—quet.*
It is not clear; it is not proven.
Cicero. Pro Cluentio 28.76.

Non mala nulla meretrix est. *none ma—la null—la meh—reh—treeks est.*
There is no whore who is not bad.
Plautus. Miles Gloriosus iii. 3.21.

Non mihi mille placent; non sum desultor amoris. *none mi—hee mill—leh plack—ent; none sum day—sult—or a—moh—riss.*
A thousand girls do not charm me; I am no inconstant person in love.
Ovid. Amorum 1.3.15.

Non multa, sed multum. *none mull—ta, sed mull—tum.*
Not many things, but much.
Pr.

Non mutat sapiens consilium . . . ideo numquam illum paenitentia subit. *none moot—at sap—i—aynce cone—sill—i—um . . . id—eh—oh num—quam ill—lum pie—nit—en—ti—a sub—it.*
The wise man does not change his opinion . . . and therefore he never suffers regret.
Seneca. De beneficiis 4.34.

[120]

Non nobis, Domine, non nobis. *none noh—beece, dom—in—eh, none noh—beece.*
Not unto us, O Lord, not unto us.
Vulgate. Ps. 115.1.

Non oculi tacuere tui. *none ock—ul—ee tack—u—ay—reh tu—ee.*
Your eyes were not silent.
Ovid. Amorum 2.5.17.

Non omnes arbusta juvant. *none om—nace ar—bust—a yu—want.*
Trees do not delight all persons.
Virgil. Ecl. 4.2.

Non omnia possumus omnes. *none om—ni—a poss—sum—uss om—nace.*
We cannot all do all things.
Virgil. Ecl. 8.63.

Non omnis moriar, multaque pars mei/Vitabit Libitinam. . . .
none om—niss mo—ri—ar, mul—ta—queh parse mi—hee wee—tah—bit lib—it—ee—nam.
I shall not all die.
I shall not altogether die; a great part of me will escape Libitina (death).
Horace. Odes Book 3.30.6.

. . . Non possum ferre, Quirites,/Graecam urbem. . . . *none poss—sum fer—eh, qui—ree—tace, grie—kam ur—bem.*
I cannot bear, O Roman citizens, to see the city (of Rome) made Grecian.
Juvenal. Sat. 3.60.

. . . Non pronuba Juno/non Hymenaeus adest, non illo Gratia lecto./
Eumenides stravere torum. . . . *none proh—nub—a you—noe none him—en—eye—uss ad—est, none ill—loe grah—ti—a leck—toh; ewe—men—id—ace strah—way—reh to—rum.*
Juno presiding over marriage was not present, nor Hymen (god of marriage), nor any of the Graces at that bed; the Eumenides (the Furies) strewed that wedding couch.
Ovid. Metam. Book 6. lines 428-9 and 431.

Non pudeat dicere, quod non pudet sentire. *none pud—eh—at dee—keh—reh, quod none pud—et sen—tee—reh.*
Do not be ashamed to say what you are not ashamed to think.
Anon.

Non propter vitam faciunt patrimonia quidam,/sed vitio caeci propter

[121]

patrimonia vivunt. *none prop—tear wee—tam fack—i—unt pat—rim—oh—ni—a quee—dam, sed wit—i—oh kye—key prop tear pat—rim—oh—ni—a wee—wunt.*
Some men make fortunes, but not to enjoy them; for, blinded by avarice, they live to make fortunes.
Juvenal.

Non quam diu, sed quam bene vixeris refert. *none quam di—oo, sed quam ben—ah wix—eh—riss reh—fairt.*
It matters not how long you have lived, but how well.
Seneca (adapted).

Non satis est pulchra esse poemata; dulcia sunto,/et quocunque volent animum auditoris agunto. *none sat—iss est pull—cra ess—seh po—ay—mat—a; dull—ki—a sunt—oh, et quoh—cun—queh wol—ent an—im—um ow—dee—toh—riss ag—unt—oh.*
It is not enough that poems be pretty; they must be sweet, and move at will the mind of the hearer.
Horace. De Arte Poetica, 99.

Non scribit, cujus carmina nemo legit. *none scree—bit, coo—yuss car—min—a nay—mo leg—it.*
He is not a writer whose poems no one reads.
Martial.

Non semper erit aestas. *none sem—per eh—rit eye—stahss.*
It will not always be summer.
Tr. of Hesiod.

Non sequitur. *none seh—quit—ur.*
It does not follow.

Non solent quae abundant vitiare scripturas. *none soll-ent quie ab—un—dant wit—i—ah—reh scrip—too—rahss.*
Redundancy does not invalidate deeds.
Law.

Non sum ego qui fueram: mutat via longa puellas. Quantus in exiguo tempore fugit amor! *none sum egg—o quee fu—eh—ram: moot—at we—a long—ga pu—ell—lahss. quan—tuss in ex—ig—u—oh tem—por—eh foo—git am—or!*
I am not what I was: a far journey can change a girl's heart. How great a love it was, and in how short a time has it fled!
Propertius. Elegies 1.12.11f.

Non sum qualis eram, bonae/sub regna Cinarae. . . . *none sum quah—liss eh—ram, bon—eye sub regnah kin—a—rye.*
I am not what I formerly was, when the good Cinara was my queen.
Horace. Odes Book 4.1.3.

Non tali auxilio, nec defensoribus istis/tempus eget. *none tah—lee owk—sil—i—oh, neck day—fane—soh—rib—uss iss—teece tem—puss egg—et.*
Not such help as that, nor such defenders as those, does the time stand in need of.
Virgil. Æneid 2.521.

. . . Non tam portas intrare patentes/quam fregisse juvat. . . .
none tam por—tahss in—tra—reh pat—ent—ace quam fray—giss—seh yu—wat.
It does not delight him so much to enter open doors as to have forced them open.
Lucan. Pharsalia Book 2.444.

Non teneas aurum totum quod splendet ut aurum. *none ten—eh—ahss ow—rum toe—tum quod splen—det ut ow—rum.*
Do not hold everything as gold which shines like gold.
Alanus de Insulis.

Non usitata, nec tenui ferar/Penna. *none oo—sit—ah—tah, neck tew—u—ee feh—rar pen—nah.*
Not on an accustomed, nor yet on a feeble wing shall I be borne.
Horace. Odes Book 2.20.1.

Non versiones sed eversiones. *none wear—si—oh—nace sed a—wear—si—oh—nace.*
Not versions but perversions.
St. Jerome (of the versions of Scripture).

Non zelus, sed caritas. *none zay—luss, sed cah—rit—ahss.*
Not your good words but your charity.
Mediaeval Pr.

Nonumque prematur in annum. *noh—num—queh prem—ah—tur in ann—num.*
Let it (what you have written) be kept back until the ninth year.
Horace. De Arte Poetica 388.

Nos duo turba sumus. *noce du—oh tur—ba sum—uss.*
We two (Deucalion and Pyrrha, after the deluge) form a multitude.
Ovid. Metam. 1, 355.

Nos haec novimus esse nihil. *noce hike noh—wim—uss ess—seh ni—hill.*
We have known these things to be nothing.
Martial.

Nos patriae fines et dulcia linquimus arva. *noce pat—ri—eye fee—nace et dull—ki—a lin—quim—uss arr—wa.*
We leave the boundaries of our native land and our beloved fields.
Virgil. Eclogues 1.3.

Nosce tempus. *noce—keh tem—puss.*
Know your time.
Pr.

Nosse omnia haec, salus est adolescentulis. *nohss—seh om—ni—a hike, sal—ooce est ad—ol—ess—ken—tull—iss.*
It is safety to young men to know all these things.
Terence. Eunuchus v. 4.18.

Nostri nosmet poenitet. *noh—stree noce—met poy—nit—eh.*
We despise what belongs to us.
Terence. Phormio i. 3.20.

Novus homo. *noh—wuss hom—oh.*
A new man (one who has risen).
Pr.

Noxiae poena par esto. *nox—i—eye poy—na parr ess—toe.*
Let the punishment be equal with the offence.
Cicero. De Legibus Book 3.20.

Nudo detrahere vestimenta me jubes. *noo—doh day—tra—heh—reh west—im—en—ta may yub—ace.*
You command me to strip a naked person.
Plautus. Asinaria i. 1.78.

Nugus addere pondus. *noo—geese ad—deh—reh pon—duss.*
To lend weight to trifles.
Horace. Ep. Book 1.19.42.

Nulla dies abeat quin linea ducta supersit. *null—la di—ace ab—eh—at queen lee—neh—a duck—ta sup—air—sit.*
Let no day pass without some line being left behind it.
Proverbial verse referring to industry; cf. the following.

[124]

Nulla dies sine linea. *null–la di–ace sin–eh lee–neh–ah.*
Not a day without a line.
Pliny, Nat. Hist. 35.36.12.

Nulla est sincera voluptas;/sollicitique aliquid laetis intervenit. . . .
null–la est sin–kay–ra wol–up–thass; soll–lick–it–ee–queh al–i–quid
lie–teece in–tear–wen–it.
There is no unalloyed pleasure; some tinge of anxiety mingles with our
joys.
Ovid. Metam. Book 7.453.

Nulla fugae ratio, nulla spes: omnia muta, Omnia sunt deserta, ostentant
omnia letum. *null–la fug–eye rat–i–oh, null–la space: om–ni–a moot–a,*
om–ni–a sunt dace–air–ta, oss–tent–ant om–ni–a lay–tum.
There is no way to escape, no hope: everything is silent, everything deserted,
everything points to death.
Catullus. Poem 64.186f.

Nulla gens est, quae non aut ita sublata sit, ut vix exstet, aut ita domita,
ut quiescat, aut ita pacata, ut victoria nostra imperioque laetetur.
null–la gainss est, quie none out it–a sub–lah–ta sit, ut wix ex–stet, out
it–a dom–it–a, ut qui–ace–cat, out it–a pah–kah–ta, ut wick–toe–ri–
ah noss–trah im–peh–ri–oh–queh lie–tay–tur.
There is no nation which has not been either destroyed so that it scarcely
survives, or so subdued that it is at rest, or so pacified that it rejoices in
our victory and empire.
Cicero. Deprovinciis consularibus 12/31.

Nulla placere diu, vel vivere carmina possunt,/quae scribuntur aquae
potoribus. . . . *nulla plack–ay–reh di–oo, well we–weh–reh car–min–a*
poss–sunt, quie scree–bun–tur a–quie poe–toe–rib–uss.
No verses can please long, or live, which are written by water drinkers.
Horace. Ep. Book 1.19.2.

Nulla potentia supra leges esse debet. *null–la pot–en–ti–a sup–rah*
lay–gace ess–seh deb–et.
No power ought to be above the laws.
Cicero. (See "Pro Domo sua." 17.43.)

Nulla salus bello; pacem te poscimus omnes. *null–la sa–loose bell–loh;*
pah–kem tay poss–ki–muss om–nace.
There is no safety in war; we all entreat thee for peace.
Virgil. Æneid 11.362.

Nulla scabies scabiosior superstitione. *null—la scab—i—ace scab—i—oh—si or sup—air—stit—i—oh—neh.*
No itch is more infectious than superstition.
Jovian. Pont. Ant. Dial.

Nullam rem citiorem apud homines esse, quam famam, reor.
null—lam rem kit—i—oh—rem ap—ud hom—in—ace ess—seh, quam fah—mam, reh-oar.
I believe there is nothing amongst mankind swifter than rumour.
Plautus. Fragm. From a play lost.

Nulli negabimus, nulli differemus justitiam. *null—lee neg—ah—bim—uss, null—lee diff—feh—ray—muss yass—ti—ti—am.*
To no one will we deny justice, to no one will we delay it.
Magna Charta.

Nulli nocendum. *null—lee nock—en—dum.*
No one should be injured.
Phaedrus. Fab. Book 1.26.1.

Nulli secundus. *null—lee seck—un—duss.*
Second to none.
Livy, etc.

Nullis fraus tuta latebris. *null—lease frowse too—ta lat—ay—breece.*
Fraud is safe in no hiding place.
Camerarius.

Nullius boni sine socio jucunda possessio. *null—lee—us bonn—ee sin—eh sock—i—oh you—cun—da poss—sess—si—oh.*
A pleasant possession is of no good without a comrade.
Seneca. Ep. 6.

Nullum anarchia majus est malum. *null—lum arn—ack—ia ma—yus est ma—lum.*
There is no evil greater than anarchy.
Pr.

Nullum est jam dictum, non dictum sit prius. *null—lum est yam dict—tum, quod none dict—tum sit pri—uss.*
There is no saying now which has not been said before.
Terence. Eunuchus. Prologue. 41.

Nullum magnum malum quod extremum est. *null—lum mag—num mal—um quod extr—ee—mum est.*

No evil is great which is the last.
Cornelius Nepos.

Nullum quod tetigit non ornavit. *null—lum quod tett—ig—it none or—*
nah—wit.
He touched nothing which he did not adorn.
Epitaph by Dr. Johnson on Goldsmith.

Nullum sine auctoramento malum est. *null—lum sine—eh owk—toh—rah—*
men—toe mal—um est.
There is no evil without its compensation.
Seneca. Epist. 69.

Nullus dolor est quem non longinquitas temporis minuat ac molliat.
null—luss doll—or est quem none long—ging—quit—ahss tem—por—iss
min—u—at ack moll—li—at.
There is no grief which length of time does not lessen and soften.
Servius Sulpicius, in Cicero, Epistulae ad Familiares 4.5.6.

Nullus semel ore receptus Pollutas patitur sanguis mansuescere fauces.
null—luss sem—ell oh—reh reck—ep—tuss poll—loot—ahss pat—it—ur
sang—gwiss mahn—sway—skeh—reh fow—case.
No-one who has once let the blood of his kinfolk pass his lips allows his
throat to grow less blood thirsty.
Lucan. Pharsalia 1.331.

Numquid vitae mimum commode peregisset? *num—quid wee—tie mee—*
mum com—mod—ay peh—ray—giss—set.
Whether he had not well played his part in the comedy of life?

Nunc dimittis servum tuum, Domine. *nunc dee—mit—tiss sair—vum*
tu—um, dom—in—eh.
Now, O Lord, lettest thou thy servant depart.
Vulgate. St. Luke 2.29.

Nunc est bibendum, nunc pede libero/pulsanda tellus. . . .
nunc est bib—en—dum, nunc ped—eh lee—beh—ro pul—sand—a tell—loose.
Now is the time for drinking, and now with sportive foot to beat the earth.
Horace. Odes Book 1.37.1.

Nunc frondent sylvae, nunc formosissimus annus. *nunc fron—dent sill—wye,*
nunc for—moh—siss—sim—uss an—nuss.
Now (in Spring) the woods are in leaf, now the year is in its greatest beauty.
Virgil. Eclogues 3.57.

Nunc mihi summa licet contingere sidera plantis: Sive dies seu nox venerit, illa mea est! Nec mihi rivalis firmos subducit amores: Ista meam norit gloria canitiem. *nunc mih—he sum—ma lick—et con—ting—gheh—reh seed—eh—ra plan—teece: see—weh di—ace sue nox way—neh—rit, ill—la meh—a est! neck mih—he ree—wah—liss fihr—moce sub—doo—kit am—oh—race: iss—ta meh—am noh—rit gloh—ri—a cah—nit—i—em.*
Now I may set my feet upon the highest stars: whether day or night come, she is mine! No rival can take my love away, it is so sure. Today's splendour will be with me when my hair is white with age.
Propertius. Elegies 1.8.43-46.

Nunc scio quid sit amor. *nunc ski—oh quid sit a—more.*
Now I know what love is.
Virgil. Eclogues 8.43.

Nunc sine me plena fiunt convivia mensa, Nunc sine me tota janua nocte patet. *nunc sin—eh may plain—ah fee—unt con—wee—we—a main—sah, nunc sin—eh may toe—tah yah—nu—a nock—teh pat—et.*
Now there are feasts laid on full tables, but none for me; now your door stands open all night, but not for me.
Propertius. Elegies 2.16.5f.

Nunquam in vita fuit mihi melius. *nun—quam in wee—tah fu—it mi—hee mel—i—us.*
Never in my life were things better with me.
Plautus.

. . . Nunquam nimis curare possunt suum parentem filiae. *nun—quam nim—iss coo—rah—reh poss—sunt soo—um pa—ren—tem feel—iae.*
Daughters can never take too much care of their father.
Plautus.

Nunquam potest non esse virtuti locus. *nun—quam pot—est none ess—seh wihr—too—tee lock—uss.*
There can never be want of room for virtue.
Seneca.

Nunquam se minus otiosum esse quam cum otiosus; nec minus solum quam cum solus esset. *nun—quam say min—uss oh—ti—oh—sum ess—seh quam cum oh—ti—oh—suss; neck min—uss soh—lum quam cum soh—luss ess—set.*
That he was never less at leisure than when at leisure; nor that he was ever less alone than when alone.
Cicero. De Off. Book 3.1. Quoted by Cicero as a saying of Scipio Africanus.

[128]

Nunquam tuta fides. *nun—quam too—ta fid—ace.*
Confidence is never safe. (The Oxford text has: "Nusquam tuta fides."
Nowhere is confidence safe.)
Virgil. Æneid 4.373.

Nunquam vidi vultum minus nuptialem. *nun—quam wee—dee woll—tum
min—uss nup—ti—ah—lem.*
Never have I seen a less marriage-like face.
Erasmus. Gamos.

Nutrimentum spiritus. *noo—trim—en—tum spee—rit—uss.*
Food for the soul.
Inscription on Berlin State Library.

O curas hominum! O quantum est in rebus inane! *oh coo—rahss hom—
in—um! oh quan—tum est in ray—buss in—ah—neh!*
O human cares! Oh what emptiness there is in the affairs of men!
Persius. Sat. 1.1.

O domus antiqua, heu, quam dispari dominare domino.
*oh dom—uss an—tee—qua, heu, quam diss—pa—ree dom—in—ah—reh
dom—in—oh.*
O ancient house! alas, how unlike is thy present master to thy former one.
Cicero.

O fallacem hominum spem! *oh fall—lah—kem hom—in—um spem!*
Oh, how deceitful is the hope of men!
Cicero.

O famuli turpes, servum pecus! *oh fam—ul—ee tur—pace, sair—wum peck—uss!*
O base servants, O servile herd!
Lucan. Pharsalia Book 6.150.

O formose puer, nimium ne crede colori. *oh for—moh—seh pu—air, nim—i—
um nay cray—deh co—loh—ree.*
O beautiful boy, do not trust too much to outward complexion.
Virgil. Eclogues 2.17.

O fortunatam natam, me consule, Romam. *oh for—too—nah—tam nah—tam, may cone—sul—eh, roc—mum.*
O fortunate Rome, born when I was Consul (a line ridiculed for its presumption and its cacophony).
Attributed to Cicero by Juvenal, Sat. 10. 122.

O fortunatos nimium, sua si bona norint,/Agricolas! *oh for—too—nah—toce nim—i—um, su—a see bon—a noe—rint, ag—rick—ol—ahss!*
O how happy beyond measure would be the husbandmen if they knew their own good fortune.
Virgil. Georgics 2.453.

O homines ad servitutem paratos! *oh hom—in—ace ad sair—wit—oo—tem pa—rah—toce!*
O men made for slavery! (A saying of Tiberius).
Tacitus. Annals Book 3.65.

O hominis impudentem audaciam! *oh hom—in—iss im—pud—en—tem ow—dah—ki—am!*
O the shameless audacity of man!
Terence. Heautontimorumenos ii. 3.72.

O litus vita mihi dulcius, o mare! Felix Cui licet ad terras ire subinde meas! *oh lee—tuss wee—tah mih—he dull—ki—uss, oh ma—reh! fay—leeks cuee lick—et ad tehr—rahss ee—reh sub—in—deh meh—ahss!*
O shore dearer to me than life! O sea! Happy am I who have leave at last to come to my own country!
Petronius.

O magna vis veritatis, quae contra hominum ingenia, calliditatem, soller-tiam contraque fictas omnium insidias facile per se ipsa defendat! *oh mag—na weece way—rit—ah—tiss, quie con—trah hom—in—um ing—ghen—i—a, cal—lid—it—ah—tem, sol—lehr—ti—am con—trah—queh fick—tahss om—ni—um in—sid—i—ahss fack—ill—eh say pehr say ip—sa day—fen—dat.*
O how great is the power of truth, which against the inventiveness, cunning, and ingenuity of men and against all falsehood and trickery can easily defend itself unaided!
Cicero. Pro Caelio 26/63.

O major tandem, parcas, insane, minori! *oh mah—yore tan—dem, par—kahss, in—sah—neh, min—oh—ree!*
O greater madman, pray have mercy upon a lesser one!
Horace. Sat. Book 2.3.326.

O matre pulchra filia pulchrior. *oh mah—treh pull—crah fee—li—a pull—cri—or.*
O more beautiful daughter of a beautiful mother.
Horace. Odes Book 1.16.1.

O miseras hominum mentes! O pectora caeca! *oh miss—eh—rahss hom—in—um men—tace! oh peck—to—ra kie—ka!*
Oh, how wretched are the minds of men, how blind their hearts!
Lucretius. De Rerum Nat. Book 2.14.

O miseri, quorum gaudia crimen habent! *oh miss—eh—ree, quoh—rum gowd—i—a cree—men hab—ent.*
O wretched men, whose joys are mixed with crime!
Pseudo—Gallus. Maximianus 1.180.

O mors, cur mihi sera venis? *oh morse, coor mih—he say—ra wen—iss?*
O death, why do you come so late to me?
Propertius. Elegies 2.13.50.

. . . O munera nondum/Intellecta Deum. . . . *oh moo—neh—ra none—dum in—tell—lect—a deh—um.*
O gifts of the gods, not yet understood.
Lucanus. Pharsalia Book 5.525.

O nimium, nimiumque oblite tuorum! *oh nim—i—um, nim—i—um—queh ob—lee—teh to—oh—rum!*
O too, too forgetful of your own kin.
Ovid. Heroides 1.41.

O noctes, coenaeque Deum! *oh nock—tace, coy—nye—queh deh—um!*
O nights and banquets of the gods!
Horace. Sat. Book 2.6.65.

O nomen dulce libertatis! *oh noe—man dull—keh lee—bear—tah—tiss!*
O sweet name of liberty!
Cicero. In Verrem Book 5.63.162.

O passi graviora! *oh pass—ee gra—wi—oh—ra!*
O ye who have suffered greater woes.
Virgil. Æneid 1.199.

O praeclarum diem, cum ad illud divinum animorum consilium coitumque proficiscar, cumque ex hac turba et colluvione discedam!
oh pri—clah—rem di—em, cum ad ill—ud di—wee—num an—im—oh—rum

[131]

cone—sil—i—um co—it—um—queh pro—fick—iss—car, cum—queh ex hahn
turbah—et coll—iu—wi—oh—neh dis—kay—dam!
O greatest of days, when I shall hasten to that divine assembly and gathering of souls, and when I shall depart from this crowd and rabble of life!
Cicero. De Senectute 23.85.

O quam contempta res est homo nisi supra humana se erexerit.
oh quam con—temp—ta race est hom—oh niss—ee sup—rah hoo—mah—na
say ay—rex—eh—rit.
O how contemptible a thing is man unless he can raise himself above what is human.
Seneca. Nat. Quaest. Book 1. Pref.

O quanta species cerebrum non habet! *oh quan—ta speck—i—ace keh—reb—*
rum none hab—et!
O that such beauty should be so devoid of understanding!
Phaedrus.

O, quid solutis est beatius curis! *oh, quid so—loot—eece est beh—ah—ti—uss*
coo—reece!
Oh, what more blissful than cares set at rest!
Catullus. 31.7.

O sacer, et magnus vatum labor! Omnia fato/Eripis, et populis donas
mortalibus aevum. *oh sack—er, et mag—nuss wat—um lab—or! om—ni—a*
fah—toe ay—rip—uss, et pop—ul—eece doe—nahss mor—tah—lib—uss
eye—wum.
O sacred and great achievement of the poets! You wrest all things from fate, and give lasting existence to mortal peoples.
Lucan. Pharsalia Book 9.980.

O sancta simplicitas! *oh sanc—ta sim—plee—chit—ahss.*
O holy simplicity.
John Huss. At the stake 1415.

O, si sic omnia! *oh, see seek om—ni—a!*
Oh, if all things were thus! *or* Oh, if all things had thus been done!

O tempora! O mores! *oh temp—o—ra! oh moh—race!*
O times! O manners!
Cicero, In Catilinam 1.1.

Obiter dicta. *ob—it—er dick—ta.*
Remarks by the way.

Oblatam occasionem tene. *ob—lah—tam ock—kah—si—oh—nem ten—eh.*
Seize an opportunity when it is offered.
Cicero.

Obscurum per obscurius. *op—scoo—rum pair op—scoo—ri—uss.*
Something obscure (explained) by something more obscure.
Pr.

Obsecro, tuum est? vetus credideram. *op—seck—ro, tu—um est? wet—uss*
cray—did—eh—ram.
Really, is it yours? I had supposed it was something old.
Pr. Addressed to a plagiarist.

Obsequio vinces. *op—seck—wi—oh win—case.*
By deference you shall prevail.

Obstupui, stereruntque comae, et vox faucibus haesit.
op—stup—u—ee, stet—eh—runt—queh com—eye, et wohkss fow—kib—uss
hie—sit.
I was astounded, my hair stood on end, and my voice stuck in my throat.
Virgil. Æneid 2.774. and 3.48.

Occidat dum imperet. *ock—key—dat dum im—peh—ret.*
Let him kill me, so long as he is emperor!
Agrippina, of her son Nero. Tacitus. Annals 14.9.

Occisissimus sum omnium qui vivunt. *ock—key—siss—sim—uss sum*
om—ni—um quee wee—wunt.
Of all men living I am the most completely beaten down.
Plautus. Casina iii. 5.53.

Occultare morbum funestum. *ock—cult—ah—reh more—bum*
foo—nest—um.
To hide disease is fatal.
Pr.

Oderint dum metuant. *ode—eh—rint dum met—u—ant.*
Let them hate so long as they fear.
Cicero. Pro Sextio 48 and Philippic 1.

Oderunt peccare boni virtutis amore. *oh—day—runt peck—cah—reh bon—ee*
wihr—too—tiss a—moh—re.
The good hate to sin through love of virtue.
Horace. Ep. 1.16.52.

Odi et amo. Quare id faciam, fortasse requiris./Nescio: sed fieri sentio, et excrucior. *oh—dee et am—oh. quah reh id fack—i—am, for—tass—seh re- quee—riss. ness—ki—oh: sed fi—eh—ree sent—i—oh, et ex—cruc—i—or.*
I hate and I love. Why do I do so, you perhaps ask. I cannot say; but I feel it to be so, and I am tormented.
Catullus. Carmen 85.

Odi profanum vulgus et arceo./Favete linguis. . . . *oh—dee proh—fah—num wool—guss et ark—eh—oh. fa—way—teh lin—gweece.*
I hate the uncultivated crowd and keep them at a distance. Favour me by your tongues (keeping silence).
Horace. Odes Book 3.1.

. . . Odia qui nimium timet,/Regnare nescit. . . . *od—i—a quee nim—i—um tim—et reg—nah—reh ness—kit.*
He who fears hatred over much, does not know how to rule.
Seneca. OEdipus iii. 703.

Odium theologicum. *od—i—um theh—o—log—ic—um.*
Theological rancour.
Pr.

Ohe! Jam satis est. . . . *o—hay! yam sat—iss est.*
Ho there! there is now enough.
Horace, Sat. Book 1.5.12; Martial, Epig. Book 4.91.1; Plautus etc.

Olet lucernam. *o—let luck—air—nam.*
It smells of the lamp.
Pr.

Oleum adde camino. *ol—eh—um add—deh ca—mee—noh.*
To add fuel to the fire. (Proverbial expression.)
Horace. Sat. Book 2.3.321.

Olla male fervet. *oll—a ma—lay fair—wet.*
The pot boils badly (*i.e.* things do not go favourably).
Pr. Petronius 38.13.

Omne aevum curae; cunctis sua displicet aetas. *om—neh eye—wum coo—rye; cunc—teece su—a diss—plick—et eye—tahss.*
Cares possess every age; their own age is distasteful to all.
Ausonius.

Omne animal seipsum diligere. *om—neh an—im—al say—ip—sum dee—lig—eh—reh.*

[134]

Every animal loves itself.
Cicero. De Finibus Book 5.10.

Omne pulchrum amabile. *om—neh pull—crum a—mah—bill—eh.*
Everything beautiful is lovable.
Pr.

Omne solum forti patria est. *om—neh sol—um for—tee pat—ri—a est.*
To a brave man every land is a native land.
Ovid. Fast. 1.393.

Omnes composui. *om—nace com—poss—u—ee.*
I have settled them all (in their funeral urns).
Horace. Sat. Book 1.9.28.

Omnes hi metuunt versus, odere poetas. *om—nace hee met—u—unt*
wear—sooce, oh—day—reh po—ay—thass.
All these fear verses and hate poets.
Horace. Sat. Book 1.4.33.

Omnes in malorum mari navigamus. *om—nace in ma—loh—rum ma—ree*
nah—wig—ah—muss.
We are all embarked on a sea of troubles.
Pr.

Omnes oedem cogimur; omnium/versatur urna serius ocius/sors exitura,
et nos in aeternum/exsilium imposita cymbae. *om—nace eh—oh—dem*
coe—gim—ur; om—ni—um wear—sah—tur ur—na say—ri—uss oh—ki—uss
sorss ex—it—oo—ra, et noce in eye—tear—num ex—ill—i—um im—poss—it—
oo—ra kim—bye.
We are all compelled by the same force; the lot is cast into the urn, sooner
or later to be drawn forth, to send us to the boat [of Charon] for our
eternal exile.
Horace. Odes Book 2.3.25.

Omnes, quibu' res sunt minu' secundae, magi' sunt, nescio quo modo/
suspiciosi: ad contemeliam omnia accipiunt magis:/Propter suam im-
potentiam se semper credunt negligi. *om—nace, quib—u race sunt min—u*
seck—un—die, ma—ghi sunt, ness—ki—oh quoh mod—oh suss—pick—i—oh—
see: ad con—tum—ay—li—am om—ni—a ack—kip—i—unt mag—iss: prop—ter
su—am im—pot—ent—i—am see semp—er cre—dunt neg—lee—gee.
All men in less prosperous circumstances are by some means, I know not
how, suspicious: they take all things more readily as of the nature of an
insult; and believe that they are always being neglected on account of their
helplessness.
Terence. Adelphi iv. 3.14.

[135]

Omnes sapientes decet conferre et fabulari. *om—nace sap—i—ent—ace deck—et cone—fair—reh et fah—bul—ah—ree.*
It becomes all wise men to confer and hold converse.
Plautus. Rudens ii. 3.8.

Omni malo punico inest granum putre. *om—nee mah—loe poo—nick—oh in—est grah—num put—reh.*
In every pomegranate there is a rotten pip.
Pr.

Omnia bonos viros decent. *om—ni—a bon—oce wi—roce deck—ent.*
All things are becoming to good men.
Pr.

Omnia Castor emis, sic fiet ut omnia vendas. *om—ni—a cass—tor em—iss, seek fi—et ut om—ni—a wen—dahss.*
You buy all things, Castor, so it will come to pass that you will have to sell all things.
Martial. Epig. Book 7.97.

Omnia conando docilis sollertia vicit. *om—ni—a cone—an—doe dock— ill—iss soll—lair—ti—a wee—kit.*
Ready cleverness has overcome all things by determination.
Manilius. 1.95.

Omnia desuper. *om—ni—a day—sup—er.*
All things are from above.
Pr.

Omnia fert aetas, animum quoque. . . . *om—ni—a fairt eye—tahss, an—im— um quo—queh.*
Age carries all things away, even the mind.
Virgil. Eclogues 9.51.

Omnia inconsulti impetus coepta, initiis valida, spatio languescunt.
om—ni—a in—cone—sul—tee im—pet—uss coyp—ta, in—it—i—eece wal—id—a, spat—i—oh lang—gwesk—unt.
All undertakings of ill—considered impulse, though strong in their beginnings, languish with time.
Tacitus. Hist. Book 3.58.

Omnia mala exempla ex bonis initiis orta sunt. *om—ni—a mal—a ex—em— pla ex bon—eece in—it—i—eece or—ta sunt.*
All bad examples of anything came originally from good beginnings.
Sallust. Catilina 51.

[136]

Omnia mutantur, nihil interit. *om—ni—a moo—tant—ur, ni—hill in—teh—rit.*
All things change, nothing perishes.
Ovid. Metam. 15.165.

Omnia praeclara rara. *om—ni—a pry—clah—ra rah—ra.*
All things which excel are rare.
Cicero.

Omnia praesumunter rite et solemniter esse acta. *om—ni—a pry—soo—nun—tur ree—teh et sol—em—nit—er ess—seh ack—ta.*
All things are presumed to have been done with due observance and custom.
Law.

. . . Omnia Romae/Cum pretio. . . . *om—ni—a roh—mye cum pret—i—oh.*
All things at Rome have their price.
Juvenal. Sat. 3.183.

Omnia serviliter pro dominatione. *om—ni—a sair—wee—lit—air proh dom—in—ah—ti—oh—neh.*
Everything servilely for the sake of power.
Tacitus. Hist. Book 1.36.

Omnia subjecisti sub pedibus ejus, oves et boves. *om—ni—a sub—yah—kiss—tee sub ped—ib—uss ay—yuss, o—vace et bo—vace.*
Thou has put all things under his feet, sheep and oxen.
Vulgate. Ps. 8.7.

Omnia venalia Romae. *om—ni—a way—nah—li—a roe—mye.*
All things are saleable at Rome.
Sallust. Jugurtha 8.

Omnia vincit amor, nos et cedamus amori. *om—ni—a wink—it a—more, noce et kay—dah—muss a—moh—ree.*
Love conquers all, and let us too yield to love.
Virgil. Eclogues 10.69.

Omnibus bonis expedit rempublicam esse salvam. *om—nib—uss bon—eece ex—ped—it rem—pub—lick—am ess—seh sal—wam.*
It is to the interest of all good men that the commonwealth should be safe.
Cicero. Philippics 13.8.16.

Omnibus idem. *om—nib—uss ee—dem.*
To all men the same.
Virgil. Æneid 10.112.

[137]

. . . Omnibus urbs est/Fons et origo malis. . . . *om—nib—uss urps est fohnss et o—ree—goe mal—eece.*
The city is the fount and origin of all evils.
Johannes Baptista Mantuanus.

Omnis fama a domesticis emanat auctoribus. *om—niss fah—ma ah dom—ess—tick—eeyce eh—man—at owk—toh—rib—uss.*
All report of us emanates from our servants (*lit.* from our familiars).
Cicero (adapted). De Petitione Consulatus, 6.

Omnis feret omnia tellus. *om—niss feh—ret om—ni—a tell—looce.*
Every land shall produce all things that it requires.
Virgil. Eclogues 4.39.

Omnis sors ferendo superanda est. *om—niss source feh—ren—doe sup—eh—ran—da est.*
Every lot is to be overcome by endurance.
Pr.

Omnium artium domina [eloquentia]. *om—ni—um art—i—um dom—in—a [ay—lo—quent—ti—a].*
[Eloquence] the mistress of all the arts.
Tacitus. Dialogus de Oratoribus 32.

Omnium enim rerum principia parva sunt. *om—ni—um en—im ray—rum prin—kip—i—a parr—wa sunt.*
For the beginnings of all things are small.
Cicero. De Finibus 5.21.58.

Omnium horarum homo. *om—ni—um hoe—rah—rum hom—oh.*
A man of all hours (*i.e.* ready for anything).
Pr. Quintilian. Book 6.3.

Omnium rerum, heus, vicissitudo est! *om—ni—um ray—rum, huce, wick—iss—sit—oo—doh est!*
Mark this, that there is change in all things.
Terence. Eunuchus 2.2.45.

Onus probandi. *on—uss pro—ban—dee.*
The burden of proof.
Law.

. . . Operosa parvus/Carmina fingo. *op—eh—roe—sa parr—wuss car—min—a fin—goe.*
A small man, I fashion laborious songs.
Horace. Odes Book 4.2.31.

Opinio veritate major. *op—ee—ni—oh way—rit—ah—teh mah—yore.*
Supposition is greater than truth.

Opprobrium medicorum. *op—proh—bi—um med—ick—oh—rum.*
The reproach of physicians (diseases said to be incurable).
Pr.

Optima quaeque dies miseris mortalibus aevi/Prima fugit; subeunt morbi,
tristisque senectus;/Et labor et durae rapit inclementia mortis.
*op—tim—a quie—queh di—ace miss—eh—reece more—tah—lib—uss eye—wee
pree—ma fugit; sub—eh—unt more—bee, triss—tiss—queh sih—neck—tuss;
et lab—or et doo—rye rap—it in—clay—men—ti—a more—tiss.*
The best day of life flies quickest to unhappy mortals; diseases and sad old
age creep on us; and labour and the rigour of cruel death seize our bodies.
Virgil. Georgics 3.66.

Optimi consiliarii mortui. *op—tim—ee cone—sill—i—ah—re more—tu—ee.*
The dead are the best advisers.
Pr. Referring to books.

Opum furiata cupido. *op—um fu—ri—ah—ta cup—ee—doh.*
The mad lust for wealth.
Ovid. Fast. Book 1.211.

Orandum est, ut sit mens sana in corpore sano. *oh—ran—dum est, ut sit
maynce sah—na in core—po—reh sah—noe.*
A sound mind in a sound body is a thing to be prayed for.
Juvenal. Sat. 10.356.

Orate pro nobis. *oh—rah—teh proh noe—beece.*
Pray for us.
Vulgate. 2 Thess. 3.1.

Orci habet galeam. *ore—key hab—et gal—eh—am.*
He has the helmet of Orcus (*i.e.* of Pluto, whose helmet rendered the
wearer invisible).
Pr.

Ore rotundo. *oh—reh ro—tun—doh.*
With a good delivery (*lit.,* with round mouth).
Horace. De Arte Poetica 323.

Ore tenus. *oh—reh ten—uss.*
From the mouth only; oral evidence.
Law.

[139]

Os dignum aeterno nitidum quod fulgeat auro,/Si mallet laudare Deum;
cui sordida monstra/Praetulit, et liquidam temeravit crimine vocem.
oce dig—num eye—tear—noe nit—id—um quod full—geh—at ow—roe, see
mahl—let low—dah—reh deh—um; cu—ee sore—did—a moan—stra pry—tul—
it, et li—quid—am tem—eh—rah—wit cree—min—eh woe—kem.
A splendid countenance worthy to shine in lasting gold, if he had preferred
to praise our God; to whom he preferred base monsters, and defiled his
fluent voice with sin.
Prudentius. (Referring to the anti-Christian.)

Os, orare, vale, communio, mensa negatur. *oce, oh—rah—reh, wal—ay,*
com—moon—i—oh, main—sa neg—ah—tur.
Speech, prayer, greeting, intercourse, food are denied.
Sentence of Excommunication.

Otiosa sedulitas. *oh—ti—oh—sa say—dull—it—ahss.*
Idle industry.

Otiosis nullus adstitit Deus. *oh—ti—oh—seece null—lus ad—stit—it deh—uss.*
No diety stands by the idle.
Pr.

Otium cum dignitate. *oh—ti—um cum dig—nit—ah—teh.*
Ease (or leisure) with dignity.
Cicero. In the form "Cum dignitate otium". Pro P. Sexto 45.98.

Otium naufragium castitatis. *oh—ti—um now—frag—i—um cass—ti—tah—tiss.*
Idleness is the shipwreck of chastity.
Pr.

P

Pabulum Acherontis. *pah—bull—um a—keh—ron—tiss.*
Food of Acheron (*i.e.* of the grave; spoken of one fit to die).
Plautus. Casina Act ii. 1.11.

Pabulum animi. *pah—bull—um an—im—ee.*
The food of the mind (knowledge).
Pr.

Pacta conventa. *pack—ta con—went—a.*
Conditions agreed upon.
Pr.

Palinodiam canere. *pal—in—ode—i—am can—eh—reh.*
To recant (*Lit.* 'to sing a palinode'.)
Macrobius. Sat. 7.5.

Pallentesque habitant Morbi, tristisque Senectus,/Et Metus et malesuada
Fames, et turpis Egestas. *pall—len—tace—queh hab—it—ant more—bee,*
trist—iss—queh seh—nect—tuss, et met—uss et mal—eh—swah—da fam—ace,
et turpis egg—ess—tahss.
Pale Disease dwells there, and sad Old Age, and Fear, and Famine persuad-
ing to evil, and hateful Want.
Virgil. Æneid 6.275.

Pallida mors aequo pulsat pede pauperum tabernas,/Regumque turres. . . .
pall—lid—a morse eye—quoh pull—sat ped—eh pow—peh—rum tab—air—
nahss, ray—gum—queh tur—race.
Pale death knocks with impartial foot at the cottages of the poor and at
the towers of kings.
Horace. Odes Book 1.4.13.

Palmam qui meruit ferat. *pal—mam quee meh—ru—it feh—rat.*
Let him bear the palm who has deserved it.
Motto of Lord Nelson.

Par negotiis neque supra erat. *parr neg—oh—ti—eece neh—queh sup—rah*
eh—rat.
He was equal to his business but not beyond it.
Tacitus. Annals Book 6.39.

Par nobile fratrum. *parr noe—bill—eh frah—trum.*
A noble pair of brothers.
Horace. Sat. 2.3.243.

Parens patriae. *pa—raynce pat—ri—eye.*
Parent of his country. (*See* "Pater patriae.")
Pliny. Book 7.

Pari passu. *pair—eye pas—you.*
With equal step (*i.e.* proceeding side by side at the same pace).
Pr.

Paritur pax bello. *pa—rit—ur pahx bell—loe.*

[141]

Peace is produced by war.
Cornelius Nepos.

Pars minima est ipsa puella sui. *parse min—im—a est ip—sa pu—ell—la su—ee.*
The girl herself is the least part of herself.
Ovid. Rem. Amoris. 344.

Pars sanitatis velle sanari fuit. *parse sah—nit—ah—tiss well—leh sah—nah—
ree fu—it.*
It was a sign of health that he was willing to be cured.
Seneca. Hippolytus i. 249.

Partibus locare. *parr—tib—us lock—ah—reh.*
To let on sharing terms.
Law.

Parturient montes; nascetur ridiculus mus. *parr—tur—i—ent mon—tace;
nah—skay—tur ree—dick—ul—uss moose.*
The mountains are in labour; an absurd mouse will be born.
Horace. De Arte Poetica 139.

Parva leves capiunt animos. *parr—wa leh—wace cap—i—unt an—im—oce.*
Small things captivate light minds.
Ovid. Ars Amat. Book 1.159.

Pascitur in vivis livor; post fata quiescit,/Cum suus, ex merito, quemque
tuetur honos./Ergo etiam, cum me supremus adederit ignis,/Vivam: parsque
mei multa superstes erit. *pass—kit—ur in wee—weece lee—wore; post fah—
ta qui—ace—kit, cum su—us, ex meh—rit—oh, quem—queh tu—ay—tur
hon—oce. air—go et—yam, cum may sup—ray—muss ad—aid—eh—rit ig—niss,
wee—wam: parse—queh meh—ee mull—ta sup—air—stess eh—rit.*
Malice feeds on the living; after life is over it rests, whilst honour preserves
everyone according to his desert. Therefore, indeed, when the funeral flame
has consumed me, I shall live; and a great part of me shall survive me.
Ovid. Amorum Book 1.15.39.

Passibus ambiguis, Fortuna volubilis errat,/Et manet in nullo certa tenaxque
loco. *pass—sib—uss am—big—u—eece, for—too—na wol—oo—bill—iss air—rat,
et man—et in null—loh care—ta ten—ahx—queh lock—oh.*
Volatile Fortune wanders with uncertain steps, and remains in no place
with any assured or lasting stay.
Ovid. Trist. 5.8.15.

Pater familias. *pat—er fam—ill—i—ahss/pay—ter fam—ill—i—ass.*
Father of a family.
Roman Law.

Pater noster, qui es in coelis. *pat—er noss—ter, quee ace in chay—lease.*
Our Father, which art in heaven.
Vulgate. St. Matt. 6.9.

Pater patriae. *pat—er pat—ri—eye.*
Father of his country.
Juvenal. Sat. 8.244. Cicero etc.

Patientia laesa fit furor. *pat—i—ent—i—a lie—sa fit fu—roar.*
Patience abused becomes madness.
Pr.

Patientissimus veri. *pat—i—en—tuss—sim—uss way—ree.*
Most patient of the truth; willing to endure plain-speaking.
Tacitus. Dialogues de Oratoribus 8.

Patitur qui vincit. *pat—it—ur quee wink—it.*
He suffers who conquers.
Pr.

Patriae solum omnibus carum est. *pat—ri—eye sol—um om—nib—uss
ca—rum est.*
The soil of our native land is dear to us all.
Cicero (adapted). See Or. in Catil. 4.

. . . Pauca Catonis/Verba, sed a pleno venientia pectore veri.
*pow—ca cat—oh—niss wear—ba, sed ah play—noh wen—i—en—ti—a pect—to—
reh way—ree.*
The words of Cato were few but proceeding from a heart full of truth.
Lucan. Pharsalia Book 9.188.

Pauci vident morbum suum, omnes amant. *pow—key wid—ent more—bum
su—um, om—nace am—ant.*
Few see their own disease, all love it.
Pr.

Paulo majora canemus. *pow—loh mah—yoh—ra can—ay—muss.*
Let us sing of somewhat greater matters.
Virgil. Eclogues. 4.1.

Paulo post futurum. *pow—loh post fu—too—rum.*
A little after the future, *i.e.* indefinitely remote.

Pauperies immunda domus procul absit. *pow—peh—ri—ace im—mun—da
dom—ooce pro—cull ap—sit.*

[143]

May foul poverty be far from your home.
Horace. Ep. Book 2.2.199.

Pauperis est numerare pecus. *pow—peh—riss est num—eh—rah—reh peck—uss.*
It is natural for a poor man to count his flock.
Ovid. Metam. 13.824.

Paupertas omnium artium repertrix. *pow—pair—tahss om—ni—um arr—ti—um re—pair—treeks.*
Poverty is the discoverer of all the arts.
Apollonius. De Magia p. 285.35.

Pax vobiscum. *pahx woe—bee—scum.*
Peace be with you.
Vulgate. Genesis 43.23. etc.

Peccavi. *peck—cah—wee.*
I have sinned.
Vulgate. St. Luke 15.21.

Pectus est quod disertos facit. *peck—tuss est quod di—sair—toce fack—it.*
It is the heart which makes men eloquent.
Quintillian 10.7.

Pecunia regimen est rerum omnium. *peck—oo—ni—a reg—im—en est ray—rum om—ni—um.*
Money is the ruling spirit of all things.
Publilius Syrus.

Pecuniae obediunt omnia. *peck—oo—ni—ay ob—ay—di—unt om—ni—a.*
All things are obedient to money.
Vulgate. Ecclesiastes 10.19.

Pecuniam accipere docuimus. *peck—oo—ni—am ack—kip—eh—reh dock—u—im—uss.*
We have taught them to accept money.
Tacitus. Germania 15.

Pecuniam in loco negligere, maximum interdum est lucrum.
peck—oo—ni—am in lock—oh neg—lig—eh—reh, max—im—um in—tear—dum est luck—rum.
To despise money on occasion is now and then a very great gain.
Terence. Adelphi ii. 2.8.

Pedibus compensari pecuniam. *ped—ib—uss com—pain—sah—ree peck—oo—ni—am.*
Money is balanced by feet: *i.e.* either, 'money is made by hard work' or, 'more distant property costs more'.
A saying of Cato, cited by Cicero, Pro Flacco 39/72, in the second sense.

Pejor est bello timor ipse belli. *pay—yore est bell—loh tim—or ip—seh bell—lee.*
Worse than war is the fear of war.
Seneca. Thyestes 572.

Pejor odio amoris simulatio. *pay—yore odd—i—oh a—moh—riss sim—ul—ah—ti—oh.*
Pretence of love is worse than hatred.
Pliny the Younger. Paneg. Traj. 85.

Pelion imposuisse Olympo. *pay—li—on im—poss—u—iss—seh o—lim—poe.*
To pile Pelion upon Olympus.
Horace. Odes Book 3.4.52.

Pellitur e medio sapientia, vi geritur res, Spernitur orator bonus, horridus miles amatur. *pell—lit—ur ay med—i—oh sap—i—en—ti—a, wee gheh—rit—ur race, spare—nit—ur oh—rah—tor bon—uss, horr—rid—uss mee—less am—ah—tur.*
Wisdom is thrown out of the centre, affairs are run by force, the good orator is scorned, the rough soldier is loved.
Ennius, Annals 8, fr.275, cited by Cicero, Pro Murena 14/30.

. . . Pendent opera interrupta. . . . *pen—dent op—eh—ra in—tear—rup—ta.*
The work is suspended through interruption.
Virgil. Æneid 4.88.

. . . Penitus toto divisos orbe Britannos. *pen—it—uss toe—toe dee—wee—soce or—beh brit—an—noce.*
The Britons, separated from almost the whole world.
Virgil. Eclogues 1.67.

Perdet te pudor hic. *pair—det tay pud—or heek.*
This modesty will be the ruin of you.
Martial. Epig. Book 10.98.11.

Per ardua ad astra. *per ar—du—a ad ast—ra.*
To the stars through difficulties.
Motto.

Per incuriam. *per in—coo—ri—am.*
Through carelessness.
Pr.

Per mare, per terras. *per ma—reh, per tear—rahss.*
By sea and by land.
Ovid. Heroides 7.88.14.101.

Per saltum. *per sal—tum.*
By a leap.
Pr.

Per scelera semper sceleribus tutum est iter. *per skell—eh—ra sem—per skell—eh—rib—uss too—tum est it—er.*
The safe way to crime is always through crime.
Seneca. Agamemnon ii. 115.

Per stirpes. *per steer—pace.*
According to the original stock.
Law.

Per undas et ignes fluctuat nec mergitur. *per un—dahss et ig—nace fluct—u—at neck mare—git—ur.*
Through waves and flames she is tossed about but not submerged.
Matthew of Paris.

Per varios casus, per tot discrimina rerum. *per wa—ri—oce cah—sooce, per tot diss—cree—min—a ray—rum.*
Through various chances and so many dangers.
Virgil. Æneid 1.204.

Percunctare a peritis. *per—cunc—tah—reh ah peh—rit—eece.*
Seek information from the experienced.
Cicero. In Somn. Scip. 1.

Perdet te pudor hic. *pair—det tay pud—or heek.*
This modesty will be the ruin of you.
Martial. Epig. Book 10.98.11.

Perdis, et in damno gratia nulla tuo. *pair—diss, et in dam—noh grah—ti—a null—la tu—oh.*
You lose, and have no thanks in your loss.
Ovid. Ars Amat. 1.434.

Pereant amici, dum una inimici intercidant. *peh—reh—ant am—ee—key,*

dum oo—nah in—im—ee—key int—er—key—dant.
Let our friends perish, provided that our enemies fall with them.
Cicero. Proverb condemned by him.

Pereunt et imputantur. *peh—reh—unt et im—put—ant—ur.*
They (the hours) pass by, and are put to our account.
Martial. Epig. Book 5.21.13.

Perfer et obdura; dolor hic tibi proderit olim. *pair—fer et ob—doo—rah;*
dol—or heek tib—ee pro—deh—rit oh—lim.
Endure and persist; this pain will turn to your good by and by.
Ovid. Amorum Book 3.11.7.

Perfer et obdura; multo graviora tulisti. *pair—fer et ob—doo—rah; mul—toe*
gra—wi—oh—ra tul—us—tee.
Endure and persist; you have borne heavier fortunes by far.
Ovid. Tristia Book 5.11.7.

Perfervidum ingenium Scotorum. *pair—fair—wid—um in—gen—i—um*
scot—oh—rum.
The very ardent disposition of the Scots.
Pr.

Perfida, sed quamvis perfida, cara tamen. *pair—fid—a, sed quam—weece*
pair—fid—a, cah—ra tem—en.
She is false, but however false, she is still dear.
Tibullus. Book 3.7.24.

Perfidiosus est amor. *pair—fid—i—oh—suss est a—mor.*
Love is perfidious.
Plautus. Cistellaria i. 1.75.

. . . Pergis pugnantia secum/Frontibus adversis componere? . . . .
pair—giss pug—nan—ti—a say—cum front—ib—uss ad—wear—seece
com—poe—neh—reh?
Do you persist in trying to reconcile things at variance with themselves,
with natures opposed to each other?
Horace. Sat. Book 1.1.102.

Pericula qui audet, ante vincit quam accipit. *peh—reek—ul—a quee ow—det,*
ant—eh win—ket quam ack—kip—it.
He who dares dangers overcomes them before he incurs them.
Publilius Syrus.

Pericula timidus etiam quae non sunt videt. *peh—reek—ul—a tim—id—uss et—yam quie none sunt wid—et.*
The timid sees dangers which do not even exist.
Publilius Syrus.

. . . Perierunt tempora longi/Servitii. *peh—ri—ay—runt tem—po—ra long—ghee sair—wit—i—ee.*
The time of my long bondage has passed.
Juvenal. Sat. 3.124.

. . . Perjuria ridet amantum/Juppiter. . . . *pair—you—ri—a ree—det a—man—tum yup—pit—er.*
At lovers' perjuries Jupiter laughs.
Tibullus. Book 4.7.17.

Persicos odi, puer, apparatus. *pair—sick—oce oh—dee, pu—er, ap—pa—rah—tooce.*
Persian luxury, boy, I hate.
Horace.

Perspicuitas in verbis praecipuam habet proprietatem. *pair—spick—u—it—ahss in wear—beece pry—kip—u—am hab—et prop—ri—et—ah—tem.*
Clearness is the most important matter in the use of words.
Quintilian. 8.2.1.

Pia desideria. *pi—a day—see—deh—ri—a.*
Pious wishes.
Title of work pub. in Antwerp, 1627, by Hermann Hugo, a Jesuit 1588-1639.

Pia fraus. *pi—a frowse.*
A pious fraud.
Ovid. Met. 9.711.

Pia vota. *pi—a woe—ta.*
Pious prayers.
Variant of "Pia desideria."

. . . Pictoribus atque poetis/Quidlibet audendi semper fuit aequa potestas. *pick—toe—rib—uss at—queh po—ay—teece quid—lib—et ow—den—dee sem—per fu—it eye—qua pot—est—ahss.*
To poets and painters alike there has always been a capacity for daring anything.
Horace. De Arte Poetica 9.

Pietas fundamentum est omnium virtutum. *pi—et—ahss fun—dah—men—tum est om—ni—um wihr—too—tum.*
Piety is the foundation of all virtues.
Cicero. Pro Plancio 12.

Pinguis venter non gignit sensum tenuem. *pin—gwiss went—er none gig—nit sane—sum ten—u—em.*
A fat belly does not produce a fine sense.
St. Jerome.

Pirata est hostis humani generis. *peer—ah—ta est hoss—tiss hoo—mah—nee gen—eh—riss.*
A pirate is an enemy of the human race.
Coke.

Piscator ictus sapiet. *pisk—ah—tor ick—tuss sap—i—et.*
The fisherman when stung will grow wise.
Pr.

Piscem natare doces. *pisk—em nah—tah—reh dock—ace.*
You are teaching a fish to swim.
Pr.

Placeat homini quidquid Deo placuit. *plack—eh—at hom—in—ee quid—quid deh—oh plack—u—it.*
Let that which has pleased God please man.
Seneca.

Placet ille meus mihi mendicus, suus rex reginae placet. *plack—et ill—leh meh—uss mi—hee men—dee—cuss, su—us rakes ray—ghee—nye plack—et.*
That beggar of mine pleases me, as her king pleases a queen.
Plautus. Stichus i. 2.

Platonem non accepit nobilem philosophia sed fecit. *plat—oh—nem none ack—kay—pit no—bill—em fil—oss—off—i—a sed fay—kit.*
Philosophy did not find Plato noble, it made him so.
Seneca. Epist. 44.

Plausibus ex ipsis populi, laetoque favore,/Ingenium quodvis incaluisse potest. *plow—sib—uss ex ip—seece pop—ul—ee, lie—toe—queh fa—woh—reh, in—gen—i—um quod—weece in—cal—u—iss—seh pot—est.*
Any nature whatsoever might warm with the very applause of the people, and their wild enthusiasm.
Ovid. Ep. ex Ponto 3.4.29.

Plausus tunc arte carebat. *plow—suss tunc ar—teh ca—ray—bat.*
In those days applause was without art.
Ovid. Ars Amat. Book 1.113.

Plerumque gratae divitibusque vices. *play—rum—queh grah—tie dee—wit—ib—uss—queh wick—ace.*
Change is generally pleasing to the rich.
Horace. Odes Book 3.29.13.

Pluma haud interest. *ploo—mah howd in—teh—rest.*
It matters not a feather (*i.e.* there is not the difference of a feather).
Plautus. Mostellaria ii.1.60.

Plures amicos mensa quam mens concipit. *ploo—race a—meek—oce main—sa quam maynce con—kip—it.*
The table attracts more friends than the mind.
Publilius Syrus.

Plures crapula quam gladius. *ploo—race crah—pull—a quam glad—i—uss.*
Drunkenness kills more than the sword.
Pr.

Pluribus intentus, minor est ad singula sensus. *ploo—rib—uss in—ten—tuss, min—or est ad sing—gull—a sane—suss.*
Our perception, when intent on too many things, is less able to grasp matters singly.
Pr.

. . . Plurima sunt quae/Non audent homines pertusa dicere laena.
ploo—rim—a sunt quie none ow—dent hom—in—ace pair—too—sah dee—keh—reh lie—nah.
There are many things which men dare not say when their clothes are in holes.
Juvenal. Sat. 5.130.

Pluris est oculatus testis unus, quam auriti decem;/Qui audiunt, audita dicunt: qui vident plane sciunt. *ploo—russ est ock—ul—ah—tuss test—iss oo—nuss, quam ow—ree—tee deck—em; qui ow—di—unt, ow—dee—ta deek—unt: qui wid—ent plah—nay ski—unt.*
One eye—witness is better than ten hearsay; Those who hear, tell what they hear: but those who see truly know.
Pr.

Plus aliis de te quam tu tibi credere noli. *plooce al—i—eece day tay quam too tib—ee cray—deh—reh noh—lee.*

[150]

Do not believe others concerning yourself more than you believe yourself.
Cato. 1.14.

Plus dolet quam necesse est qui ante dolet quam necesse est.
plooce dol—et quam neck—ess—seh est quee ant—eh dol—et quam neck—ess—seh est.
He grieves more than he needs, who grieves before he needs.
Seneca. Epist. 95.

Plus ratio quam vis caeca valere solet. *plooce rat—i—oh quam weece key—ca wal—ey—reh sol—et.*
Reason is apt to be of more avail than blind force.
Gallus. Elegy 2. ad fin.

Poenas garrulus iste dabit. *poy—nahss gar—rul—uss iss—teh dab—it.*
That talkative fellow will be punished.
Ovid. Amorum Book 2.2.60.

Poesis est vinum daemonum. *po—ay—siss est vee—num day—mon—um.*
Poetry is devil's wine.
St. Augustine.

Poeta nascitur, non fit. *po—ay—ta nah—skit—ur, non fit.*
A poet is born, not made.
Pr. See "Nascimur".

. . . Poetica surgit/Tempestas. *po—ay—tick—a sur—git tem—pest—ahss.*
A poetical tempest arises.
Juvenal. Sat. 12.24.

Polypi mentem obtine. *po—lip—ee men—tem ob—tin—ay.*
Get the faculty of the polypus (supposed to be able to change its colour to suit its surroundings).
Pr.

Pomifer autumnus. *poe—mi—fer ow—tum—nuss.*
Fruit-bearing autumn.
Horace. Odes Book 4.7.11.

Ponderanda sunt testimonia, non numeranda. *pon—deh—rand—a sunt test—im—oh—ni—a, none num—eh—rand—a.*
Testimonies are to be weighed, not counted.
Pr.

. . . Pone irae frena modumque,/Pone et avaritiae. . . . *poe—neh ee—rye*

[151]

frah—na mod—um—queh, poe—neh et a—wah—rit—i—eye.
Place a curb and a drag on your passion; put a restraint also on your avarice.
Juvenal. Sat. 8.88.

Pone metum; valeo. *poe—neh met—um; wal—eh—oh.*
Dismiss your fear; I am well.
Ovid. Tristia Book 5.2.3.

Pone seram; cohibe; sed quis custodiet ipsos/Custodes? Cauta est, et ab
illis incipit uxor. *poe—neh sih—ram; co—hib—ay; sed quiss cust—ode—i—et
ip—sose cust—ode—ace? cow—ta est, et ab ill—lease in—kip—it uck—soar.*
Fasten the bolt; restrain her; but who will guard the guards themselves?
Your wife is cunning, and begins with them.
Juvenal. Sat. 6.347.

Pons Asinorum. *pons ass—in—oar—um.*
The asses' bridge.
Traditional name of the fifth theorem of Euclid.

. . . Ponto nox incubat atra;/Intonuere poli, et crebris micat ignibus aether.
*pon—toe nox in—cub—at ah—tra; in—ton—u—ay—reh poll—ee, et cray—
breece mick—at ig—nib—uss eye—thair.*
Black night broods over the deep; the sky thunders, and the air sparkles
with innumerable fires.
Virgil. Æneid 1.89.

Porro meditatus innoxios casus incertus vel etiam adversus culpae non
potest addicere. *por—roe med—it—ah—tooce in—nox—i—oce cah—suss
in—care—tuss well etyam ad—wear—suss cull—pie none pot—est ad—dee—
keh—reh.*
Moreover, when the intention is innocent, an accident or even bad luck
cannot make it blameworthy.
Apuleius. Metamorphoses 3.14.

Porro unum est necessarium. *por—roe oo—num est neck—ess—sah—ri—um.*
Still there is one thing needful.
Vulgate. St. Luke 10.42. Motto of Duke of Wellington.

Portatur leviter quod portat quisque libenter. *pore—tah—tur leh—wit—er
quod pore—tat quiss—queh lib—en—ter.*
What anyone bears willingly he bears easily.
Pr.

Possum nil ego sobrius. *poss—sum neel egg—oh soe—bri—uss.*
I, for my part, can do nothing when sober.
Martial. Ep. Book 11.7.12.

[152]

Possunt quia posse videntur. *poss—sunt qui—a poss—seh wid—en—tur.*
They can, because they think they can.
Virgil. Æneid 5.231.

Post acclamationem bellicam jacula volant. *post ack—clah—mah—ti—oh—
nem bell—lick—em yack—ull—a woll—ant.*
After the shout of war the darts begin to fly.
Pr.

Post Diluvium. *post dee—lu—wi—um/dye—lew—vi—um.*
Subsequent to the flood (denoted by the initials P.D.).
Pr.

Post equitem sedet atra cura. *post eh—quit—em sed—et ah—tra coo—ra.*
Behind the horseman sits black care.
Horace. Odes Book 3.1.40.

Post hoc; ergo propter hoc. *post hoke; air—go prop—ter hoke.*
After this; therefore on account of this.
Pr.

Post malam segetem serendum est. *post mal—am seg—et—em seh—ren—dum
est.*
After a bad crop you should sow.
Seneca. Ep. 81.1.

Post mortem nulla voluptas. *post more—tem nul—la wol—up—tahss.*
No pleasure after death.
*Epicurean Maxim. Part of epitaph of Sardanapalus, as given by Sir. D. Lyndesay, "The
Monarche" (1556).*

Post proelia praemia. *post proy—li—a pry—mi—a.*
After battles rewards.
Pr.

Post tot naufragia portum. *post tot now—frag—i—a pore—tum.*
After so many shipwrecks, the harbour.
Pr.

Postremo in scelera simul ac dedecora prorupit postquam remoto pudore
et metu suo tantum ingenio utebatur. *poss—tray—moe in skel—eh—ra
sim—ul ack day—deck—oh—ra proh—roo—pit posst—quam ray—moe—toe
pud—oh—reh et met—oo su—oh tan—tum ing—ghen—i—oh oo—tay—bah—tur.*
In the end he (Tiberius Caesar) rushed into both crime and depravity at

once, and, when shame and fear had gone, he expressed only his own real nature.
Tacitus. Annals 6.51.

Potentiam cautis, quam acribus consiliis, tutius haberi. *pot—en—ti—am cow—teece, quam ah—crib—uss cone—sil—i—eece, too—ti—uss hab—ay—re.*
Power is to be possessed more safely by cautious counsel than by severity.
Tacitus. Annals Book 11.29.

. . . Potuit fortasse minoris/Piscator, quam piscis, emi. . . . *pot—u—it fore—tass—seh min—oh—riss pisk—ah—tor, quam pisk—iss, em—ee.*
The fisherman could perhaps be bought for less than the fish.
Juvenal. Sat. 4.26.

Praecipuum munus annalium reor, ne virtutes sileantur, utque pravis dictis factisque, ex posteritate et infamia metus sit. *pry—kip—u—um moon—us an—nah—li—um reh—or, nay wihr—too—tace sil—eh—an—tur, ut—queh prah—weece dict—teece fack—teece—queh, ex poss—teh—rit—ah—teh et in—fah—mi—ah met—uss sit.*
I consider it to be the chief office of history that the virtuous qualities of men be not unrecorded, and that evil words and deeds may incur the fear of posterity and future ill report.
Tacitus. Annals Book 3.65.

Praemia virtutis honores. *pry—mi—a wihr—too—tiss hon—oh—race.*
Honours are the rewards of virtue (or of valour).
Pr. (See Cicero. Brutus, 81.281.)

Praemonitus, praemunitus. *pry—mon—it—uss, pry—moon—eat—uss.*
Forewarned, forearmed.
Pr.

Praesens numen, inempta salus. *pry—saynce noo—men, in—emp—ta sal—ooce.*
Unbought health, a deity presiding over the affairs of men.
Claudian. Idyll, 6.76.

Praesentemque refert quaelibet herba Deum. *pry—sen—tem—queh reh—fairt quie—lib—et hair—ba deh—um.*
And every herb reveals a present God.
Anon.

Praesis ut prosis. *pry—siss ut proh—siss.*
Be first that you may be of service.
Pr.

Praestant aeterna caducis. *pry—stant eye—tear—na cad—oo—keece.*
Things eternal are better than things which are transitory.
Pr.

Praestat amicitia propinquitati. *pry—stat am—ee—kit—i—a proh—pin—quit—ah—tee.*
Friendship excels relationship.
Pr.

Praestat cautela quam medela. *pry—stat cow—tay—la quam med—ay—la.*
Precaution is better than cure.
Coke.

Praestat otiosum esse quam male agere. *pry—stat oh—ti—oh—sum ess—seh quam mal—eh ag—eh—reh.*
It is better to be idle than to do wrong.
Pr.

Praeter speciem stultus es. *pry—ter speck—i—em stul—tuss ace.*
You are a bigger fool than you look.
Plautus. Mostellaria iv. 2.48.

Praetulit arma togae, sed pacem armatus amavit. *pry—tul—it arr—ma tog—eye, sed pah—kem ar—mah—tuss a—mah—wit.*
He preferred arms to civil office, but when armed he loved peace.
Lucan. Pharsalia 9.199.

Pretio parata pretio vendita justitia. *pret—i—oh pa—rah—ta pret—i—oh wen—dit—a yust—it—i—a.*
Justice put up at a price is sold at a price.
Quoted by Bacon, Essay "Of a King."

Pretium ob stultitiam fero. *pret—i—um ob stul—ti—ti—am feh—roe.*
I gain the reward of my folly.
Terence. Andria iii. 5.4.

Prima caritas incipit a seipso. *pree—ma cah—rit—ahss in—kip—it ah say—ip—soe.*
Charity first begins with one's self (*i.e.* at home).
Pr.

Prima docet rectum sapientia. *pree—ma dock—et rect—tum sap—i—ent—i—a.*
Wisdom first teaches that which is right.
Juvenal. Sat. 13.189.

[155]

Primo dede mulieris consilio, secundo noli. *pree—moe ded—eh mul—i—eh—riss cone—sil—i—oh, seck—un doe noe—lee.*
Take the first advice of a woman and not the second.
Gilbertus Cognatus Noxeranus.

Primus in orbe Deos fecit timor. *pree—muss in orb—eh deh—oce fay—kit tim—or.*
Fear first made gods in the world.
Statius. Theb., 3, 661. Also attrib. to Petronius by Fulgentius-Mythol. Bk. 1. ch. 1.

Primus inter pares. *pree—muss in—ter pah—race/pry—muss in—ter pair—ease.*
First among equals.
Pr.

Principia probant non probantur. *prin—kip—i—a prob—ant none prob—ant—ur.*
First principles prove and are not proved.
Law.

Principibus placuisse viris non ultima laus est. *prin—kip—ib—uss plack—u—iss—seh wi—reece none ul—tim—a louse est.*
It is not the least praise to have pleased distinguished men.
Horace. Ep. Book 1.17.35.

Principis est virtus maxima nosse suos. *prin—kip—iss est wihr—tooce max—im—a noce—seh so—oce.*
It is a very great virtue in a chief to have known his own followers (or subjects).
Martial. Epig. Book 8.15.8.

Pristinae virtutis memores. *priss—tee—nye wihr—too—tiss mem—o—race.*
Mindful of the valour of former days.
Sallust. Catilina 60.

Privilegium est quasi privata lex. *pree—will—ay—gi—um est qua—si pree—wah—ta lakes.*
Privilege is as it were a private law.
Law.

Privilegium non valet contra rempublicam. *pree—will—ay—gi—um none wal—et con—trah rem—pub—lick—am.*
Privilege does not avail against the commonwealth.
Law.

Pro alieno facto non est puniendus. *proh al—i—ay—noe fack—toe none*

est poon—i—end—uss.
A man is not to be punished for another man's actions.
Law.

Pro aris et focis. *proh ah—reece et fock—eece.*
For altars and hearths.
Cicero. De Natura Deorum 3.40.94.

Pro patria, pro liberis, pro aris atque focis suis. *proh pat—ri—ah, proh lee—beh—reece, proh ah—reece at—queh fock—eece su—eece.*
On behalf of their country, their children, their altars and their hearts.
Sallust.

Pro rege, grege, et lege. *proh ray—geh, greg—eh, et la—geh.*
For king, people, and law.
Motto.

Proba merx facile emptorem repperit. *prob—a mairks fack—il—eh emp—toh—rem rep—peh—rit.*
Good merchandise easily finds a buyer.
Plautus. Poenulus i. 2.128.

Probitas laudatur et alget. *prob—it—ahss lowd—ah—tur et al—get.*
Integrity is praised and starves.
Juvenal. Sat. 1.74.

Probo bona fama maxima est hereditas. *prob—oh bon—a fah—ma max—im—a est hay—rit—dit—ahss.*
To an upright man a good reputation is the greatest inheritance.
Publilius Syrus.

Probum patrem esse oportet, qui gnatum suum/Esse probiorem quam ipse fuerit, postulet. *prob—um pat—rem ess—seh op—ore—tet, quee gnah—tum su—um ess—seh prob—i—oh—rem quam ip—seh fu—eh—rit, post—ul—et.*
It behoves the father to be virtuous who desires his son to be more virtuous than he has been.
Plautus. Pseudolus Act i. 5.24.

Procax otii et potestatis temperantior. *prock—ahx oh—ti—ee et pot—est—ah—tiss tem—peh—ran—ti—or.*
Shameless in his spare time, restrained in office. (Of M. Salvius Otho)
Tacitus. Annals 13.47.

Procul hinc, procul este, severae! *prock—ul hink, prock—ul ess—teh, seh—way—rye.*

Hence, far hence, ye prudes!
Ovid. Amorum Book 2.1.3.

Procul, O procul este, profani! *prock–ul, oh prock–ul ess–teh, pro–fah–nee!*
Keep far off, far off, ye profane ones!
Virgil. Æneid 6.258.

. . . Procul omnis esto/Clamor et ira! *prock–ul om–niss ess–toe clah–mor
et ee–ra!*
Far off be tumult and wrath!
Horace. Odes Book 3.8.15.

Prodigus et stultus donat quae spernit et odit;/Haec seges ingratos tulit,
et feret omnibus annis. *proh–dig–uss et stul–tuss doh–nat quie spare–nit
et oh–dit; hike seg–ess in–grah–toce tul–it, et–feh–ret om–nib–uss
an–neece.*
The prodigal and fool give what they despise and hate; this seed has produced,
and ever will produce in all time, a crop of ungrateful persons.
Horace. Ep. Book 1.7.20.

Proditionem amo, sed proditorem non laudo. *proh–dit–i–oh–nem
am–oh, sed proh–dit–oh–rem none lowd–oh.*
I love the treason, but I do not praise the traitor.
Tr. from Plutarch.

Proditor pro hoste habendus. *proh–dit–or proh hoss–teh hab–end–uss.*
A traitor is to be regarded as an enemy.
Cicero. Adapted. See "Pro Sulla" 31.88 and "De Finibus," 3.19.64.

Proditores, etiam iis quos anteponunt, invisi sunt. *proh–dit–oh–race,
et–yam i–eece quoce ant–eh–poe–nunt, in–wee–see sunt.*
Betrayers are hated even by those whom they benefit.
Tacitus. Annals Book 1.58.

Projice tela manu, sanguis meus. *proh–yick–eh tay–la man–oo,
san–gwiss meh–uss.*
Put away the weapon from your hand, you who are my own flesh and
blood.
Virgil. Æneid 6.835.

Projicit ampullas et sesquipedalia verba,/Si curat cor spectantis tetigisse
querela. *pro–yick–it am–pull–lahss et sess–quip–ed–ah–li–a wear–ba,
see coo–rat cor speck–tan–tiss tet–ig–iss–seh queh–ray–lah.*
He lays aside bombast and words a foot-and-a-half long, if his object is to

[158]

move the heart of the bystander with his complaint.
Horace. De Arte Poet. 97.

Properium humani ingenii est odisse quem laeseris. *prop—ri—um hoo—mah—nee ghen—eh—riss est ode—iss—seh quem lice—eh—riss.*
It is characteristic of human nature to hate him whom you have injured.
Tacitus. Agricola 42.

Proque sua causa quisque disertus erat. *proh—queh su—ah cow—sah quiss—queh diss—air—tuss eh—rat.*
Everyone was eloquent in behalf of his own cause.
Ovid. Fast. 4.112.

Protinus apparet quae arbores frugiferae futurae. *proh—tin—uss ap—pah—ret quie ar—boh—race froo—giff—eh—rye fut—oo—rye.*
It will soon be seen which trees will be fruitful.
Pr.

. . . Proximus ardet/Ucalegon. . . . *prox—im—uss ar—det oo—cal—eg—ohn.*
The house of Ucalegon, your next-door neighbour, is burning.
Virgil. Æneid 2.311.

Proximus sum egomet mihi. *prox—im—uss sum egg—o—met mi—hee.*
I am myself my own nearest of kin; I am dearest to myself.
Terence. Andria iv. 1.12.

Prudens futuri temporis exitum/Caliginosa nocte premit Deus,/Ridetque, si mortalis ultra/Fas trepidat. *prude—aynce fu—too—ree tem—po—riss ex—it—um cah—lee—ghin—oh—sah nock—teh prem—it deh—uss, ree—det—queh, see more—tah—liss ul—trah fahss trep—ee—dat.*
The wise god covers with the darkness of night the issues of the future, and laughs if a mortal is anxious beyond what is right.
Horace. Odes Book 3.29.30.

Prudens in flammam ne manum inicito. *proo—daynce in flam—mam nay man—um in—yick—it—oh.*
If you are prudent, do not thrust your hand into the fire.
Proverb quoted by St. Jerome.

Prudens quaestio dimidium scientae. proo-·daynce kwie—sti—oh dim—eh—dee—um ski—ent—eye.
To know what to ask is already to know half.
Mendel.

Psallere et saltare elegantius quam necesse est probae. *psall—leh—reh et sal—tah—reh ay—leg—ant—i—uss quam neck—ess—seh est prob—eye.*
She (Sempronia) was wont to play and to dance more skillfully than is necessary in an honest woman.
Sallust. Catilina 25.

Puellis nuper idoneus. *pu—ell—leece noo—per i—doh—neh—uss.*
Fitted for girls; a ladies' man.
Horace. Odes Book 3.26.1.

Pugna suum finem, cum jacet hostis, habet. *pug—na su—um fee—nem, cum yack—et hoss—tiss, hab—et.*
The battle has its ending when the enemy is down.
Ovid. Trist. 3.5.34.

Pugnam sperate parati. *pug—nam spay—rah—teh pa—rah—tee.*
Being ready, hope for the battle.
Virgil. Æneid 9.158.

. . . Pulchra/Edepol pecunia dos est. . . . *pull—cra ed—ep—ol peck—oo—ni—a dose est.*
By Heaven, money is a beautiful gift.
Plautus. Epidicus ii. 1.10.

Pulchra comis annisque decens et candida vultu Dulce quiescenti basia blanda dabas. Si te jam vigilans non unquam cernere possum, Somne, precor, jugiter lumina nostra tene. *pull—cra com—eece an—neece—queh dech—aynce et can—did—a wool—too dull—cheh qui—ace—ken—tee bah—si—a bland—a dab—ahss. see tay yam vi—jill—ahnce none un—quam chair—neh—reh poss—sum, som—neh, preck—ore, yu—jit—ehr loom—in—a noss—tra ten—ay.*
Lovely-haired, young, and fair of face, you sweetly gave me tender kisses as I slept. If now I am awake I may never look on you, – Sleep, I beg you, hold my eyes closed for ever!
Manuscript of St. Remy, Rheims, 9th cent.

Pulchrorum autumnus pulcher. *pull—croh—rum ow—tum—nuss pull—ker.*
The autumn of the beautiful is beautiful.
Quoted by Bacon: Essay, "Of Beauty."

Pulvis et umbra sumus. *pull—wiss et um—bra sum—uss.*
We are but dust and shadow.
Horace. Odes Book 4.7.16.

Punctum comparationis. *punk—tum com—pa—rah—ti—oh—niss.*
The point (or standard) of comparison.

Punitis ingeniis gliscit auctoritas, neque aliud externi reges aut qui eadem
saevitia usi sunt nisi dedecus sibi atque illis gloriam peperere.
*poon—ee—teece ing—ghen—i—eece glee—skit owk—toe—rit—ahss, neh—queh
al—i—ud ex—tehr—nee ray—gace out quee eh—ah—dem sye—wit—i—ah
oo—see sunt niss—ee day—deck—uss sib—ee at—queh ill—lease gloh—ri—am
pep—eh—ray—reh*
When genius is punished its influence grows, and all that foreign kings or
those who practise similar cruelty have brought about, is infamy for
themselves and renown for their victims.
Tacitus. Annals 4.35.

Quadrupedante putrem sonitu quatit ungula campum. *quad—rup—ed—ant—
eh put—rem son—it—oo quat—it ung—gull—a cam—pum.*
The hoof with its four-footed reverberation shakes the crumbling field.
Virgil. Æneid 8.596.

Quae caret ora cruore nostro? *quie ca—ret oh—ra cru—oh—reh noss—troh?*
What shore is without our blood? (*i.e.* unstained by the blood of our
soldiers).
Horace. Odes Book 2.1.36.

Quae dant, quaeque negant, gaudent tamen esse rogatae. *quie dant, quie—
queh neg—ant, gow—dent tam—en ess—seh rog—ah—tie.*
Whether they give or refuse, it delights women just the same to have been
asked.
Ovid. Ars Amat. Book 1.345.

Quae dant, quaeque negant, gaudent tamen esse rogatae. *quie dant, quie—
queh neg—ant, goud—ent tam—en ess—seh rog—ah—tie.*
Whether they give or refuse, women are glad to have been asked.
Ovid. Ars amatoria I.

Quae dubitationis tollendae causa contractibus inferuntur, jus commune
non laedunt. *quie dub—it—ah—ti—oh—niss toll—lend—eye cow—sah con—*

tract—ib—uss in—feh—run—tur, yooce com—moo—neh none lie—dunt.
Things introduced into contracts for the sake of removing doubt, do not
affect injuriously any common law right.
Law.

Quae e longinquo magis placent. *quie ay long—ghin—quoh mag—iss
plack—ent.*
Things from afar please us the more.
Pr. Founded on passage following.

Quae ex longinquo in majus audiebantur. *quie ex long—ghin—quoh in
mah—yuss ow—di—ay—ban—tur.*
Which coming from afar were reported of in exaggerated style.
Tacitus. Annals Book 4.23.

Quae fuerant vitia mores sunt. *quie fu—eh—rant wit—i—a moh—race sunt.*
What used to be vices are become fashions.
Seneca.

Quae infra nos nihil ad nos. *quie in—frah noce ni—hill ad noce.*
Things which are below us are nothing to us.
Pr.

Quae legi communi derogant stricte interpretantur. *quie lay—ghee com—
moon—ee day—rog—ant strick—tay in—ter—pret—ant—ur.*
Things which restrict the common law are to be interpreted rigidly.
Law.

Quae lucis miseris tam dira cupido? *quie luke—iss miss—eh—reece tam
dee—ra cup—ee—doh?*
Why is there this cruel craving for light (*i.e.* life) in the wretched?
Virgil. Æneid 6.721.

Quae nescieris, ut bene nota refer. *quie ness—ki—eh—riss, ut beh—neh
noh—ta reh—fer.*
What you are ignorant of, relate as if you knew it well.
Ovid. Ars Amat. Book 1.222.

Quae nimis adparent retia, vitat avis. *quie nim—iss ad—pah—rent ray—ti—a
wee—tat a—wiss.*
The bird avoids the snares which show too conspicuously.
Ovid. Rem. Amor. 516.

. . . Quae non prosunt singula, multa juvant. *quie none proh—sunt sing—
gull—a, mul—ta yu—want.*

Things which are not of value singly, are useful collectively.
Ovid. Rem. Amor. 420.

Quae prosunt omnibus artes. *quie proh—sunt om—nib—uss arr—tace.*
The arts, which profit all men.
Motto of Surgeons' Company.

Quae regio in terris nostri non plena laboris? *quie reg—i—oh in tear—reece noss—tree none play—na lab—oh—reece?*
What region in the world is not full of our labour?
Virgil. Æneid 1.460.

Quae sint, quae fuerint, quae mox ventura trahantur. *quie sint, quie fu— eh—rint, quie mox wen—too—ra tra—han—tur.*
The things which are, which have been, which may happen in time to come.
Virgil. Georgics 4.393.

Quae te dementia cepit? *quie tay day—men—ti—a kay—pit?*
What madness has taken possession of you?
Virgil. Eclogues 6.47.

Quae tibi, quae tali reddam pro carmine dona? *quie ti—bee, quie tah—lee, red—dam proh carr—min—eh doh—na?*
What gifts shall I give to you, what gifts, in reward for such a song?
Virgil. Eclogues 5.81.

Quae uncis sunt unguibus ne nutrias. *quie un—keece sunt un—gwi—buss nay noo—tri—ahss.*
Do not foster animals with hooked claws.
Pr.

Quaenam discors foedera rerum Causa resolvit? Quis tanta deus Veris statuit bella duobus? *quie—nam disc—orce foy—deh—ra ray—rum cow—sa ress—ol—wit? quiss tan—ta deh—uss way—reece stat—u—it bell—la du—oh—buss?*
What inharmonious cause breaks open the treaties of the universe? What god ordained so great a battle between two truths?
Boethius.

Quaerenda pecunia primum est; Virtus post nummos. *quie—ren—da peck— oo—ni—a pree—mum est; wihr—tooce post num—moce.*
Getting money is the first thing; virtue comes after cash.
Horace. Epistles 1.1.53f.

. . . Quaeque ipse miserrima vidi,/Et quorum pars magna fui. . . .
quie—queh ip—seh miss—air—rim—a wee—dee, et quoh—rum parse mag-na fu—ee.
Most unhappy events which I myself saw, and in which I was myself a chief participator.
Virgil. Æneid 2.5.

Quaerens quem devoret. *quay—raynce quem day—vo—ret.*
Seeking whom he may devour.
Vulgate. 1 Pet. 5.8.

Quaeritur, Sitne aequum amicos cognatis anteferre? *quie—rit—ur, sit—neh eye—quum a—mee—cose cog—nah—teece an—te—fair—reh?*
It is asked, Is it not right to prefer friends to relatives?
Cicero.

Quales sunt summi civitatis viri, talis est civitas. *quah—lace sunt sum—mee key—wit—ah—tiss wi—ree, tah—liss est key—wit—ahss.*
Such as are the leading men of the State, such is the State itself.
Cicero. (adapted).

Qualis artifex pereo. *quah—liss arr—ti—fex peh—reh—oh.*
What an artist dies with me.
Nero. (Last words, attr. by Suetonius Nero, 49.1.)

Quam bene vivas, non quamdiu, refert. *quam beh—neh wee—wahss, none quam—di—oo re—fairt.*
How well you live matters, and not how long.
Seneca. Ep. 101.

Quamlibet infirmas adjuvat ira manus. *quam—lib—et in—fear—mahss, ad—yoo—wat ee—rah mahn—oss.*
Anger assists hands however weak.
Ovid.

Quam parva sapientia regatur! *quam parr—wah sap—i—ent—i—ah reg—ah—tur!*
With how little wisdom [the world] is governed!
Quoted by Dr. Arbuthnot in letter to Swift, 1732-3, "Quam pauca sapientia mundus regitur." Cf. also 'An Nescis'.

. . . Quam saepe forte temere/Eveniunt, quae non audeas optare. . . .
quam sigh—peh for—teh tem—eh—reh ay—wen—i—unt, quie none ow—deh—ahss op—tah—reh.
How often things happen by chance which you would not dare to hope for.
Terence. Phormio, v. 1.31.

Quam temere in nosmet legem sancimus iniquam! *quam tem–eh–re in noce–met lay–gem san–kim–uss in–ee–quam!*
How rashly we sanction a law unfair to ourselves!
Horace. Sat. Book 1.3.67.

Quam veterrimus homini optimus est amicus! *quam wet–air–rim–uss hom–in–ee op–tim–uss est a–meek–uss!*
How much the best of a man's friends is his oldest friend!
Plautus. Truc. i. 2.71.

Quamvis diducere amantes Non queat invitos Juppiter ipse duos. *quam–weece deed–oo–keh–reh am–an–tace none queh–at in–wee–toce yup–pit–ehr ip–seh du–oce.*
Although Jupiter himself could not separate two lovers against their will.
Propertius. Elegies 2.7.3f.

Quando jus domini regis et subditi concurrunt, jus regis·praeferri debet. *quan–doh yooce dom–in–ee ray–giss et sub–dit–ee con–cur–runt, yooce ray–giss pry–fair–ree day–bet.*
Where the king's right and the right of a subject are at variance, the king's right should be preferred.
Law.

Quando terra iter facere possis, ne mari facias. *quan–doh tear–ra it–er fack–eh–reh poss–siss, nay ma–ree fack–i–ahss.*
Whenever you can make your journey by land, do not make it by sea.
Apostolius. 1653 ed. Cent. 2. pr. 54.

Quando ullum invenient parum? *quan–doh ull–lum in wen–i–et pa–rum?*
When shall another equal to him be found?
Horace. Odes Book 1.24.8.

Quandoque bonus dormitat Homerus. *quan–doh–que bon–uss dor–mee–tat hom–ay–russ.*
Sometimes the good Homer grows drowsy.
Horace. De Arte Poetica 359.

Quanto plura recentium, seu veterum revolvo, tanto magis ludibria rerum mortalium cunctis in negotiis observantur. *quan–toe ploo–ra reck–ent–i–um, sue wet–eh–rum reh–wol–woe, tan–toe mag–iss lood–ib–ri–a ray–rum more–tah–li–um conc–teese in neg–oh–ti–eece op–sair–wan–tur.*
The more I turn over in my mind the affairs of modern times or of ancient times, the more do I see the mockery of human affairs in all transactions.
Tacitus. Annals Book 3.18.

Quanto sibi in proelio minus pepercissent, tanto tutiores fore.
quan–toh si–bee in proy–li–oh min–uss pep–air–kiss–sent, tan–toe toot–i–oh–race fo–reh.
The less careful they were of themselves in battle, the safer they were.
Sallust. Jugurtha 104.

Quanto spei est minus, tanto magis amo. *quan–toe speh–ee est min–uss, tan–toe mag–iss am–oh.*
The less hope there is, the more do I love.
Terence. Eunuchus v. 9.23.

Quantum nobis nostrisque haec fabula de Christo profuerit, notum est.
quan–tum noh–beece noss–treece–queh hike fah–bull–ah day Criss–toh pro–fu–eh–rit, noe–tum est.
It is well known how much this story about Christ has profited us and ours.
Attrib. to Leo X 1475-1521.

Quantum quisque ferat, respiciendus erit. *quan–tum quiss–queh feh–rat, ress–pick–i–end–uss eh–rit.*
Each man will be worthy of regard according to what he brings with him.
Ovid. Amorum 1.8.38.

Quare, dum licet, inter nos laetemur amantes: Non satis est ullo tempore longus amor. *quah–ray, dum lick–et, in–tehr noce lie–tay–mur am–an–tace: none sat–iss est ull–loh tem–por–eh long–guss am–or.*
Wherefore, while we may, let us love and be glad together: love is too short for any length of time.
Propertius. Elegies 1.19.25f.

Quare fremuerunt Gentes? *quah–ray frem–u–ay–runt jen–tace?*
Why do the nations rage?
Vulgate. Ps. 2.1.

Quare nec talis dignantur visere coetus, Nec se contingi patiuntur lumine claro. *quah–ray neck tah–lease dig–nan–tur wee–seh–reh coy–tooce, neck say con–ting–ghee pat–i–un–tur loom–in–eh clah–roe.*
Wherefore they (the gods) neither deign to visit the company of man, nor let the clear light of day touch them.
Catullus. Poem 64.407f.

Quem Juppiter [*or* Deus] vult perdere, dementat prius. *quem yup–pit–er (deh–uss) woolt pair–deh–reh day–men–tat pri–uss.*
Whom Jupiter [*or* God] wishes to ruin, he first drives mad.
Found in James Duport's "Homeri Gnomologia" Cambridge 1660, p. 282. James Duport

1606-1679 was Professor of Greek, Magdalene Coll. Cambridge. It has been pointed out
that "dementat", as an active verb is not classical. See "Stultum facit."

Quem di diligunt adulescens moritur. *quem dee dee—lig—unt ad—ul—ace—*
kaynce mo—rit—ur.
He whom the gods favour dies young.
Plautus. Bacchides 4.816.

Quem metuunt, oderunt. *quem met—oo—unt, oh—day—runt.*
They hate whom they fear.
Ennius. Thyestes.

Qui alterum incusat probri, eum ipsum se intueri oportet. *quee al—teh—rum*
in—coo—sat prob—ree, eh—um ip—sum say in—tu—ay—ree op—or—tet.
He who accuses another man of shameful conduct should take care to keep
himself blameless.
Plautus. Truc. i. 2.58.

Qui amat, tamen hercle si esurit, nullum esurit. *quee am—at, tam—en*
hair—cleh see ay—soo—rit, null—lum ay—soo—rit.
He who is in love, even if he is hungry in sooth, is not hungry at all.
Plautus.

Qui ante diem periit: sed miles, sed pro patria. *quee an—teh di—em peh—*
ri—it: sed mi—lace, sed proh pat—ri—ah.
Who died before his day: but as a soldier, but for his native land.
Anon.

Qui Bavium non odit, amat tua carmina, Maevi. *quee ba—wi—um none*
oh—dit, a—mat tu—a carr—min—a, my—wee.
He who does not hate Bavius (a third-rate poet), loves your poems Maevius.
Virgil. Ecl. 3.90.

. . . Qui bellus homo, Cotta, pusillus homo est. *quee bell—luss ho—moh,*
cot—ta, pu—sill—luss ho—moh est.
He, Cotta, who is a pretty man (an effeminate fop), is a paltry man.
Martial. Epig. Book 1.10.

Qui bene imperat, paruerit aliquando necesse est. *quee beh—neh*
im—peh—rat, pa—ru—eh—rit a—li—quan—doh neck—ess—seh est.
It is necessary that he who commands well, should have at some time
obeyed.
Cicero. De Legibus Book 3.2.

Qui cadit a syllaba cadit a tota causa. *quee cad—it ah sil—lab—ah cad—it ah toe—tah cow—sah.*
He who fails in one small particular, fails in the whole action.
Law Maxim.

Qui cum triste aliquid statuit, fit tristis et ipse;/Cuique fere poenam sumere poena sua est. *quee cum triss—teh al—i—quid stat—u—it, fit triss—tiss et ip—seh; cu—ee—queh feh—ray poy—nam soo—meh—reh poy—na su—a est.*
One who, when he resolves upon a sad decision, becomes sad also himself; and to whom it is almost a punishment to inflict punishment.
Ovid. Ep. ex Pont. 2.2.119.

Qui Curios simulant, et Bacchanalia vivunt. *quee cu—ri—oce sim—ul—ant, et back—cah—nah—li—a wee—wunt.*
Who pretend to be men of the austere pattern of Curius, and who live the life of Baccanals.
Juvenal. Sat. 2.3.

Qui desiderat pacem, praeparet bellum. *quee day—see—deh—rat pah—kem, pry—pah—ret bell—lum.*
Who desires peace, let him make ready for war.
Vegetius. De Re Militari 3. Prologue.

Qui facit per alium facit per se. *quee fact—it per al—i—um fack—it per say.*
He who does a thing by another's agency does it himself.
Coke.

Qui fert malis auxilium, post tempus dolet. *quee fairt ma—leece owk—sil—i—um, post tem—puss dol—et.*
He who renders succour to the wicked, grieves for it after a time.
Phaedrus. Fab. Book 4.18.1.

Qui genus jactat suum aliena laudat. *quee gen—uss yack—tat su—um al—i—ay—na loud—at.*
He who boasts of his descent, praises the deeds of another.
Seneca.

Qui gravis es nimium, potes hinc jam lector abire. *quee gra—wiss ace nim—i—um, pott—ess hinc yam lect—or ab—ee—reh.*
Reader, who is too seriously disposed, you may take yourself far away hence.
Martial. Epig. Book 11.17.

Qui histrionibus dat, daemonibus sacrificat. *quee hist—ri—oh—nib—uss dat, day—moan—ib—uss sack—rif—ick—at.*

Who gives to actors sacrifices to devils.
Peter Cantor. Ch. 47.

Qui invenit verba quibus deberent loqui. *quee in—way—nit wear—ba quib—*
uss day—bay—rent lo—quee.
Who has invented words which deserve to be quoted.
Cited by Voltaire. Pref. to Irene.

Qui legitis flores et humi nascentia fraga,/Frigidus, O pueri, fugite hinc,
latet anguis in herba. *quee leg—it—iss floh—race et hum—ee nah—skent—i—a*
frah—ga, free—gid—uss, oh pu—eh—ree, fug—it—eh hinc, lat—et an—gwiss in
hair—bah.
O boys, who pluck the flowers and strawberries springing from the ground,
flee hence; a cold snake lies hidden in the grass.
Virgil. Eclogues 3.92.

Qui mare teneat, eum necesse est rerum potiri. *quee ma—reh ten—eh—at,*
eh—um neck—ess—seh est ray—rum pot—ee—ree.
He who has possession of the sea must of necessity be master of the
situation.
Ascribed to Cicero.

Qui monet quasi adjuvat. *quee mon—et qua—see ad—yu—wat.*
He who advises, as it were helps.
Plautus. Curculio Act. iii. 1.89.

Qui mores hominum multorum vidit et urbes. *quee moh—race hom—in—*
um mul—toh—rum wee—det et ur—bace.
Who saw the manners of many men and their cities.
Horace. De Arte Poetica, 142. (Trans. of Homer, Odyssey 1.3.)

Qui neminem habet inimicum, eum nec amicum habet quenquam.
quee nay—min—em hab—et in—im—ee—cum, eh—um neck a—mee—cum
hab—et quen—quam.
He who has no enemy, has not any friend.
Pr.

Qui nescit dissimulare, nescit regnare. *quee ness—kit diss—sim—ul—ah—reh,*
ness—kit rayg—nah—reh.
Who does not know how to dissemble, does not know how to reign.
Attrib. by Lipsius "Politica sive civilis Doctrina." Bk. 4, ch. 14 to the Emperor Frederick.

Qui nescit dissimulare nescit vivere. *quee nes—kit diss—sim—ul—ah—reh,*
ness—kit wee—weh—reh.
Who does not know how to dissemble does not know how to live.

[169]

Quoted by R. Burton (Anat. Melan., Pt. 1, 2.3. subs. 15) as a saying of "that Emperor," which according to A.R. Shilleto (1848-1894) meant the Emperor Frederick Barbarossa (c. 1123-1190) with whom it was "a favourite maxim." The saying is quoted in the above form, as a proverb, by Palingenius (Zodiacus Vitae), Book 4.684).

Qui nil molitur inepte. *quee nee moh—lee—tur in—ep—tay.*
One who never undertakes anything ineffectually.
Horace. De Arte Poetica, 140. (Referring to Homer).

Qui non est hodie, cras minus aptus erit. *quee none est hoh—di—ay, crahss min—uss ap—tuss eh—rit.*
He who is not prepared to-day, will be less so to-morrow.
Ovid. Rem. Amor. 94.

Qui nunc jacet horrida pulvis, Unius hic quondam servus amoris erat. *quee nunc yack—et horr—rid—a pull—wiss, oo—ni—uss heek quon—dam sehr—wuss am—oh—riss eh—rat.*
He that now lies here as vile dust, was once the slave of one single love.
Propertius. Elegies 2.13.35f.

Qui non prohibet quod prohibere potest, assentire videtur. *quee none pro—hib—et quod proh—hib—ay—reh pot—est, ass—sent—ee—reh wid—ay—tur.*
He who does not prevent what he has the power to prevent, is regarded as assenting to it.
Law.

Qui non vetat peccare cum possit, jubet. *quee none wet—at peck—cah—reh cum poss—sit, yub—et.*
He who does not forbid sin when he can, encourages it.
Seneca. Troades ii. 291.

. . . Qui novit mollissima fandi/tempora. . . . *quee noh—wit moll—liss—sim—a fahn—dee tem—po—ra.*
Who knew the most effective time for speaking.
Virgil (adapted). Æneid 4.293.

Qui omnes despicit, omnes displicet. *quee om—nace day—spick—it, om—nace diss—plick—et.*
He who despises all, displeases all.
Albertano of Brescia, 13th cent.

Qui parcit virgae, odit filium suum. *quee parr—kit wihr—guy, oh—dit fee—li—um su—um.*

He that spareth the rod hateth his own son.
Vulgate. Prov. 13.24.

Qui patitur vincit. *quee pat—it—ur win—kit.*
He who suffers conquers.
Pr.

Qui pessime canit, primus incipiet. *quee pess—im—ay can—it, pree—mus in—kip—i—et.*
He who sings worst will begin first.
Pr.

Qui potest mulieres vitare, vitet. *quee pot—est mull—i—eh—race wee—tah—reh, wee—tet.*
He who can avoid women, let him avoid them.
Plautus. Stichus i. 2.

Qui prior est tempore, potior est jure. *quee pri—or est tem—po—reh, pot—i—or est you—reh.*
He who is first in time has the advantage in right.
Coke.

Qui pro innocenti dicit satis est eloquens. *quee proh in—nock—en—tee dee—kit sat—iss est a—lock—waynce.*
He who speaks on behalf of an innocent man is eloquent enough.
Publilius Syrus.

Qui seipsum laudat, cito derisorem inveniet. *quee say—ip—sum lowd—at, kit—o day—ree—soh—rem in—wen—i—et.*
He who praises himself will soon find someone to deride him.
Publilius Syrus.

Qui silet est firmus. *quee sill—et est fear—muss.*
He who holds his tongue is strong.
Ovid. Rem. Amor. 697.

Qui simulat verbis, nec corde est fidus amicus;/Tu quoque fac simile, et sic ars deluditur arte. *quee sim—ull—at wear—beece, neck cor—deh est fee—dus a—meek—uss; too quo—queh fack sim—ill—eh, et seek arss day—lood—it—ur arr—teh.*
If one pretends with his words, and at heart is not a true friend, do you do the same to him, and so art will be foiled by art.
Cato.

[171]

Qui spe aluntur pendent non vivunt. *quee spay a—lun—tur pen—dent none wee—wunt.*
Those who are fed on hope do not live but hang on.
Pr.

Qui terret plus ipse timet. *quee tear—ret plooce ip—seh tim—et.*
He who terrifies others is more afraid himself.
Claudian. 4. Consul. Honorii 290.

. . . Qui timide rogat/Docet negare. . . . *quee tim—id—ay rog—at dock—et neg—ah—reh.*
He who asks faint-heartedly teaches how to refuse.
Seneca. Hippolytus ii. 593.

Qui uti scit, ei bona. *quee ut—ee skit, eh—ee bon—a.*
He has wealth who knows how to use it.
Pr.

Quia perire solus nolo, te cupio perire mecum. *qui—a peh—ree—reh sole—uss noh—loh, tay cup—i—oh peh—ree—reh may—cum.*
Because I do not wish to perish alone, I desire you to perish with me.
Plautus. Epidicus Act i. 1.71.

. . . Quibus in solo vivendi causa palato est. *quib—uss in soh—loh wee—wen—dee cow—sa pa—lah—toe est.*
Whose reason of living is in their palate alone.
Juvenal. Sat. 11.11.

Quicquid agunt homines, votum, timor, ira, voluptas,/Gaudia, discursus, nostri est farrago libelli. *quick—quid ag—unt hom—in—ace, woe—tum, tim—or, ee—ra, wol—up—tahss, Gowd—i—a diss—cur—sooce, noss—tree est far—rah—go lib—ell—lee.*
Whatever men do, wishes, fears, anger, pleasure, joys and different pursuits, of these is the hotch-potch of our book.
Juvenal. Sat. 1.85.

Quicquid dignum sapiente bonoque est. *quick—quid dig—num sap—i—en—teh bon—oh—queh est.*
Whatsoever is worthy of a good and wise man.
Horace. Ep. Book 1.4.5.

Quicquid multis peccatur inultum est. *quick—quid mul—teece peck—cah—tur in—ul—tum est.*
Whatsoever sin is committed by many remains unpunished.
Lucan. Pharsalia Book 5.257.

Quicquid plantatur solo, solo ceditur. *quick—quid plan—tah—tur so—loh,
so—loh kay—dit—ur.*
Whatever is placed into the soil belongs to the soil.
Law.

Quicunque, ubique sunt, qui fuere, quique futuri sunt posthac,/Stulti,
stolidi, factui, fungi, bardi, blenni, buccones,/Solus ego omnes longo anteeo
stultitia et moribus indoctis. *quee—cun—queh, ub—ee—queh sunt, quee
fu—ay—reh, quee—queh fut—oo—ree sunt post—hahk, stul—tee, stol—id—ee,
fat—u—ee, fun—ghee, bar—dee, blen—nee, buck—coe—nace, soh—luss egg—o
om—nace long—goe an—teh—eh—oh stool—ti—ti—ah et moh—rib—uss
in—dock—teece.* Whoever and wherever they are, have been, or ever shall be
in time to come, fools, blockheads, duffers, idiots, dunderheads, dullards,
blunderers, I alone far exceed them all in folly and want of sense.
Plautus. Bacchides v.i.

Quicunque vult salvus esse. *quee—cun—queh woolt sal—vuss ess—seh.*
Whosoever will be saved.
Athanasian Creed.

Quid ad farinas? *quid ad fa—ree—nahss?*
How will this bring you meal? (*i.e.* What profit will it bring you?).
Pr.

Quid caeco cum speculo? *quid kye—coe cum speck—ul—oh!*
What has a blind man to do with a mirror?
Pr.

. . . Quid crastina volveret aetas/Scire nefas homini. . . . *quid crahss—tin—a
wol—weh—ret eye—tahss skee—reh neh—fahss hom—in—ee.*
It is not lawful for man to know what the morrow may bring round.
Satius. Thebaid 3.562.

Quid datur a Divis felici optatius hora? *quid dat—ur ah dee—weece fay—lee—
key op—tah—ti—uss hoe—rah?*
What is there given by the gods more to be desired than a happy hour?
Catullus. Carm. 62.30.

Quid deceat, quid non, obliti. *quid deck—ch at, quid none, ob—lee—tee.*
Persons forgetful of what is right and of what is not.
Horace. Ep. Book 1.6.62.

Quid dignum tanto feret hic promissor hiatu? *quid dig—num tan—toe
feh—ret heek proh—miss—sor hi—ah—too?*

What will this boaster produce worthy of such inflated language?
Horace. De Arte Poetica 138.

Quid domini facient, audent cum talia fures? *quid dom—in—ee fack—i—ent, ow—dent cum tah—li—a foo—race?*
What will not the masters do, when their rascals dare to do such things?
Virgil. Eclogues 3.16.

Quid ego ex hac inopia nunc capiam? *quid egg—o ex hahk in—op—i—a nunc cap—i—am?*
What am I now to take out of all this scarcity?
Terence. Phormio i. 3.14.

Quid enim aliud est natura quam deus? *quid en—im al—i—ud est nah—too—ra quam deh—uss?*
For what else is Nature but God?
Seneca. De beneficiis 4.7.

Quid est autem turpius quam senex vivere incipiens? *quid est ow—tem tur—pi—uss quam sen—ex wee—weh—reh in—kip—i—aynce?*
What is more disgraceful than an old man just beginning to live?
Seneca.

Quid facies odio, sic ubi amore noces? *quid fack—i—ace od—i—oh, seek ub—i a—moh—reh nock—ace?*
What will you do in your hatred, when you are so cruel in your love?
Ovid. Heroides 21.56.

Quid facis, infelix? Perdis bona vota! *quid fack—is, in—fay—leeks? pair—diss bon—a woe—ta!*
What are you doing, unhappy one? You are losing our good wishes.
Ovid. Amorum 3.2.71.

Quid faciunt pauci contra tot milia fortes? *quid fack—i—unt pow—key con—trah tot mee—li—a for—tace?*
What can a few brave men do against so many thousands?
Ovid. Fast. 2.219.

Quid habet pulchri constructus acervus? *quid hab—et pull—cree cone—struck—tuss a—care—wuss?*
What is there of beauty in a piled-up heap (of money)?
Horace. Sat. Book 1.44.

Quid leges sine moribus/Vanae proficiunt? . . . *quid lay—gace sin—eh moh—rib—uss wah—nye pro—fick—i—unt?*

[174]

Of what use are empty laws without morals?
Horace. Odes Book 3.24.35.

Quid magis est durum saxo, quid mollius unda?/Dura tamen molli saxa cavantur aqua. *quid mag—iss est doo—rum sax—oh, quid moll—li—uss un—dah? doo—ra tam—en moll—ee sax—a ca—wan—tur a—quah.*
What is more hard than rock, what is softer than the wave? Yet hard rocks are hollowed by the soft water.
Ovid. Ars Amat. Book 1.475.

Quid non speremus amantes? *quid none spay—ray—muss a—man—tace?*
What may we not hope for when we are in love?
Virgil. Eclogues 8.26.

. . . Quid nos dura refugimus/Ætas? Quid intactum nefasti/Liquimus? *quid noce doo—ra reh—foo—gim—uss eye—tahss? quid in-tack—tum ne—fass—tee lee—qui—muss?*
What have we, a hardened age, avoided? What have we left untouched, impious that we are?
Horace. Odes Book 1.35.34.

Quid nunc? *quid nunc?*
What now? (A newsmonger or inquisitive person.)
Pr.

Quid pro quo. *quid proh quoh.*
Something for something. (An equivalent in return.)
Pr.

Quid si nunc coelum ruat? *quid see nunc coe—lum ru—at?*
What if the heavens should now fall?
Terence. Heautontimorumenos iv. 3.41.

Quid tibi cum pelago? Terra contenta fuisses. *quid tib—ee cum pel—ag—oh? tear-rah con—ten—ta fu—iss—sace.*
What have you to do with the sea? You should have been content with land.
Ovid. Amorum 3.8.49.

Quid turpius quam illudi? *quid tur—pi—uss quam ill—loud—ee?*
What is viler than to be laughed at?
Cicero. De Amicitia.

Quid victor, gaudes? Haec te victoria perdet. *quid wick—tor, gowd—ace? hike tay wick—toe—ri—a pair—det.*

Why, victor, does thou exult? This victory will be your ruin.
Ovid. Fast. 2.811.

Quid violentius aure tyranni? *quid wi—ol—ent—i—uss ow—reh ti—ran—nee?*
What is more furious than the ear of a tyrant?
Juvenal. Sat. 4.86.

Quidquid Amor jussit, non est contemnere tutum. *quid—quid amor yuss—sit,
none est con—tem—neh—reh too—tum.*
Whatsoever love has ordained it is not safe to despise.
Ovid. Heroides 4.11.

Quidquid id est, timeo Danaos, et dona ferentes. *quid—quid id est, tim—
eh—o dan—a—oce, et doe—na feh—ren—tace.*
Whatever it be, I fear the Greeks even when bringing gifts.
Virgil. Æneid 2.49.

Quidquid praecipies, esto brevis; ut cito dicta/Percipiant animi dociles,
teneantque fideles;/Omne supervacuum pleno de pectore manat.
*quid—quid pry—kip—i—ace, ess—toe breh—wuss; ut kit—o dick—ta pair—
kip—i—ant an—im—ee dock—ill—ace, ten—eh—ant—queh fid—ay—lace;
om—neh sup—air—wack—u—um play—noh day peck—to—reh mah—nat.*
Whatever you teach, be brief, for minds grasp with readiness what is said
shortly, and retain it firmly; all that is unnecessary overflows from the
charged mind.
Horace. De Arte Poetica 335.

Quidquid principes faciunt praecipere videntur. *quid—quid prin—kip—ace
fack—i—unt pry—kip—eh—reh wid—en—tur.*
Whatsoever princes do they seem to command it.
Quintilian. Declam. 3.

. . . Quin corpus, onustum/Hesternis vitiis, animum quoque praegravat una,/
Atque adfligit humo divinae particulam aurae. *queen core—puss, on—ust—
um hess—tear—neece wit—i—eece, an—im—um quoh—queh pry—grah—wat
oo—nah, at—queh ad—flee—git hum—oh dee—wee—nye par—tick—ul—am
ow—rye.*
So that the body, laden with the vices of yesterday weighs down also the
soul at the same time, and fastens a particle of God's heaven into the earth.
Horace. Sat. Book 2.2.77.

Quis fallere possit amantem? *quiss fall—leh—reh poss—sit—a—man—tem?*
Who can deceive a lover?
Virgil. Æneid 4.296.

Quis furor est census corpore ferre suo? *quiss fu—ror est cane—suss cor—po—reh fair—reh su—oh?*
What sort of madness is it to carry one's fortune upon one's body.
Ovid. Ars Amat. Book 3.172.

Quis separabit? *quiss say—pa—rah—bit?*
Who shall separate?
Motto of Order of St. Patrick.

. . . Quis talia fando . . . Temperet a lacrimis? . . . *quiss tah—li—a fahn—doh tem—peh—ret ah lack—rim—eece?*
Who in telling such things can refrain from tears?
Virgil. Æneid 2.6. and 8.

Quis caelum posset nisi caeli munere nosse, Et reperire deum nisi qui pars ipse deorum? *quiss kye—lum poss—set niss—e kye—lee moon—eh—reh noce—seh, et rep—eh—ree—reh deh—um niss—e quee parse ip—seh deh—oh—rum?*
Who could know the heavens save by the gift of heaven, and find God unless he is himself part of the gods?
Manilius. Astronomica 2.115.

Quis color ille vadis, seras cum propulit umbras Hesperus et viridi perfudit monte Mosellam? Tota natant crispis juga moribus et tremit absens Pampinus et vitreis vindemia turget in undis. *quiss col—or ill—leh wa—deece, say—rahss cum proh—pull—it um—brahss hess—peh—russ et wih—rid—ee pehr—food—it mon—teh moss—ell—lam? toe—ta nat—ant crisp—eece yug—a moe—tib—uss et trem—it ap—saynce pam—pin—uss et wit—reh—eece win—day—mi—a tur—get in un—deece.*
What is that colour in the waters, when the evening star has brought on the shades of evening and bathed the Moselle in the green hillside? The heights all swim with quivering movements and the absent vine-leaves tremble, and the grapes swell in the glassy waves.
Ausonius. Mosella.

Quis legem dat amantibus? Major lex amor est sibi. *quiss lay—ghem dat am—ant—ib—uss? mah—yore lakes am—or est sib—ee.*
Who can give a law to lovers? Love is a greater law to itself.
Boethius.

Quis tulerit Gracchos de seditione querentes? *quiss tul—eh—rit grack—coce day say—dit—i—oh—neh queh—ren—tace?*
Who shall endure the Gracchi [two brothers famous for ambition and unscrupulousness] complaining about sedition?
Juvenal. Sat. 2.24.

[177]

Quicumque casus temporum illorum nobis vel aliis auctoribus noscent, praesumptum habeant, quoties fugas et caedes jussit princeps, toties grates dcis actas, quaeque rerum secundarum olim, tum publicae cladis insignia fuisse. *quee—cum—queh cah—sooce tem—por—um ill—loh—rum noh—beece well al—i—eece owk—toe—rib—uss noh—skent, pry—sump—tum hab—eh— ant, quot—i—ace fug—ahss et kye—dace youss—sit preen—keps, tot—i—ace grah—tace deh—eece act—ahss, quie—queh ray—rum seck—un—dah—rum oh—lim, tum pub—lick—eye clah—diss in—sig—ni—a fu—iss—seh.*
Anyone learning about the events of those days (the last years of Nero) from us or from other writers may make the assumption that whenever the emperor ordered banishment or murder the gods were given thanks, and what had once been signs of good fortune were taken as disasters to the State.
Tacitus. Annals 14.64.

Quis custodiet ipsos custodes? *quis coos—toh—dee--et ip—soce coos—toh— dace?*
Who is guarding the guards themselves?
Juvenal.

Quisnam hominum est, quem tu contentum videris uno/Flagitio? *quiss—nam hom—in—um est, quem too con—ten—tum wee—deh—riss oo—noh flah—git—i—oh?*
What man can you find anywhere who is contented with one crime only?
Juvenal. Sat. 13.243.

Quisnam igitur liber? Sapiens, sibi qui imperiosus;/Quem neque pauperies, neque mors, neque vincula terrent;/Responsare cupidinibus, contemnere honores/Fortis; et in seipso totus teres atque rotundus. *quiss—nam ig—it—ur lee- ber? sap—i—aynce, sib—ee quee im—peh—ri—oh—suss; quem neh—queh pow—peh—ri—ace, neh—queh morse, neh—queh wink—ul—a tear—rent; ress—pone—sah—reh cup—ee—din—ib—uss, con—tem—neh—reh hon—oh—race for—tus; et in sayip—soh toe—tuss teh—ress at—queh ro—tun—duss.*
Who then is free? The wise man who is lord over himself; whom neither poverty nor death, nor chains alarm; strong to withstand his passions and to despise honours, and who is completely finished and rounded off in himself.
Horace. Sat. Book 2.7.83.

Quisque suos patimur manes. *quiss—queh su—oce pat—im—ur mah—nace.*
Each of us suffers his own punishment in the lower world.
Virgil. Æneid 6.743.

Quo bene coepisti, sic pede semper eas. *quoh beh—neh coyp—iss—tee, seek ped—eh sem—per eh—ahss.*

In the path where you have begun well, may you always continue to tread.
Ovid. Tristia Book 1.9.66.

Quo jure, quaque injuria. *quoh you—reh quah—queh in—you—ri—ah.*
By any sort of right or wrong.
Terence. Andria i. 3.9.

Quo me, Bacche, rapis, tui/Plenum? *quoh may, back—keh, rap—iss, tu—ee*
play—num?
Whither, O Bacchus, wilt thou lead me, full of thee?
Horace. Odes Book 3.25.1.

Quo moriture ruis? majoraque viribus audes? *quoh mo—rit—oo—reh ru—iss?*
mah—yoh—ra—queh wee—rib—uss ow—dace?
Where are you rushing, O man about to perish? And why do you attempt
things beyond your power?
Virgil. Æneid 10.811.

Quo res cunque cadent, unum et commune periclum,/Una salus ambobus
erit. . . . *quoh race cun—queh cad—ent, oo—num et com—moon—eh peh—*
reek—lum, uo—na sal—ooce am—boh—buss eh—rit.
However things may befall, there shall be to both of us one common danger,
one source of safety.
Virgil. Æneid 2.709.

Quo ruitis, generosa domus? Male creditur hosti./Simplex nobilitas, perfida
tela cave! *quoh ru—it—iss, geh—neh—roe—sa dom—uss? mal—eh cray—pit—*
ur hoss—tee. sim—plex noh—bill—it—ahss, pair—fid—a tay—la ca—way!
O high-born house, to what ruin are you impelled? It is evil to trust the
enemy. O simple nobility, beware of treacherous weapons!
Ovid. Fast. 2.225.

Quo tamen adversis fluctibus ire paras? *quoh tam—en ad—wear—seece*
fluct—ib—uss ee—reh pa—rahss?
Where then are you trying to go against the adverse waves?
Ovid. Heroides Ep. 7.40

Quo timoris minus est, eo minus ferme periculi est. *quoh tim—oh—riss*
min—uss est, eh—oh min—uss fair—may peh—ree—cul—ee est.
The less there is of fear, so much the less generally is there of danger.
Livy. 22.5.

. . . Quocirca vivite fortes,/Fortiaque adversis opponite pectora rebus.
quoh—kihr—ca wee—wit—eh for—tace, for—ti—a—queh ad—wear—seece
op—pone—it—eh pect—to—ra ray—buss.

[179]

On that account live as brave men, and oppose brave hearts to adverse fate.
Horace. Sat. Book 2.2.135.

Quomodo sedet sola civitas plena populo! *quoh—mod—oh sed—et soh—la chee—vit—ahss plain—a pop—ull—oh!*
How doth the city sit solitary, that was full of people!
Vulgate, Lamentations 1.1: first lession of Tenebrae on Maundy Thursday.

Quod absurdum est. *quod ap—sur—dum est.*
Which is absurd.
Euclid. (Tr.)

Quod certaminibus ortum, ultra metam durat. *quod care—tah—min—ib—uss ore—tum, ul—trah may—tam doo—rat.*
What is begun in strife lasts beyond our measurement.
Velleius Paterculus.

Quod eorem minimis, mihi. *quod ee—oh—rum min—im—eece, mi—hee.*
What (you have done) to the least of them (you have done) to me.
Motto. Adapted from the Vulgate, St. Matthew, 25.40.

Quod erat demonstrandum (*or* faciendum). *quod eh—rat day—moan— strand—um (or fack—i—end—um).*
Which was to be shown (or done).
Euclid. (Tr.)

Quod est venturum, sapiens ut praesens cavet. *quod est wen—too—rum, sap—i—aynce ut pry—saynce ca—wet.*
The wise man is on his guard against what is to come as if it were the present.
Publilius Syrus.

Quod in corde sobrii, id in lingua ebrii. *quod in core—deh soh—bri—ee, id in lin—gwah ay—bri—ee.*
What is kept in the heart of a man sober is in the tongue of a man drunk.
Pr.

Quod licet Jovi non licet bovi. *quod lick—et yo—wee none lick—et bo—wee.*
What is lawful to Jupiter is not lawful to the ox.
Pr.

Quod naturalis ratio inter omnes homines constituit, . . . vocatur jus gentium. *quod nah—too—rah—liss rah—ti—oh in—ter om—nace hom—in—ace cone— stit—u—it, wock—ah—tur yooce gent—i—um.*
That which natural reason has established amongst all men is called the law of nations. *Gaius. Inst. Jur. Civ. 1.1.*

[180]

Quod non fecerunt barbari fecerunt Barberini. *quod none fay–chair–unt bar–ba–ree fay–chair–unt bar–beh–ree–nee.*
What the barbarians did not, the Barberini have done.
Attrib. to Carlo Castelli 1565-1639.

Quod non opus est, asse carum est. *quod none op–uss est, ass–seh cah–rum est.*
That which is not required is dear at a farthing.
Cato. As quoted by Seneca. Ep. 94.

Quod nunc ratio est, impetus ante fuit. *quod nunc rat–i–oh est, im–pet–uss an–teh fu–it.*
What is now reason was formerly impulse.
Ovid. Rem. Amor. 10.

Quod scripsi, scripsi. *quod scrip–see, scrip–see.*
What I have written, I have written.
Vulgate. St. John 19.22.

Quod senior loquitur, omnes consilium putant. *quod sen–i–or lo–quit–ur, om–nace cone–sil–i–um put–ant.*
What an elder speaks all imagine to be good advice.
Publilius Syrus.

Quod sors feret, feremus aequo animo. *quod sorce feh–ret, feh–ray–muss eye–quoh an–im–oh.*
What fortune offers let us accept with unmoved mind.
Terence. Phormio i. 2.88.

Quod tam grande sophos clamat tibi turba togata, Non tu, Pomponi, cena diserta tua est. *quod tam grand–eh soff–oss clah–mat tib–e tour–ba tog–ah–ta, none too, pom–pone–ee, cane–a diss–air–ta tu–a est.*
When your crowd in evening dress hails you so loudly as a sage, it is not you, Pomponius, but your dinner that is eloquent.
Martial. Epigrams 6.

Quod timeas citius quam quod speres evenit. *quod tim–eh–ahss kit–i–uss quam quod spay–race ay–wen–it.*
That which you fear happens sooner than that which you hope.
Publilius Syrus.

Quod tuum est, teneas tuum. *quod tu–um est, ten–eh–ahss tu–um.*
What is thine own hold as thine own.
Plautus. Cistellaria iv. 2.105.

Quod vide. *quod vie–de.*
Which see (generally written *q.v.*).

Quod vocis pretium? *quod woe–kiss pret–i–um?*
What is the price of your voice? (referring to a barrister's fee).
Juvenal. Sat. 7.119.

Quodcunque ostendis mihi sic, incredulus odi. *quod–cun–queh oss–ten–diss mi–hee seek, in–cray–dull–uss oh–dee.*
Whatever you display before me in such a way, I, disbelieving, hate.
Horace. De Arte Poetica 188.

Quodsi me lyricis vatibus inseres, Sublimi feriam sidera vertice.
quod–see may li–rick–eece wah–tib–uss in–seh–race, sub–lee–mee feh–ri–am seed–eh–ra wear–tick–eh.
But if you include me among the lyric poets, I shall strike the stars with my exalted head.
Horace. Odes 1.1.35f.

Quondam etiam victis redit in praecordia virtus. *quon–dam et–yam wick–teece red–it in pry–core–di–a wihr–tooce.*
Sometimes valour returns even to the hearts of the conquered.
Virgil. Æneid 2.367.

Quot homines, tot sententiae; suus cuique mos. *quot hom–in–ace, tot sen–ten–ti–eye; su–us cu–ee–queh moce.*
So many men, so many opinions; everyone has his own fancy.
Terence. Phormio ii. 3.14.

Quot linguas calles, tot homines vales. *quot ling–gwahss cal–lace, tot om–in–ace va–lace.*
You are worth as many men as you know languages.
Attributed to Charles V.

Quotidie morimur. *quot–ee–di–ay mo–rim–ur.*
We are dying daily (or day by day).
Seneca. Ep. 24.

Quousque tandem abutere, Catilina, patientia nostra? *quoh–uss–queh tan–dem ab–oo–teh–reh, cat–ill–ee–na, pat–i–en–ti–ah noss–trah?*
How far, Catiline, will you abuse our patience?
Cicero. In Catilinam 1.1.

R

Radit usque ad cutem. *rah—dit uss—queh ad cut—em.*
He shaves to the very skin.
Pr.

Rara avis in terris, nigroque simillima cygno. *rah—ra a—wiss in tear—reece,*
nig—roe—queh sim—ill—lim—a kig—noh.
A rare bird upon the earth, and exceedingly like a black swan.
Juvenal. Sat. 6.165.

Rara est adeo concordia formae/Atque pudicitiae. *rah—ra est ad—eh—oh*
con—cor—di—a for—my at—queh pud—ee—kit—i—eye.
So rare is the agreement between beauty and modesty.
Juvenal. Sat. 10.297.

Rarum est enim ut satis se quisque vereatur. *rah—rum est en—im ut sat—iss*
say quiss—queh weh—reh—ah—tur.
For it is rare that anyone reverences himself enough.
Quintillian 107.

Rara temporum felicitate, ubi sentire quae velis, et quae sentias dicere licet.
rah—ra tem—po—rum fay—lick—it—ah—teh, ub—i sen—tee—reh quie wel—iss,
et quie sen—ti—ahss dee—keh—reh lick—et.
The happiness of the times being extraordinary, when it was lawful to
think what you wished, and to say what you thought.
Tacitus. Hist. Book 1.1.

Rarus sermo illis, et magna libido tacendi. *rah—russ sair—moh ill—lease,*
et mag—na lib—ee—do tack—end—ee.
Rare is their speech and great their passion for silence.
Juvenal. Sat. 2.14.

Ratio justifica. *rat—i—oh yuss—tiff—ic—a.*
Reason acting justly (justifying).
Pr.

Ratio suasoria. *rat—i—oh swah—soh—ri—a.*
The persuasive reason.
Quintillian.

. . . Re ipsa repperi,/Facilitate nihil esse homini melius, neque clementia.
ray ip—sah rep—peh—ree, fack—ill—it—ah—teh ni—hill ess—seh hom—in—ee
mel—i—uss, neh—queh clay—men—ti—ah.
By personal experience I have discovered that nothing is more valuable to
a man than courtesy and mildness.
Terence. Adelphi v. 4.7.

Rebus cunctis inest quidam velut orbis. *ray—buss cunc—teece in—est*
quee—dam well—ut ore—biss.
In all things there is a kind of law of cycles.
Tacitus. Annals Book 3.55.

Rebus sic stantibus. *ray—buss seek stan—tib—uss.*
Such being the state of things.

Recipiunt feminae sustentacula a nobis. *re—kip—i—unt fay—min—eye*
suss—ten—tah—cul—a ah noh—beece.
Women receive supports from us.
Motto of the Pattenmakers' Company.

Recusatio judicis. *reck—oo—sah—ti—oh you—dick—iss.*
Objection taken to the judge.
Law.

Reddite ergo quae sunt Caesaris, Caesari, et quae sunt Dei, Deo.
red—dit—eh air—go quay sunt chay—sa—riss, chay—sa—ree;
et quay sunt deh—ee, deh—oh.
Render, therefore, unto Caesar the things which are Caesar's, and unto
God the things that are God's.
Vulgate. St. Matthew 22, 21.

Redire ad nuces. *red—ee—reh ad nuc—ace.*
To return to the nuts; to resume childish amusements.
Pr.

Recte enim Graeci praecipiunt non tentanda quae effici omnino non
possint. *reck—tay en—im gry—key pry—kip—i—unt none ten—tan—da quie*
eff—fick—ee om—nee—noh none poss—sint.
The Greeks rightly warn us not to attempt what cannot be done at all.
Quintilian. Institutes 4.5.17.

. . . Redituraque nunquam/Libertas. . . . *red—it—oo—ra—queh nun—quam lee—bear—tahss.*
And Liberty, never again to return.
Lucan. Pharsalia Book 7.444.

Reductio ad absurdum. *red—uck—ti—oh ad ap—sur—dum.*
Reduction (of an argument) to an absurdity.
cf., Quod Absurdum Est!

Rege incolumi, mens omnibus una est;/Amisso, rupere fidem.
ray—geh in—col—um—ee, maynce om—ni—buss oo—nah est; ah—miss—soh, roo—pay—reh fid—em.
The king being safe they are all of one mind; but when he is lost they break concord.
Virgil. Georgics 4.212.

Reges ex nobilitate, duces ex virtute sumunt. *ray—gace ex noh—bill—it—ah—teh, duck—ace ex wihr—too—teh soo—munt.*
They (the Germans) choose their kings on the ground of birth, their commanders on the ground of courage.
Tacitus. Germania 7.

Regia, crede mihi, res est succurrere lapsis. *ray—gi—a, cray—deh mi—hee, race est suck—cur—reh—reh lap—seece.*
It is a kingly action, believe me, to come to the help of those who are fallen.
Ovid. Ep. ex Pont. 2.9.11.

Regius morbus. *ray—gi—uss more—buss.*
The king's evil; the royal disease (in classical authors, jaundice).

Relicta non bene parmula. *ray—lick—ta none ben—eh parr—mull—ah.*
Having wrongly left my buckler behind.
Horace. Odes Book 2.7.10.

Rem peragit nullam, Sertorius incipit omnes. *rem peh—rag—it null—lam, sair—toe—ri—us in—kip—it om—nace.*
Sertorius does nothing thoroughly, but he begins everything.
Martial. Epig. Book 3.79.

Rem tu strenuus auge. *rem too stray—nu—us ow—gay.*
Endeavour vigorously to increase your property.
Horace. Ep. Book 1.7.71.

Remis adjice vela tuis. *ray—meece ad—yick—eh way—la tu—eece.*

[185]

Add sails to your oars.
Ovid. Rem. Amor. 790.

Remis ventisque. *ray—meece went—eece—queh.*
With oars and wind.
Pr.

Requiem aeternam dona eis, Domine. *reh—qui—em ay—tear—nam doh—
nah eh—eece, dom—in—eh.*
Give them eternal rest, O Lord.
Introit Anthem of Masses for the dead.

Requiescant in pace. *reh—qui—ay—scant in pah—cheh.*
May they rest in peace.
Order of the Mass For the Dead.

Res amicos invenit. *race a—meek—oce in—wen—it.*
Money finds friends.
Plautus.

Res in cardine est. *race in carr—din—eh est.*
The affair is hanging upon the hinge (is in a critical condition).
Pr.

Res severa est verum gaudium. *race seh—way—ra est way—rum gow—di—um.*
True joy is a serious matter.
Seneca. Ep. 23.4.

Res unius aetatis. *race oo—nee—uss eye—tah—tiss.*
An affair of only one age (one generation).
Law.

Respicite caeli spatium . . . et aliquando desinite vilia mirari.
*ress—pick—it—eh kye—lee spat—i—um . . . et al—ick—wan—doe day—sin—
it—eh wee—li—a mee—rah—ree.*
Look at the expanse of the skies . . . and cease at last from wondering at
worthless things.
Boethius. De consolatione philosophiae 3.8.

. . . Respondes, ut tuus est mos,/pauca. *ress—pond—ace, ut tu—us est
moce, pow—ca.*
You reply, as your custom is, in few words.
Horace. Sat. Book 1.6.60.

Responsum est, quod Angli vocarentur. At ille, 'Bene,' inquit, 'nam et angelicam habent faciem, et tales angelorum in caelis decet esse coheredes'. *ress—pone—sum est, quod ang—glee wock—ah—rent—ur. at ill—leh, 'ben—eh,' ink—wit, 'nam et ang—ghel—i—cam hab—ent fack—i—em, et tah—lace ang—ghel—oh—rum in kye—lease deck—et ess—seh co—hay—ray—dace'.*
He (Pope Gregory I 'the Great') was answered, that they were called Angles. But he said, 'It is well, for they have the countenance of angels, and also it is fitting that such men should be equal heirs with the angels in heaven.'
Bede. Ecclesiastical History 2.1.

Resurgam. *reh—sur—gam.*
I shall rise again.
Epitaph inscribed on the west front of St. Paul's Cathedral, London.

. . . Revocate animos, maestumque timorem/Mittite. *reh—wock—ah—teh an—im—oce, mice—tum queh tim—oh—rem mit—ti—teh.*
Recall your courage, and lay aside this gloomy fearfulness.
Virgil. Æneid 1.202.

Rex non potest fallere nec falli. *rakes none pot—est fal—leh—reh neck fal—lee.*
The king cannot deceive or be deceived.
Pr.

Rex nunquam moritur. *rakes nun—quam mo—rit—ur.*
The king never dies.
Law.

Ridetur chorda qui semper oberrat eadem. *ree—day—tur core—dah quee sem—per ob—air—rat eh—ah—dem.*
He is laughed at who always blunders with the same string.
Horace. De Arte Poet. 356.

Risum teneatis, amici? *ree—sum ten—eh—ah—tiss, a—meek—ee?*
Can you withhold your laughter, my friends?
Horace. De Arte Poetica 5.

Roma locuta est; causa finita est. *roh—ma lock—oo—ta est; cow—sa fee—nee—ta est.*
Rome has spoken; the case is ended.
St. Augustine. Sermons, Book 1.

Romae, Lutetiae, ac Venetiae, nemo quicquid miratur. *roh—may, loot—ate—si—ay, ac ven—ate—si—ay, nay—moh quick—quid mee—rah—tur.*

At Rome, Paris, and Venice, no one wonders at anything.
Mediaeval saying.

Romanos vicimus, ab Horatio victi sumus. *roh—mah—noce week—im—uss,
ab ho—rah—ti—oh wick—tee sum—uss.*
We have vanquished the Romans; we are vanquished by Horatius (Cocles).
Valerius Maximus Book 3.2.1.

Rudis indigestaque moles. *rud—iss in—dee—guest—a—queh moh—lace.*
An unwrought, confused mass (*i.e.* chaos).
Ovid. Matam. 1.7.

Rus in urbe. *rooce in ur—beh.*
Country in town.
Martial. Epig. Book 12.57.12.

Rustica gens est optima flens et pessima gaudens. *rooce—tick—a gaynce est
op—tim—a flaynce et pess—sim—a gowd—aynce.*
Country-folk are best when weeping and worst when rejoicing.
Pr.

. . . Saepe illi dixerat Almo,/Nata, tene linguam; nec tamen illa tenet.
*sigh—peh ill—lee dix—eh—rat al—moh, nah—ta, ten—ay ling—gwam; neck
tam—en ill—la ten—et.*
Often had Almo said to her, "Daughter, hold thy tongue": yet still she
held it not.
Ovid. Fast. 2.601.

Saepe nihil inimicus homini quam sibi ipse. *sigh—peh ni—hill in—im—ee—
cuss hom—in—ee quam sib—ee ip—seh.*
Often nothing is a man's enemy but himself.
Cicero.

Saepe sub attrita latitat sapientia veste. *sigh—peh sub at—tree—tah lat—it—at
sap—i—en—ti—a west—eh.*
Wisdom often lies concealed beneath a threadbare garment.
Pr. Founded on Caecilius.

[188]

Saepe viri fallunt; tenerae non saepe puellae. *sigh—peh wi—ree fall—lunt; ten—eh—rye none sigh—peh pu—ell—lie.*
Men often deceive; but gentle maidens not often.
Ovid. Ars Amat. Book 3.31.

Saepius ventis agitatur ingens/Pinus, et celsae graviore casu/Decidunt turres; feriuntque summos/Fulgura montes. *sigh—pi—uss wen—teece ag—it—ah—tur in—gaynce peen—uss, et kel—sigh gra—wi—oh—reh cah—soo day—key—dunt tur—race; feh—ri—unt—queh sum—moce ful—gur—a mon—tace.*
The huge pine is shaken by the winds more often, and the high towers fall with a heavier fall, and the lightening strikes the highest peaks of the mountains.
Horace. Odes Book 2.10.9.

Saevis tranquillus in undis. *sigh—weece tran—quill—luss in un—deece.*
Undisturbed among the savage waves.
Motto of William I. of Orange.

Saltare elgantius, quam necesse est probae. *sal—tah—reh ay—leg—ant—i—uss, quam neck—ess—seh est prob—eye.*
She (Sempronia) could dance more skilfully than an honest woman need.
Sallust. Catiline 25.

Savit amor ferri, et scelerata insania belli. *sah—wit a—more fair—ree, et skel—eh—rah—ta in—sah—ni—a bell—lee.*
The love of the sword rages, and the guilty madness of war.
Virgil. Æneid 7.461.

Saevitque animis ignobile vulgus. *sigh—wit—queh an—im—eece ig—noh—bill—eh wool—guss.*
And the low-born crowd rage in their minds.
Virgil. Æneid 1.149.

Salus populi suprema est lex. *sal—ooce pop—ul—ee sup—ray—ma est lakes.*
The health (or safety) of the people is the highest law.
Cicero. De Legibus Bk. 3.3.8.

Salve, magna parens frugum, Saturnia tellus,/Magna virum!
sal—way, mag—na pa—raynce froo—gum, sah—tur—ni—a tell—looce, mag—na wi—rum.
Hail! land of Saturn (Italy), great parent of fruits, great parent of men!
Virgil. Georgics 2.173.

Salvus sum, jam philosophatur. *sal—wuss sum, yam fill—oss—off—ah—tur.*

I am safe, he is now philosophising.
Plautus. Pseudolus Act iv. 2.18.

Sapere isthac aetate oportet, qui sunt capite candido. *sap—eh—reh ist—hahk eye—tah—teh op—ore—tet, quee sunt cap—it—eh can—did—oh.*
Those who have white heads ought at that age to be wise.
Plautus.

Sapiens dominabitur astris. *sap—i—aynce dom—in—ah—bit—ur ass—treece.*
A wise man will overrule the stars.
Pr.

Sapienti sat. *sap—i—en—tee sat.*
Sufficient for a wise man.
Plautus. Persa iv. 7.19.

Sapientia, quae sola libertas est. *sap—i—en—ti—a, quie soh—la lee—bear—tahss est.*
Wisdom, which is the only liberty.
Seneca. Ep. 37.

Sapientia vino obumbratur. *sap—i—en—ti—a, wee—noh ob—um—brah—tur.*
Wisdom is obscured by wine.
Pliny the Elder.

Sat cito si sat tuto. *sat kit—o see sat too—toe.*
Quickly enough if safely enough.
One of Lord Eldon's favourite maxims.

Sartor resartus. *sar—tor ress—art—uss.*
The patched-up tailor.
Title of work by Carlyle 1833.

Sat est disertus pro quo loquitur veritas. *sat est diss—air—tuss proh quoh lo—quit—ur way—rit—ahss.*
He is eloquent enough for whom truth speaks.
Publilius Syrus.

Satis dives qui pane non indiget. *sat—iss de—wace quee pah—neh none in—dig—et.*
He is rich enough who does not want bread.
St. Jerome. Epist. 125.

Satis quod sufficit. *sat—iss quod suff—fick—it.*
What suffices is enough.   *Pr.*

... Scabiem tantam et contagia lucri. *scab—i--em tan—tam et con—tah—gi —a luck—ree.*
So great an itch and disease for gain.
Horace. Ep., 1.12.14.

Sceleris in scelere supplicium est. *skel—eh—riss in skel—eh—reh sup—plick— i—um est.*
The punishment of crime is in the crime.
Seneca. Epist. 97.

Scientia popinae. *ski—en—ti—a pop—ee—nye.*
The science of the cookshop.
Seneca. Consol. ad Helv. 10.

Scimus te prae litteras fatuum esse. *skee—muss tay pry lit—teh—rahss fat— oo—um ess—seh.*
We know that you are mad with learning.
Petronius.

Scinditur incertum studia in contraria vulgus. *skin—dit—ur in—care—tum stud—i—a in con—trah—ri—a wool—guss.*
The unstable multitude is cleft into opposite courses.
Virgil. Æneid 2.39.

Scio: tu coactus tua voluntate es. *ski—oh: too co—act—uss tu—ah wol—un— tah—teh ace.*
I am aware that you are compelled by your own will.
Terence. Andria iv. 1.34.

Scire facias. *sigh—re fay—shi—ass.*
Make it known.
Law. (Title of a writ).

Scit Caesar poenamque peti, veniamque timeri. *skit kye—sar poy—nam—queh pet—ee, wen—i—am—queh tim—ay—ree.*
Caesar knew that punishment was sought and pardon feared.
Lucan. Pharsalia Book 2.512.

Scit uti foro. *skit oo—tee fo—roe.*
He knows how to avail himself of the market.
Terence. Phormio i. 2.29.

Scitum est inter caecos luscum regnare posse. *skee—tum est in—ter kye— coce luss—cum rayg—nah—reh poss—seh.*

[191]

It is well–known that among the blind the one-eyed man may be king.
Erasmus. Adagia.

Scribe aliquid magnum. *scree–beh al–i–quid mag–num.*
Write something great.
Martial. Epig. Book 1.108.2.

Scriptorum chorus omnis amat nemus et fugit urbes. *scrip–toe–rum co–russ om–niss a–mat nem–uss et fug–it ur–bace.*
The whole band of writers loves the groves and flees from cities.
Horace. Ep. 2.2.77.

Secundas fortunas decent superbiae. *sec–un–dahss for–too–nahss deck–ent sup–air–bi–eye.*
Proud bearing is appropriate to prosperous fortunes.
Plautus. Stichus ii. 2.

Securus judicat orbis terrarum. *say–coo–russ you–dick–at ore–biss tear–rah–rum.*
The world judges with sure judgment.
St. Augustine. Letter on the Donatist Schism viz. Contra Episs. Parmen., 3.24.

Sed de me ut sileam. *sed day may ut sill–eh–am.*
But to say nothing of myself.
Ovid. Ep. ex Pont. Book 1.2.147.

Sed fugit interea, fugit irreparabile tempus. *sed fu–git in–teh–reh–ah, fug–it ir–rep–a–rah–bill–eh tem–puss.*
But meanwhile time flies; it flies never to be regained.
Virgil. Georgics 3.284.

Sed mulier cupido quod dicit amanti in vento et rapida scribere oportet aqua. *sed mull–i–air cup–id–oh quod dee–kit am–ant–ee in wen–toe et rap–id–ah scree–beh–reh op–ore–tet ack–wah.*
But what a woman says to her eager lover should be written in wind and running water.
Catullus. Poem 70.3f.

Sed piger ad poenas Princeps, ad praemia velox. *sed pig–er ad poy–nahss prin–keps, ad pry–mi–a way–loaks.*
But let the ruler be slow in punishing, swift in rewarding.
Ovid. Ep. ex Pont. Book 1.2.123.

Sed plures nimia congesta pecunia cura/Strangulat. *sed ploo–race nim–i–ah con–guess–ta peck–oo–ni–a coo–rah strang–gull–at.*

But money amassed with excessive care chokes many.
Juvenal. Sat. 10.12.

Sed scelus hoc meriti pondus et instar habet. *sed skel—uss hoke meh—rit—ee pond—uss et in—star hab—et.*
But this offence possesses the dignity and the form of a good deed.
Ovid. Heroides 2.30.

Sed summa sequar fastigia rerum. *sed sum—ma seh—quar fass—tee—gi—a ray—rum.*
But I will trace the footsteps of the chief events.
Virgil. Æneid 1.342.

Sed taciti fecere tamen convicia vultus. *sed tack—it—ee fay—kay—reh tam—en con—week—i—a wool—tuss.*
But still her silent looks loudly reproached me.
Ovid. Amorum 1.7.21.

Semen est sanguis Christianorum. *say—men est sang—gwiss criss—ti—ah—noh—rum.*
The blood of Christians is as seed.
Tertulian. Apol. 17. (usually quoted as 'The blood of the martyrs is the seed of the church')

Semper Augustus. *sem—per ow—guss—tuss.*
Always Augustus (always an enlarger of the empire).
Symmachus.

Semper bonus homo tiro est. *sem—per bon—uss hom—oh tee—roe est.*
A good man is always a beginner.
Martial. Epig. Book 12.51.

Semper eadem. *sem—per eh—a—dem.*
Ever the same.
Motto of Queen Elizabeth I.

Semper eris pauper, si pauper es Æmiliane;/Dantur opes nulli nunc nisi divitibus. *sem—per eh—riss pow—per, see pow—per es eye—mill—i—ah—ne; dan—tur op—ace null—eye nunc niss—i dee—wit—ib—uss.*
If once you are poor, you will always be poor, Æmilianus; riches are given nowadays to none except the wealthy.
Martial. Epig. 5.82.

Semper fidelis, mutare sperno. *sem—per fid—ay—liss, moot—ah—ray spare—noh.*

Always faithful, I scorn to change.
Motto of City of Worcester.

Semper in absentes felicior aestus amantes: Elevat assiduos copia
longa viros. *sem—pehr in ap—sen—tace fay—leek—i—or ice—tuss
am—ant—ace: ay—leh—wat ass—sid—u—oce cope—i—a long—ga wih—roce.*
Women's passions are always more favourable towards absent lovers: long
possession lessens the worth of attentive lovers.
Propertius. Elegies 2.33.43f.

Semper ornare. *sem—per oar—nah—ray.*
Always to adorn.
Motto of the "Master of Cree."

Senatus Populusque Romanus. *sen—ah—tuss pop—ull—uss—queh
roe—mah—nuss.*
The Roman Senate and People.
Official Title of the Roman State.

Senem juventus pigra mendicum creat. *sen—em you—went—uss pig—ra
men—dee—cum creh—at.*
Slothful youth produces an old age of beggary.
Pr.

Seniores priores. *sen—i—oh—race pri—oh—race.*
Those who are older first.
Pr.

. . . Sequiturque patrem non passibus aequis. *seh—quit—ur—queh pat—rem
none pass—sib—uss eye—queece.*
He follows his father with unequal steps.
Virgil. Æneid 2.724.

Sera parsimonia in fundo est. *say—ra parr—sim—oh—ni—a in fun—doh est.*
Thrift is too late at the bottom of the purse.
Seneca. Ep. 1. fin.

Sermone huic obsonas. *sair—moh—neh hu—ick op—soh—nahss.*
You interrupt him with your talking.
Plautus. Pseudolus i. 2.74.

Sero domum est reversus titubanti pede. *say—roh dom—um est reh—wear—
suss ti—tub—an—tee.ped—eh.*
He has come home late with staggering foot.
Phaedrus. Fab. Book 4.14.10.

Sero sapiunt Phryges. *say—roh sap—i—unt fri—guess.*
The Phrygians become wise too late.
Pr. Used in reference to after-wit.

Serpens, ni edat serpentem, draco non fiet. *sair—paynce, nee ed—at sair—pen—tem, drack—oh none fi—et.*
Unless a serpent eats a serpent, it will not become a dragon.
Ancient Maxim.

Servare cives major est patriae patri. *sair—wah—reh key—wace mah—yor est pat—ri—eye pat—ree.*
To safeguard the citizens is the greater [achievement] of a father of his country.
Seneca. Octavia ii. 444.

Servata semper lege et ratione loquendi. *sair—wah—tah sem—per lay—geh et rat—i—oh—neh lo—quen—dee.*
The rules and principles of speech being always preserved.
Juvenal. Sat. 6.453.

Sese omnes amant. *say—say om—nace a—mant.*
All men love themselves.
Plautus. Captivi iii. 1.

Sexu femina, ingenio vir. *sex—oo fay—min—a, in—gen—i—oh wihr.*
In sex a woman, in abilities a man.

Si antiquitatem spectes, est vetustissima; si dignitatem, est honoratissima; si jurisdicitionem, est capacissima. *see ant—ee—quit—ah—tem speck—tace, est wet—ust—iss—sim—a; see dig—nit—a—tem, est hon—oh—rah—tiss—sim—a; see you—riss—dick—ti—oh—nem, est cap—ah—kiss—sim—a.*
If you regard antiquity it is the most venerable; if you look at dignity it is the most honourable; if you consider jurisdiction it has the most extended powers.
Coke, on the English House of Commons.

Si bene quid memini causae sunt quinque bibendi: Hospitis adventus, praesens sitis atque futura, Aut vini bonitas, aut quaelibet altera causa.
see ben—eh quid mem—in—ee, cow—sye sunt quing—queh bib—en—dee: hoss—pit—iss ad—wen—tuss, pry—saynce sit—iss at—queh fut—oo—ra, out wee—nee bon—it—ahss, out quie—lib—et al—teh—ra cow—sa.
If I remember correctly there are five reasons for drinking: the arrival of a guest, thirst now, or anticipated thirst, or the excellence of the wine, or any other reason you like.
Anonymous.

[195]

Si cadere necesse est, occurrendum discrimini. *see cad—eh—reh neck—ess—seh est, ock—cur—ren—dum diss—cree—min—ee.*
If it is essential that we should fall, let us face the hazard.
Tacitus. Hist. Book 1.33.

Si Deus pro nobis, quis contra nos? *see deh—uss proh noh—beece, quiss con—trah noce?*
If God is for us, who shall be against us?
Vulgate Rom. 8.31.

Si diceris "Æstuo", sudat. *see dee—keh—riss eye—stu—oh, soo—dat.*
If you should say "I am hot" he perspires.
Juvenal. Sat. 3.103.

Si foret in terris rideret Democritus. . . . *see for—et in tear—reece rid—eh—ret day—mock—rit—uss.*
If Democritus (the laughing philosopher) were on the earth he would laugh. (Sometimes the name of "Heraclitus", the "crying philosopher", is substituted for that of Democritus.)
Horace. Ep. Book 2.1.194.

Si gravis brevis, si longus levis. *see gra—wiss breh—wiss, see long—guss leh—wiss.*
If severe, short; if long, light.
Cicero. De Fin. 2.7.22.

Si incolumem servaveris, aeternum exemplar clementiae ero.
see in—col—um—em sair—wah—weh—riss, eye—tear—num ex—em—plar clay—men—ti—eye eh—roh.
If you preserve me uninjured, I (Caractacus) shall be a lasting example of your clemency.
Tacitus. Annals Book 12.37.

Si ita e republica videretur, age et feri. *see it—a ay ray—pub—lick—ah wid—eh—ray—tur, ag—eh et feh—ree.*
If it so seems, good to the republic, do it and strike.
Tacitus. Hist. 1.41. (adapted).

Si mereor in me. *see meh—reh—or in may.*
Against me — if I deserve it.
Motto on coin struck at James I's.

Si mihi pergit quae vult dicere, ea quae non vult audiet. *see mi—hee pair—git quie woolt dee—keh—reh, eh—a quie none woolt ow—di—et.*

[196]

If he persists in telling me what he wishes, he shall hear what he does not wish to hear.
Terence. Andria v. 4.17.

Si mihi quae quondam fuerat, quamque esse decebat,/Vis in amore foret, non hoc mihi namque negares. *see mi—he quie quon—dam fu—eh—rat, quam—queh ess—seh deck—ay—bat, weece in a—moh—re fo—ret, none hoke mi—he nam—que neg—ah—race.*
If the same influence in love was mine which formerly was, and which should be, you would not have denied me this thing.
Virgil. Æneid 10.613.

Si monumentum requiris, circumpsice. *see mon—u—men—tum re—quee—ris, kihr—cum—spick—eh.*
If you seek his monument, look around you.
Inscription to Sir Christopher Wren.

Si numeres anno soles et nubila toto,/Invenies nitidum saepius isse diem. *see num—eh—race an—noh soh—lace et noo—bill—a toe—toe, in—wen—i—ace nit—id—um sigh—pi—uss eess—seh di—em.*
If you count up the sunny and cloudy days in a complete year, you will find that the fine day has come more often.
Ovid. Trist. 5.8.31.

Si parva licet componere magnis. *see parr—wa lick—et com—poe—neh—reh mag—neece.*
If it is allowable to compare small things with great.
Virgil. Georgics, 4.176.

Si quid cum periculo experiri velis, in Care id potissimum esse faciendum. *see quid cum peh—reek—ull—oh ex—peh—ree—ree well—iss, in cah—reh id pot—iss—sim—um ess—seh fack—i—end—um.*
If you want to try a dangerous experiment, it is best to do it on a Carian.
Greek proverb cited by Cicero, Pro Flacco, 26/65: cf. Plato, Laches 187B.

Si quid scis me fecisse inscite aut improbe,/Si id non accusas, tu ipse objurgandus es, scio. *see quid skeece may fay—kiss—seh in—skeet—ay owt im—prob—ay, see id none ack—coo—sahss, too ip—seh ob—yur—gan—duss ess, ski—oh.*
I know that if you know that I have done anything unskillfully or badly, and have not found fault with it, you are yourself to be blamed.
Plautus. Trinummus Act i. 2.

Si quis non vult operari, nec manducet. *see quiss none woolt op—eh—rah—ree, neck man—doo—ket.*

If any one will not work, neither let him eat.
Vulgate. 2 Thess. 3.10.

Si sapias, sapias; habeas quod Di dabunt boni. *see sap—i—ahss, sap—i—ahss; hab—eh—ahss quod dee da—bunt bon—ee.*
Be wise if you are wise; possess what amount of good the gods will give you.
Plautus.

Si stimulos pugnis caedis, manibus plus dolet. *see stim—ull—oce pug—neece kye—diss, man—ib—uss plooce dol—et.*
If you beat goads with your fists, your hands suffer most.
Plautus. Truculentus iv. 2.55.

Si te nulla movet tantarum gloria rerum. *see tay null—la mo—wet tan—tah—rum gloh—ri—a ray—rum.*
If no glory appertaining to such illustrious deeds moves you.
Virgil. Æneid 4.272.

Si tibi vis omnia subjicere, te subjice rationi. *see ti—be weece om—ni—a sub—yick—eh—reh, tay sub—yick—eh rat—i—oh—nee.*
If you wish to subject all things to yourself, subject yourself to reason.
Seneca. Ep. 37.

. . . Si vis me flere, dolendum est/Primum ipsi tibi. . . .
see weece may flay—reh, dol—end—dum est pree—mum ip—see ti—be.
If you wish me to weep, you must first feel grief yourself.
Horace. De Arte Poetica 102.

Sibi benefacit qui benefacit amico. *si—be ben—eff—ack—it quee ben—eff—ack—it am—ee—coe.*
He does good to himself who does good to his friend.
Erasmus. Fam. Col.

Sibi parat malum qui alteri parat. *si—be pa—rat mal—um quee al—teh—ree pa—rat.*
He prepares evil for himself who prepares it for another.
Pr.

Sibi quisque peccat. *si—be quiss—queh peck—at.*
It is against himself that everybody sins.
Pr.

Sibi uni fortunam debet. *si—bee oo—nee for—too—nam day—bett.*
He owes his fortune to himself alone.
Pr.

[198]

Sic ait, et dicto citius tumida aequora placat. *seek ah—it, et dick—toe kit—i—uss tum—id—a eye—quo—ra plah—cat.*
Thus he speaks, and by his word he quickly pacifies the raging waters.
Virgil. Æneid. 1.142.

Sic itur ad astra. *seek ee—tur ad ass—tra.*
Thus is the journey to the stars accomplished.
Virgil. Æneid 9.641.

Sic me servavit Apollo. *seek may sair—wah—wit a—poll—loh.*
Thus did Apollo serve me.
Horace. Sat. Book 1.9.98.

Sic omnes amor unus habet decernere ferro. *seek om—nace a—mor oo—nuss hab—et day—care—neh—reh fair—roh.*
So the same love of deciding by warlike means possessed them all.
Virgil. Æneid 12.282.

Sic passim. *seek pass—im.*
So in various places.
Pr.

Sic transit gloria mundi. *seek trahn—sit gloh—ri—a mun—dee.*
So passes away the glory of the world.
Thomas à Kempis. Imit. Christi, 3.6.

Sic visum Veneri; cui placet impares/Formas, atque animos sub juga aenea/ Saevo mittere cum joco. *sic wee—sum wen—eh—ree; cu—ee plack—et im—pa—race for—mahss, at—queh an—im—oce sub yug—a a—ay—neh—a sigh—woe mitt—teh—reh cum yock—oh.*
So it seems fit to Venus; to whom it is a delight to place, with cruel humour, incongruous forms and minds under her brazen yoke.
Horace. Odes Book 1.33.10.

Sic vive cum hominibus tanquam Deus videat, et videt. *seek we—weh cum hom—in—ib—uss tan—quam deh—uss wid—eh—at, et wid—et.*
So live with men as if God saw you, and He does see you.
Seneca. Ep. 10.5.

Sic vos non vobis mellificatis apes. *seek woce none woe—beece mell—liff—ick—ah—tiss ap—ace.*
So do you bees make your honey, not for yourselves.
Virgil. (Attr.)

Sicut patribus sit Deus nobis. *see—cut pat—ree—buss sit deh—uss no—bees.*
God be with us as he was with our fathers.
Kings Bible. chapter 8. motto on the seal of the City of Boston, U.S.A.

Silent enim leges inter arma. *sill—ent en—im lay—gace in—ter ar—ma.*
For the laws are dumb in the midst of arms.
Cicero. Pro Milone 4.

Simplex munditiis. *sim—plex mun—dit—i—eece.*
Simple in her elegance.
Horace. Odes Book 1.5.5.

Sine amicitia vitam esse nullam. *sin—eh am—ee—kit—i—ah wee—tam ess—
seh null—lam.*
There is no life without friendship.
Cicero. (adapted from Ennius).

Sine die. *sine—e die—e.*
Without any fixed date. (i.e. indefinitely).

Sine ira et studio. *sin—eh ee—rah et stud—i—oh.*
Without anger and without partiality.
Tacitus. Annals 1.1.

Sine prole. *sine—e proh—le.*
Without offspring. (Frequently denoted by the initials S.P.)

Sine qua non. *sine—e quay none.*
Without which, nothing (*i.e.* an indispensable condition).

Singuli enim decipere et decipi possunt: nemo omnes, neminem omnes
fefellunt. *sing—gull—ee en—im day—kip—eh—reh et day—kip—ee poss—unt:
nay—moh om—nace, nem—in—em om—nace fe—fell—lunt.*
Individuals indeed may deceive and be deceived; but no one has ever deceived all men, nor have all men ever deceived any one.
Pliny the Younger. Panegyr. Traj. 62.

Sint Maecenates, non derunt, Flacce, Marones. *sint my—kay—nah—tace,
none day—runt, flack—keh, ma—roe—nace.*
Let there be Maecenases, Flaccus, and there will not be wanting Virgils.
Martial. Epig. Book 8.56.

Sint sales sine vilitate. *sint sal—ace sin—eh wee—lit—ah—teh.*
Let the jests be without anything vile about them.
Pr.

Siqua recordanti benefacta priora voluptas Est homini, cum se cogitat esse pium, . . . Multa parata manent in longa aetate, Catulle, Ex hoc ingrato gaudia amore tibi. *seek—wa reck—or—dan—tee ben—eh—fack—ta pri—oh—ra wol—up—tahss est hom—in—ee, cum say coe—git—at ess—seh pi—um, . . . mull—ta pa—rah—ta man—ent in long—gah eye—tah—teh, cat—ull—leh, ex hoke ing—grah—toe gow—di—a am—oh—reh tib—ee.*
If there is any pleasure for a man in recalling previous good deeds, in that he thinks he is virtuous, . . . then many delights are set by to keep for long ages, Catullus, for yourself from this thankless love.
Catullus. Poem 76.1.2.5.6.

Sisyphus in vita quoque nobis ante oculos est,/Qui petere a populo fasces, saevasque secures/Imbibit; et semper victus, tristisque recedit.
see—siff—uss in wee—tah quo—queh noh—beece an—teh ock—ul—oce est, quee pet—eh—reh ah pop—ull—oh fass—case, sigh—wahss—queh seck—oo—race im—bib—it; et sem—per wick—tuss, triss—tiss—queh re—kay—dit.
In life also we have Sisyphus before our eyes, who resolves to seek from the people the fasces and cruel axes (the supreme power); and ever retires beaten and sad.
Lucretius. De Rer. Nat. Book 3.1008.

Sit mihi fas audita loqui. *sit mi—hee fahss ow—dee—ta lo—quee.*
Let it be allowed me to speak what I have heard.
Virgil. Æneid Book 6.266.

Sit tibi terra levis! *sit ti—be ter—ra leh—wiss.*
Let the earth lie light upon you. Denoted sometimes by the initials S.T.T.L.
Monumental Inscription.

Sit venia verbis. *set wen—i—a wear—beece.*
Let my words be forgiven.
Pr.

Sociale animal est. *sock—i—ah—leh an—im—al est.*
[Man] is a social animal.
Seneca. De Benef. Book 7.1.

. . . Sol crescentes decedens duplicat umbras. *sole cray—sken—tace day—kay—daynce doo—plick—at um—brahss.*
The sun when setting makes the increasing shadows twice as large.
Virgil. Eclogues 2.67.

Solem e mundo tollunt qui amicitiam e vita tollunt. *soh—lem ay mun—doh toll—lunt quee am—ee—kit—i—am ay wee—tah toll—lunt.*

They take the sunshine from the world who take friendship from life.
Anon.

Sobria grata parum: cum bibit, omne decet. *soh—bri—a grah—ta pa—rum:*
cum bib—it, om—neh deck—et.
When sober she pleases me little: when she drinks, she is all delight.
Propertius. Elegies 4.8.30.

Soles occidere et redire possunt:/Nobis, cum semel occidit brevis lux,/
Nox est perpetua una dormienda. *so—lace ock—kid—eh—reh et red—ee—reh*
poss—sunt: noh—beece, cum sem—el ock—did—it breh—wiss lux, nox est
pair—pet—u—a oo—na dore—mi—end—a.
Suns can set and return again; with us, when once our short day has set,
there is one everlasting night of sleep.
Catullus. Carm. 5.4.

Solet sequi laus cum viam fecit labor. *sol—et seh—quee louse cum wi—am*
fay—kit lab—or.
Praise is wont to follow where labour has made the way.
Publilius Syrus.

Solo Deo salus. *sol—oh deh—oh sal—oose.*
Salvation (or safety) is from God alone.
Motto.

Solum patriae omnibus est carum, dulce, atque jucundum.
sol—um pat—ri—eye om—nib—uss est cah—rum, dool—keh, at—queh
you—cun—dum.
Dear, sweet and pleasing to us all is the soil of our native land.
Cicero. Adapted from In Catilinam 4.8.26.

Solus sapiens scit amare; solus sapiens amicus est. *soh—luss sap—i—aynce*
skit a—mah—reh; soh—lus sap—i—aynce a—meek—us est.
Only a wise man knows how to love; only a wise man is a friend.
Seneca. Epist. 81.

Solventur risu tabulae. . . . *sol—wen—tur ree—soo tab—ull—eye.*
The case will be dismissed with laughter.
Horace. Sat. Book 2.1.86.

Solvitur acris hiems. *sol—wit—ur ah—criss hi—emss.*
Sharp winter is now loosened.
Horace. Odes Book 1.4.

Solvitur ambulando. *sol—wit—ur am—bull—an—doh.*

It is settled by walking.
Pr.

Somnia me terrent veros imitantia casus;/Et vigilant sensus in mea damna mei.
*som—ni—a may tear—rent way—roce im—it—ant—i—a cah—sooce; et wig—ill—
ant sain—sooce in meh—a dam—na meh—ee.*
Dreams terrify me, depicting real misfortunes, and my senses are awake
to my losses.
Ovid. Ep. ex Pont. 1.2.45.

. . . Sonat hic de nare canina/Littera. . . . *sonn—at heek day nah—reh
can—ee—na lit—teh—ra.*
Here from the nostril sounds the "canine letter" (the letter R, the sound
resembling the snarling of a dog).
Persius. Sat. 1.109.

Sortes Virgilianae, *or* Sortes Homericae. *sor—tace wihr—gill—i—ah—nye,
(sor—tace hom—ay—rick—eye).*
Virgilian chances *or* Homeric chances.
Divination by random selection of passages from the poets.

. . . Spargere voces/In vulgum ambiguas. . . . *spar—geh—reh woe—case in
wool—gum am—big—u—ahss.*
To scatter doubtful reports amongst the crowd.
Virgil. Æneid 2.98.

Spectatum veniunt; veniunt spectentur ut ipsae. *speck—tah—tum wen—i—
unt; wen—i—unt speck—ten—tur ut ip—sigh.*
These women come to see; and they come that they may themselves be
seen.
Ovid. Ars Amat. Book 1.99.

Spem bonam certamque domum reporto. *spem bon—am care—tam—queh
dom—um rep—ore—toe.*
I bring back a good and sure hope.
Pr.

Spem vultu simulat. *spem wool—too sim—ul—at.*
He counterfeits hope in his features.
Virgil. Æneid 1.209.

Sperate, et vosmet rebus servate secundis. *spay—rah—teh, et woce—met
ray—buss sair—wah—teh seck—un—deece.*
Hope, and reserve yourself for better times.
Virgil. Æneid 1.207.

[203]

Spes addita suscitat iras. *space ad—dit—a suss—kit—at ee—rahss.*
Increase of hope kindled their passion.
Virgil. Æneid 10.263.

Spes alit agricolas. *space a—lit ag—rick—ol—ahss.*
Hope sustains the husbandmen.

Spes est salutis ubi hominem objurgat pudor. *space est sal—oo—tiss ub—i*
hom—in—em ob—yur—gat pud—or.
There is hope of salvation where shame reproaches a man.
Publilius Syrus.

Spes est vigilantis somnium. *space est wig—ill—ant—iss som—ni—um.*
Hope is the dream of a man awake.
Coke.

Spes incerta futuri. *space in—care—ta fu—too—ree.*
Hope doubtful of what is to be.
Virgil. Æneid 8.580.

. . . Spes sibi quisque. . . . *space si—be quis—queh.*
Let every man's hope be in himself.
Virgil. Æneid 11.309.

Spiritus quidem promptus est, caro autem infirma. *spee—rit—uss quid—em*
prome—ptuss est, cah—roe ow—tem in—fear—ma.
The spirit indeed is ready, but the flesh is weak.
Vulgate. St. Matthew 26.41.

Splendide mendax. *splen—did—ay men—dahks.*
Magnificently false.
Horace. Odes Book 3.11.35.

Spolia opima. *spoll—i—a op—ee—ma.*
The splendid spoils, the personal spoils of the enemy's general when slain
by the opposing commander.
Livy, etc.

Stabat Mater dolorosa. *stah—bat mah—ter doll—or—oh—sa.*
There was standing the weeping mother [Mary].
Sequence of Our Lady of Sorrows. Ascribed to Jacopone Da Todi (died 1306), also to
Innocent III.

Stabit quocunque jeceris. *stah—bit quoh—cun—queh yay—keh—riss.*
Whatever way you cast it, it will stand.

[204]

Legend on the three-legged armorial bear.

Stant belli causae. *stant bell—lee cow—sigh.*
The causes of war still remain.
Virgil. Æneid 7.553.

Stare decisis, et non movere quieta. *sta—reh day—key—seece, et none*
moh—way—reh qui—ay—ta.
To stand by decisions, and not disturb things which are settled.
Law.

Stare super vias antiquas. *sta—reh sup—er wi—ahss an—tea—quahss.*
To stand in the old-established ways.
Pr.

Stat magni nominis umbra. *stat mag—nee nome—in—iss um—bra.*
There stands the shadow of a mighty name.
Lucan. Pharsalia Book 1.135.

Stat pro ratione voluntas. *stat proh rat—i—oh—neh wol—un—tahss.*
Will stands for reason.
Adapted from Juvenal. (See "Hoc volo.")

Stemmata quid faciunt? Quid prodest, Pontice, longo/Sanguine censeri,
pictosque ostendere vultus/Majorum? *stem—mat—a quid fack—i—unt?*
quid proh—dest, pon—tick—eh, long—goh sang—gwin—eh cane—say—ree,
pick—toce—queh oss—ten—deh—reh wool—tooce mah—yoh—rum?
What do pedigrees avail? What is the profit, Ponticus, in possessing ancient
blood, and in showing the painted features of ancestors?
Juvenal. Sat. 8.1.

Stet fortuna domus! *stet for—too—na dom—ooce!*
May the fortune of the house endure.
Pr.

Stillicidi casus lapidem cavat. *still—lick—id—ee cah—suss lap—id—em*
ca—wat.
The fall of dropping water wears away the stone.
Lucretius. De Rerum Nat. 1.314.

Stimulos dedit aemula virtus. *stim—ull—oce ded—it eye—mull—a*
wihr—tooce.
Valour full of rivalry spurred him on.
Lucan.

[205]

Studia hilaritate proveniunt. *stud—i—a hill—a—rit—ah—te proh—wen—i—unt.*
Our studies are advanced by cheerfulness.
Pliny.

. . . Studium famae mihi crescit amore. *stud—i—um fah—my mi—he cray—
skit a—moh—reh.*
My application is increased by my love of fame.
Ovid. Rem. Amor. 393.

Stultitiam dissimulare non potes nisi taciturnitate. *stool—ti—ti—am diss—
sim—ul—ah—reh none pot—ess niss—i tack—it—ur—nit—ah—teh.*
You cannot conceal folly except by silence.
Pr.

Stultum est timere quod vitari non potest. *stool—tum est tim—ay—re quod
wee—tah—ree none pot—est.*
It is foolish to fear what cannot be avoided.
Publilius Syrus.

Stultum facit Fortuna quem vult perdere. *stultum fack—it for—too—na
quem woolt pair—deh—reh.*
When Fortune wishes to ruin a man she makes him a fool.
Publilius Syrus.

. . . Stultus labor est ineptiarum. *stool—tuss lab—or est in—ep—ti—ah—rum.*
Labour about trifles is foolish.
Martial 2.86.9.

Stupor mundi clerus Britannicus. *stup—or mun—dee clay—russ brit—an—
nick—uss.*
The British clergy are the astonishment of the world.
Anon.

Stupor mundi Fridericus et immutator mirabilis. *stup—or mun—dee
frid—eh—rick—uss et im—moot—ah—tor mee—rah—bill—iss.*
Frederick [the Emperor Frederick II] was the astonishment of the world
and marvellously obstinate.
Matthew Paris.

. . . Sua cuique Deus fit dira cupido? *su—a cu—ee—queh deh—uss fit dee—
ra cup—ee—doh?*
Does his own fatal passion become to each man his God?
Virgil. Æneid 9.185.

Sua cuique vita obscura est. *su—a cu—ee—queh wee—ta op—scoo—ra est.*
To everyone his own life is dark.
Pr.

Sua regina regi placet, Juno Jovi. *su—a ray—ghee—na ray—ghee plack—et, yoo—noh yo—wee.*
His own queen pleases a king, Juno pleases Jupiter.
Plautus.

Suave, mari magno, turbantibus aequora ventis,/E terra magnum alterius spectare laborem. *swah—weh, ma—ree mag—noh, tur—ban—tib—uss eye— quo—ra wen—teece, ay tair—wah mag—num al—teh—ri—uss speck—tah—reh lab—oh—rem.*
It is pleasant, when the sea is high, and the winds are dashing the waves about, to watch, from the land, the great straits of another (at sea).
Lucretius. De Rerum Nat. 2.1.

Suavis laborum est praeteritorum memoria. *swah—wiss lab—oh—rum est pry—teh—rit—oh—rum mem—oh—ri—a.*
The remembrance of past labours is agreeable.
Cicero. De Finibus 2.32.

Sub Jove frigido. *sub yo—weh free—gid—oh.*
Under the cold heaven.
Horace. Odes Book 1.1.25.

Sub rosa. *sub roe—sah/sub roe—za.*
Under the rose.
(i.e. secretly, the rose being emblematic of secrecy with the ancients. There was a legend that Cupid bribed Harpocrates, god of silence, with a rose, not to divulge the amours of Venus. Hence the host hung a rose over his tables in order that his guests might know that under it words spoken were to remain secret).

Subita amicitia raro sine paenitentia colitur. *sub—it—a am—ee—kit—i—a rah—roe sin—eh pie—nit—en—ti—ah col—it—ur.*
Sudden friendship is rarely formed without subsequent repentance.
Pr.

Sublata causa tollitur effectus. *sub—lah—tah cow—sah toll—lit—ur ef—fec— tuss.*
The cause being taken away the effect is removed.
Law.

Sublimi feriam sidera vertice. *sub—lee—mee feh—ri—am seed—eh—ra wear— tick—eh.*
I strike the stars with my head, upraised.

Horace. Odes Book 1.1.36.

Subtilis veterum judex et callidus. . . . *sub—tee—liss wet—eh—rum you—decks et call—lid—uss.*
An acute and experienced judge of things which are old.
Horace. Sat. Book 2.7.101.

Subverterent potius jura quam custodes eorem amoverent. *sub—wehr—teh—rent pot—i—uss you—ra quam cuss—toe—dace eh—oh—rum ah—mo—way—rent.*
They should overthrow the laws rather than remove their guardians. (Tiberius Caesar,)
Tacitus. Annals 4.30.

Sudor Anglicus. *soo—dor ang—lick—uss.*
The English sweating sickness.

Sui cuique mores fingunt fortunam. *su—ee cu—ee—queh moh—race fing—gunt for—too—nam.*
Every man's manners fashion his fortune.
Cornelius Nepos. Atticus 11.16.

Sum quod eris, fui quod es. *sum quod eh—riss, fu—ee quod ess.*
I am what thou wilt be, what thou art I have been.
Epitaph.

. . . Sume superbiam/Quaesitam meritis. *soo—meh sup—air—bi—am quie—see—tam meh—rit—eece.*
Assume the honourable pride acquired by merit.
Horace. Odes Book 3.10.14.

Sumite materiam vestris, qui scribitis, aequam/Viribus, et versate diu quid ferre recusent,/Quid valeant humeri. . . . *soo—mit—eh mah—teh—ri—am west—reece, quee scree—bit—iss, eye—quam wee—rib—uss, et wear—sah—teh di—oo quid fair—reh reck—oo—sent, quid wal—eh—ant hum—eh—ree.*
You who write, select a subject suited to your powers, and consider long what your shoulders are unable to bear and what they are capable of.
Horace. De Arte Poetica 38.

Summa perfectio attingi non potest. *sum—ma pair—fec—ti—oh at—ting—ghee none pot—est.*
The highest perfection cannot be attained.
Cicero.

Summa sedes non capit duos. *sum—ma say—dace none cap—it du—oce.*
The highest seat will not hold two. *Pr.*

[208]

Summum jus, summa injuria. *sum—mum yooce, sum—ma in—you—ri—a.*
Extreme law is extreme injustice.
Cicero. De Off., 1.10.33. (Quoted by him as a "trite proverb"; referred to by Terence, Heaut. v. 48.)

Summum nec metuas diem, nec optas. *sum—mum neck met—u—ahss diem, neck op—tahss.*
Neither fear your last day nor desire it.
Martial. Book 4.47.

Sunt bona mixta malis, sunt mala mixta bonis. *sunt bon—a mik—ta ma—lease, sunt mal—a mik—ta bon—eese.*
Good things are mixed with evil, evil things with good.
Pr.

Sunt enim ingeniis nostris semina innata virtutum. *sunt en—im in—gen—i— eece noss—treece say—min—a in—nah—ta wihr—too—tum.*
For in our dispositions the seeds of the virtues are implanted by nature.
Cicero. Tusc. Quaest. 3.1.

Sunt aliquid Manes: letum non omnia finit, Luridaque evictos effugit umbra rogos. *sunt al—ick—wid mah—nace: lay—tum none om—ni—a fee—nit, loo— rid—a—queh ay—wick—toce eff—fug—it umb—ra rog—oce.*
The Shades exist: death is not the end of all things, and the pallid ghost escapes from the defeated pyre.
Propertius. Elegies 4.7.1f.

Sunt et mihi carmina: me quoque dicunt/Vatem pastores, sed non ego credulus illis./Nam neque adhuc Varo videor, nec dicere Cinna/Digna, sed argutos inter strepere anser olores. *sunt et mi—he carr—min—a: may quo— queh dee—kunt wah—tem pah—stoh—race, sed none egg—o cray—dull—uss ill—lease. nam neh—queh ad—hook wah—roe wid—eh—or, neck dee—keh— reh kin—nah dig—na, sed ar—goo—toce in—ter strep—eh—reh ahn—ser o—loh—race.*
I too have my songs: me also the shepherds call a poet, but I do not give credence to them. For thus far I do not seem to say anything worthy of Varus or of Cinna, but I appear to cackle, a goose among the melodious swans.
Virgil. Eclogues 9.33.

Sunt lacrimae rerum, et mentem mortalia tangunt. *sunt lack—rim—eye ray—rum, et men—tem mor—tah—li—a tan—gunt.*
There are tears in the affairs of this life, and human sufferings touch the heart.
Virgil. Æneid 1.462.

[209]

Sunt quaedam vitiorum elementa. *sunt quie—dam wit—i—oh—rum e—lem—en—ta.*
There are certain redimentary beginnings of vice.
Juvenal. Sat. 14.123.

Super vires. *sup—er wee—race.*
Beyond one's strength.
Tacitus. Germania 43.

Supplicium mei oblivio sequeretur: at si incolumem servaveris, aeternum exemplar clementiae ero. *sup—plick—i—um meh—ee ob—lee—we—oh seck—weh—ray—tur: at see in—coll—um—em sehr—wah—weh—riss, eye—tehr—num ex—em—plar clay—men—ti—eye eh—roe.*
If you execute me, I shall be forgotten: but if you save me unharmed, I shall be an everlasting witness to your mercy. (Caratacus to the Emperor Claudius.)
Tacitus. Annals 12.37.

Suppressio veri; suggestio falsi. *sup—press—si—oh way—ree; sug—guess—ti—oh fal—see.*
Suppression of what is true; suggestion of what is false.
Pr.

Surdo narras fabulam. *sur—doe nahr—rahss fah—bull—am.*
You tell your story to a deaf ear.
Terence. Heautontimorumenos 2.1.9.

Sursum corda. *sur—sum core—da.*
Lift up your hearts.
Missal.

Suspendatur per collum. *suss—pen—dah—tur per coll—lum.*
Let him be hanged by the neck.
Law.

Sustine et abstine. *suss—tin—ay et ap—stin—ay.*
Bear and forbear.
Tr. of Epictetus.

Suum cuique decus posteritas rependit. *su—um cu—ee—queh deck—uss pos—teh—rit—ahss re—pen—dit.*
Posterity gives to each man his due.
Tacitus. Annals. Book 4.35.

Syllaba longa brevi subjecta vocatur Iambus. *sill—lab—a long—ga breh—wee sub—yeck—ta wock—ah—tur i—am—buss.*
A long syllable following a short is called an Iambus.
Horace. De Arte Poetica 251.

Tabula rasa. *tab—ul—a rah—sa.*
A smooth tablet.
Pr.

Taciturnitas stulto homini pro sapientia est. *tack—it—ur—nit—ahss stool—toe hom—in—ee proh sap—i—en—ti—ah est.*
In a foolish man silence stands for wisdom.
Publilius Syrus.

Taedium vitae. *tie—di—um wee—tie.*
Weariness of life.
Gellius. 7.18.11.

Tam facile et pronum est superos contemnere testes,/Si mortalis idem nemo sciat! . . . *tam fack—ill—eh et proh—num est sup—eh—roce con—tem—neh—reh tess—tace, see mor—tah—liss id—em nay—moh ski—at!*
It is so natural and easy to despise the gods, who are witnesses of our guilt, if only no mortal knows of it!
Juvenal. Sat. 13.75.

. . . Tam timidis quanta sit ira feris? *tam tim—id—eece quan—ta sit ee—ra feh—reece?*
Can such great rage exist in such timid creatures?
Martial. Epig. Book 4.74.

Tandem desine matrem. *tan—dem day—sin—eh mah—trem.*
At length abandon your mother.
Horace. Odes Book 1.23.11.

Tandem triumphans. *tan—dem tri—um—fahnss.*
Triumphing at last.
Motto.

[211]

Tangere ulcus. *tang—geh—reh ull—cuss.*
To touch a sore.
Terence. Phormio iv. 4.9.

. . . Tanta est quaerendi cura decoris. *tan—ta est quie—ren—dee coo—ra deck—oh—riss.*
So great is their desire for personal adornment.
Juvenal Sat. 6.501.

Tantae molis erat Romanam condere gentem. *tan—tie moh—liss eh—rat roe—mah—nam con—deh—reh gen—tem.*
So great a labour was it to found the Roman race.
Virgil. Æneid 1.33.

. . . Tantaene animis coelestibus irae? *tan—tie—neh an—im—eece coy—less—tib—uss ee—rye?*
Is there such wrath in heavenly minds?
Virgil. Æneid 1.11.

Tantum bona valent, quantum vendi possunt. *tan—tum bon—a wal—ent, quan—tum wen—dee poss—sunt.*
Goods are worth just as much as they can be sold for.
Coke.

Tantum religio potuit suadere malorum. *tan—tum ray—lig—i—oh pot—u—it swah—day—reh mal—oh—rum.*
To such a pitch of evil could religion prompt. (Spoken of the sacrifice of Iphigenia.)
Lucretius. De Rerum Nat. 1.102.

. . . Tantum series juncturaque pollet;/Tantum de medio sumptis accedit honoris. *tan—tum seh—ri—ace yunc—too—ra—queh poll—let; tan—tum day med—i—oh sump—teece ack—kay—dit hon—oh—riss.*
So great is the power of order and conjunction (in words), so much of honour is imparted to matters taken from common life.
Horace. De Arte Poetica 242.

Tantus amor florum, et generandi gloria mellis. *tan—tuss a—mor floh—rum, et gen—eh—ran—dee gloh—ri—a mel—liss.*
So great is their love of flowers and pride in producing honey.
Virgil. Georgics 4.205.

Tarda sit illa dies, et nostro serior aevo. *tar--da sit ill—la di—ace, et noss—troh say—ri—or eye—woe.*

Slow be the approach of that day, and may it come later than the age we live in.
Ovid. Metam. 15.867.

. . . Tarde quae credita laedunt/Credimus. *tar—day quie cray—dit—a lie—dunt cray—di—muss.*
We believe tardily things which, when believed, are grievous to us.
Ovid. Heroides 2.9.

Tarde sed tute. *tar—day sed too—tay.*
Slowly but safely.
Pr.

Te Deum laudamus. *tay deh—um lowd—ah—muss.*
We praise thee, O God.
Hymn attrib. to St. Ambrose, Bishop of Milan (c. 340-397).

Te, Fortuna, sequor; procul hinc jam foedera sunto:/Credidimus fatis; utendum est judice bello. *tay, for—too—na, seh—quor; proc—ul hink yam foy—deh—ra sun—toe: cray—did—im—uss fah—teece; oo—ten—dum est you—dick—eh bell—loe.*
Thee, Fortune, I follow. Away, far hence all treaties! We have trusted ourselves to fate; war be now the judge.
Lucan. Pharsalia Book 1.226.

Te hominem esse memento. *tay hom—in—em ess—seh me—men—toe.*
Remember that you are a man.
Cicero (adapted).

. . . Telum ira facit. . . . *tay—lum ee—ra fack—it.*
Wrath turns it into a weapon.
Virgil. Æneid 7.508.

. . . Telumque imbelle sine ictu/Conjecit. *tay—lum—queh im—bell—leh sin—eh ick—too con—yay—kit.*
And he threw a feeble and ineffective dart.
Virgil. Æneid. 2.544.

Temperatae suaves sunt argutiae:/Immodicae offendunt. . . . *tem—peh—rah—tie swah—wace sunt ar—goo—ti—eye: im—mod—ick—eye off—fen—dunt.*
Wit when temperate is pleasing, when unbridled it offends.
Phaedrus. Fab. Book 4. Epil. 3.

[213]

Templa quam dilecta. *temp—la quam dee—leck—ta.*
How amiable are thy temples.
Motto of the Temples, Earls of Buckingham: Adapted from the Vulgate, Ps. 84.1.

Tempora mutantur, nos et mutamur in illis. *tem—po—ra moot—an—tur, noce et moot—ah—mur in ill—lease.*
Times change and we change with them.
J. Owen (c. 1560-1622). Epigram.

Tempore difficiles veniunt ad aratra juvenci;/Tempore lenta pati frena docentur equi. *tem—po—reh diff—fick—ill—ace wen—i—unt ad a—rah—tra yu—wen—key; tem—po—reh len—ta pat—ee fray—na dock—en—tur eh—quee.*
In time the unmanageable young oxen come to the plough; in time the horses are taught to endure the restraining bit.
Ovid. Ars Amat. Book 1.471.

Temporis ars medicina fere est. *tem—po—riss arss med—ick—ee—na feh—reh est.*
The art of medicine is generally a question of time.
Ovid. Rem. Amor. 131.

Temporis illius colui fovique poetas. *tem—po—riss ill—lee—uss col—u—ee foe—wee—queh po—ay—tahss.*
I have honoured and cherished the poets of that time.
Ovid. Trist. 4.10.41.

Tempus anima rei. *tem—puss an—im—a reh—ee.*
Time is the soul of the business (*i.e.* the essence of the contract).
Pr.

Tempus edax rerum. *tem—puss ed—ahks ray—rum.*
Time, the devourer of things.
Ovid. Metam. Book 15.234.

Tempus fugit. *tem—pus fug—it.*
Time flies.
Anon.

. . . Tenet insanabile multos/Scribendi cacoethes. *ten—et in—sah—nah—bill—eh mull—toce scree—bend—ee cack—o—ay—thess.*
The incurable itch of writing possesses many.
Juvenal. Sat. 7.52.

Terra antiqua, potens armis atque ubere glebae. *tear—ra an—tee—qua, pot—aynce ar—meece at—queh oo—beh—reh glay—bye.*

[214]

An ancient land, powerful in arms and in the richness of its soil.
Virgil. Æneid 1.531.

Terra incognita. *tear—ra in—cog—nit—a.*
An unknown land.
Pr.

Terrore nominis Romani. *tear—roh—reh noh—min—iss roe—mah—nee.*
By the terror of the Roman name.
Tacitus. Annals Book 4.24.

Tertium quid. *tear—ti—um quid/ter—shi—um quid.*
Some third thing (spoken of the result of two other matters or causes).
Irenaeus (tr. from A Greek Phrase.)

Theatra stuprandis moribus orientia. *theh—ah—tra stup—ran—deece
moh—rib—uss o—ri—en—ti—a.*
Theatres springing from debauched manners.
Tertullian. Apolog. 6.

Tigridis evita sodalitatem. *tig—rid—is ay—wee—tah sod—ah—lit—ah—tem.*
Shun the companionship of the tiger.
Pr.

Time Deum, et recede a malo. *tim—ay deh—um et re—chay—deh ah mal—oh.*
Fear God, and withdraw from evil.
Vulgate. Prov. 3.7.

Timidus Plutus. *tim—id—uss. ploo—tuss.*
Plutus (wealth) is full of fear.
Old Proverb.

Timor mortis conturbat me. *tim—or more—tiss con—tur—bat may.*
The fear of death terrifies me.
From the seventh Responsory of Matins for the Dead.

. . . Timor unus erat; facies non una timoris. *tim—or oo—nus eh—rat;
fack—i—ace none oo—na tim—oh—riss.*
There was one fear; but not one and the same expression of fear.
Ovid. Ars Amat. 1.121.

Tormenta gubernat dolor, moderatur natura cujusque cum animi tum
corporis, regit quaesitor, flectit libido, corrumpit spes, infirmat metus, ut
in tot rerum angustiis nihil veritati loci relinquatur. *tor—men—ta gub—ehr—
nat doll—or, mod—eh—rah—tur nah—too—ra coo—yuss—queh cum an—im—ee*

[215]

tum cor—por—iss, regg—it quice—ee—tor, flect—it lib—ee—doe, cor—rum—pit space, in—fihr—mat met—uss, ut in tot ray—rum ang—gust—i—eece nih—hill way—rit—ah—tee lock—ee reh—link—wah—tur.
Pain is the guide when under torture, the mental and bodily qualities of each man controls it, the inquisitor directs it, desire diverts it, hope destroys it, and fear weakens it, so that in such straits there is no room for truth.
Cicero. Pro Sulla 28/78.

Tota philosophorum vita commentatio mortis est. *toe—ta fil—oss—off— oh—rum wee—ta com—men—tah—ti—oh more—teece est.*
The whole of the life of philosophers is a preparation for death.
Cicero. Tusc. Quaest. 1.30,74.

Totum mundum agit histrio. *toe—tum mun—dum ag—it hist—ri—oh.*
The actor acts the whole world (assumes every kind of character).
Pr.

. . . Totum nutu tremefecit Olympum. *toe—tum noo—too trem—eff—ay— kit ol—im—pum.*
He caused all Olympus to tremble with his nod.
Virgil. Æneid 9.106.

. . . Trahit sua quemque voluptas. *tra—hit su—a quem—queh wol—up—tahss.*
His own desire leads every man.
Virgil. Eclogues 2.65.

Transeat in exemplum. *trahn—seh—at in ex—em—plum.*
Let it stand as an example.
Pr.

Trepide concursans, occupata in otio. *trep—id—ay con—cur—sahnss, ock— cup—ah—ta in oh—ti—oh.*
A nation rushing hastily to and fro, busily employed in idleness.
Phaedrus. Fab. Book 2.5.

Tria juncta in uno. *tri—a yunc—ta in oo—noh.*
Three things joined in one.
Motto of the Order of the Bath.

Tristius est leto, leti genus. . . . *triss—ti—uss est lay—toe, lay—tee gen—uss.*
The mode of death is sadder than death itself.
Martial. Epig. Book 11.92.5.

Troja (nefas!) commune sepulcrum Asiae Europaeque, Troja virum et

virtutum omnium acerba cinis. *troh—ya (neff—ahss!) com—moon—eh sep—ull—crum ass—i—eye ewe—roe—pie—queh, troh—ya wih—rum et wihr—too—tum om—ni—um ack—air—ba kin—iss.*
Troy (O wickedness!) — the tomb shared by Asia and Europe, Troy, the bitter ashes of all men and their courage.
Catullus. Poem 68.89f.

Tu autem. *too ow—tem.*
"But thou" (a hint to be on).
From the words used by preachers at the end of their discourse, "Tu autem, Domine, miserere nobis."

Tu mihi magnus Apollo. *too mi—he mag—nuss ap—oll—loh.*
Thou art my great Apollo (my oracle).
Virgil (adapted). Eclogues 3.104.

Tu mihi solus eras. *too mi—he soe—luss eh—rahss.*
Thou wast my only one.
Ovid. Rem. Amor. 464.

Tu ne quaesieris (scire nefas) quem mihi, quem tibi/Finem Di dederint, Leuconoe.... *too nay quie—si—eh—riss (skee—reh neff—ahss) quem mi—hee, quem ti—bee fee—nem dee ded—eh—rint, lew—con—o—ay.*
Seek not thou, Leuconoe, to discover that which it is unlawful for us to know, what end the gods have assigned to me or to thee.
Horace. Odes Book 1.11.1.

Tu nihil invita dices faciesve Minerva. *too ni—hill in—wee—tah dee—case fack—i—ace—weh min—air—wah.*
You shall speak or do nothing if Minerva is unfavourable.
Horace. De Arte Poetica 385.

Tu quoque. *too quo—queh.*
You also (*i.e.* "You're another").
Ovid. Tristia 2.39.

Tu, si hic sis, aliter sentias. *too, see heek siss, al—it—er sen—ti—ahss.*
You, if you were here, would think otherwise.
Terence. Andria ii. 1.10.

Tum excidit omnis constantia. *tum ex—kid—it om—niss cone—stan—ti—a.*
Then all our endurance failed.
Petronius Arbiter.

Tunica propior pallio est. *too—nick—a prop—i—or pal—li—oh est.*
My tunic is nearer to me than my mantle.
Plautus. Trinummus v. 2.30.

Turba Remi sequitur Fortunam, ut semper, et odit/Damnatos.
tur—ba rem—ee seh—quit—ur for—too—nam, ut sem—per, et oh—dit
dam—nah—toce.
The Roman mob follows after Fortune, as it always did, and hates those
who have been condemned.
Juvenal. Sat. 10.74.

Turpe est laudari ab illaudatis. *tur—peh est lowd—ah—ree ab ill—lowd—*
ah—teece.
It is discreditable to be praised by the undeserving.
Pr.

Turpes amores conciliare. *tur—pace a—moh—race con—kill—i—ah—reh.*
To engage in disgraceful attachments.
Pr.

Turpis in reum omnis exprobratio. *turp—iss in reh—um om—niss ex—prob—*
rah—ti—oh.
All invective against a man on his trial is disgraceful.
Pr.

Turris fortissima nomen Domini. *tur—riss for—tiss—sim—a noh—men*
dom—in—ee.
The name of the Lord is a very strong tower.
Vulgate. Prov. 18.10.

. . . Tuta timens. . . . *too—ta tim—aynce.*
Fearing even things which are safe.
Virgil. Æneid 4.298.

Tutius erratur ex parte mitiori. *too—ti—uss air—rah—tur ex parr—teh*
meet—i—oh—ree.
It is safer to err on the more merciful side.
Law.

Tutum silentii praemium. *too—tum sil—ent—i—ee pry—mi—um.*
Sure is the reward of silence.
Pr.

Uberrima fides. *oo—bear—rim—a fid—ace.*
The most implicit confidence.
Pr.

Ubi dolor, ibi digitus. *ub—i dol—or, ib—i dig—it—uss.*
Where there is pain, there will the finger be.
Pr.

Ubi jus, ibi remedium. *ub—i yooce, ib—i rem—ed—i—um.*
Where there is right, there is remedy.
Law.

. . . Ubi mel, ibi apes. . . . *ub—i mel, ib—i ap—ace.*
Where the honey is, there are bees.
Plautus.

Ubi saeva indignatio cor ulterius lacerare nequit. *ub—i sigh—wa in—dig—*
nah—ti—oh cor ul—teh—ri—uss lack—eh—rah—reh neh—quit.
Where fierce indignation can no longer tear my heart.
Dean Swift's epitaph.

Ubi timor adest, sapientia adesse nequit. *ub—i tim—or ad—est, sap—i—ent—*
i—a ad—ess—seh neh—quit.
Where fear is present, wisdom cannot be.
Lactantius.

Ubi uber, ibi tuber. *ub—i oo—ber, ib—i too—ber.*
Where plenty is, there is swelling (*i.e.* unwieldiness).
Apuleius. Florid. 18.

Ulterius ne tende odiis. *ul—teh—ri—uss nay ten—deh od—i—eece.*
Do not go further with your hatred.
Virgil. Æneid 12.938.

Ultima Cumael venit jam Carminis aetas; magnus ab integro seaclorum

nascitur ordo. Jam redit et virgo, redeunt Saturnia Regna. Jam nova pro-
genies caelo demittitur alto. *ull—tim—a coo—my—el way—nit yam car-*
min—iss eye—tahss; mag—nuss ab in—teg—roe sigh—clow—rum nah—skit—
ur ore—doh. yam red—it et wihr—goh, red—eh—unt sah—tur—ni—a rayg—na,
yam no—wa proh—gen—i—ace kie—loh day—mit—ti—tur al—toh.
Now the last age of Cumaean song is come: the great cycle of the ages is
born anew. Now the virgin returns, and the reign of Saturn returns, and now
a new generation is sent down from high heaven.

Ultima Thule. *ul—tim—a thoo—lay.*
Remotest Thule.
Virgil. Georgics 1.30.

Ultra vires. *ul—tra vie—reece.*
Beyond one's power.
Law.

Una domus non alit duos canes. *oo—nah dom—uss none al—it du—oce*
can—ace.
One house does not keep two dogs.
Pr.

Un salus victis nullam sperare salutem. *oo—nah sa—loose wick—teece*
null—lam spay—rah—reh sal—oo—tem.
The one safety to the conquered is to hope for no safety.
Virgil. Æneid 2.354.

Unde fames homini vetitorum tanta ciborum? *un—deh fa—mace hom—in—*
ee wet—it—oh—rum tan—ta kib—oh—rum?
Whence has man so great a hunger for food which is forbidden?
Ovid. Metam. 15.138.

Unde quamquam adversus sontis et novissima exempla meritos miseratio
oriebatur, tamquam non utilitate publica sed in saevitiam unius absum-
erentur. *un—deh quam—quam ad—wehr—suss son—teece et no—wiss—sim—*
a ex—em—pla meh—rit—oce miss—eh—rah—ti—oh or—i—ay—bah—tur,
tam—quam none oo—till—it—ah—teh pub—lick—ah sed in sye—wit—i—am
oo—nee—uss ap—soo—meh—ent—ur.
As a result although they (the Christians) were guilty and deserved the most
extreme penalties there arose pity for them, as it was thought they were
not being exterminated for the public good but for the sake of one man's
cruelty (*sc.* Nero's).
Tacitus. Annals 15.44.

Unguibus et rostro. *un—guib—uss et roe—stroh.*
With claws and beak.
Pr.

. . . Uni aequus virtuti, atque ejus amicis. *oo—nee eye—quuss wihr—too—tee,*
at—queh ay—yuss a—meek—eece.
Friendly to virtue alone and to its friends.
Horace. Sat. Book 2.1.70.

Unica virtus necessaria. *oo—nick—a wihr—tuss neck—ess—sah—ri—a.*
Virtue only is necessary.
Pr.

Unius dementia dementes efficit multos. *oo—nee—us day—men—ti—a*
day—men—tace eff—fick—it mul—toce.
The madness of one man makes many mad.
Pr.

Unum prae cunctis fama loquatur opus. *oo—num pry cunc—teece fah—ma*
lo—quah—tur op—uss.
Report commemorates one work before all that he has done.
Martial. De Spectaculis 1.8.

Unus qui nobis cunctando restituit rem;/Non ponebat enim rumores ante
salutem. *oo—nuss quee noh—beece cunc—tan—doe ress—ti—tu—it rem;*
none poe—nay—bat en—im room—oh—race an—teh sal—oot—em.
One who by delay restored our affairs to us; for he did not esteem public
rumour above public safety.
Ennius Ap. Cicero, De Sen. 4. of Quintus Maximus. Fabius surnamed "cunctator".

Urbem lateritiam accepit, marmoream reliquit. *ur—bem lat—eh—rit—i—am*
ack—kay—pit, mar—mo—reh—am rah—lee—quit.
He (Caesar Augustus) found a city built of brick; he left it built of marble.
Suetonius (adapted). Caes. Aug. 28.

Urbem quam dicunt Romam, Meliboee, putavi,/Stultus ego, huic nostrae
similem. . . . *ur—bem quam deek—unt roe—mam, mel—ib—oy—eh, put—ah—*
wee, stool—tuss egg—o, hu—eek noss—try sim—ill—em.
The city, Meliboeus, which they call Rome, I, fool that I am, imagined to
be like this town of ours.
Virgil. Eclogues 1.20.

Urbem venalem et mature perituram, si emptorem invenerit. *ur—bem way—*
nah—lem et mah—too—reh peh—rit—oo—ram, see emp—toe—rem in—way—
neh—rit.

A city (Rome) for sale, and destined soon to disappear, if it can find a buyer.
Sallust. Jugurtha 35 fin.

Urbi pater, est urbique maritus. *ur—bee pat—er, est ur—bee—queh ma—ree—tuss.*
He is a father to the town, and a husband to the town. (Spoken of a man of intrique.)
Pr.

Urbs antiqua ruit, multos dominata per annos. *urps an—tee—qua ru—it, mull—toce dom—in—ah—ta per an—noce.*
The ancient city falls, having had dominion throughout many years.
Virgil. Æneid 2.363.

Urit mature urtica vera. *oo—rit mah—too—ray ur—tick—a way—ra.*
The true nettle stings when it is young.
Pr.

Usque adeo miserum est civili vincere bello. *uss—queh ad—eh—oh miss—eh—rum est key—wee—lee win—keh—reh bell—loh.*
To such an extent is it wretched to conquer in civil warfare.
Lucan. Pharsalia 1.361.

Ut absolvaris, ignosce. *ut ap—sol—wah—riss, ig—noh—skeh.*
Forgive that you may be forgiven.
Seneca. De Beneficiis Book 7.28.

. . . Ut ameris, ama. . . . *ut a—may—riss, a—mah.*
In order that you may be loved, love.
Martial. Epig. Book 6.11.10.

Ut homo est, ita morem geras. *ut hom—oh est, it—a moh—rem geh—rahss.*
Suit your manner to the man.
Terence. Adelphi iii. 3.78.

Ut ludas creditores, mille sunt artes. *ut lood—ahss cray—dit—oh—race, mil—leh sunt arr—tace.*
There are a thousand methods of cheating your creditors.
Erasmus. Hippeus Anippos.

Ut metus ad omnes, poena ad paucos perveniret. *ut met—uss ad om—nace, poy—na ad pow—coce pair—wen—ee—ret.*
That fear may reach all, the punishment should reach the few.
Law.

. . . Ut mos est. . . . *ut moce est.*
As the custom is.
Juvenal. Sat. 6.392.

Ut pictura poesis. *ut pick—too—ra po—ay—siss.*
As is a picture so is a poem.
Horace. De Arte Poetica 361.

Ut plerique solent, naso suspendis adunco/Ignotos. *ut play—ree—que*
sol—ent, nah—soe suss—pen—diss ad—un—coe ig—noh—toce.
As many are wont to do, you turn up your nose at men who are unknown.
Horace. Sat. Book 1.6.5.

Ut prosim. *ut proh—sim.*
That I may benefit others.

Ut quod segnitia erat, sapientia vocaretur. *ut quod sayg—nit—i—a eh—rat,*
sap—i—ent—i—a wock—ah—ray—tur.
So that what was indolence was called wisdom.
Tacitus. Hist. Book 1.49.

Ut servi volunt esse erum, ita solet esse;/Bonis boni sunt; improbi, qui
malus fuit. *ut sair—wee wol—unt ess—seh eh—rum, it—a sol—et ess—seh;*
bon—eece bon—ee sunt; im—prob—ee, quee mal—uss fu—it.
As servants wish their master to be, so he is wont to be; the good servants
have good masters; but masters are bad to a servant who has done evil.
Plautus. Mostellaria iv. 1.16.

Ut tu fortunam, sic nos te, Celse, feremus. *ut tu for—too—nam, seek noce*
tay, kel—seh, feh—ray—muss.
As you bear your good fortune, Celsus, so shall we have you in estimation.
Horace. Ep. Book 1.8.17.

Uti possidetis. *ut—ee poss—sid—ay—tiss.*
As you now have in your possession. (Used in the termination of war or
dispute, as the opposite phrase to "In statu quo.")

Utinam ne in nemore Pelio securibus Caesa accidisset abiegna ad terram
trabes . . . Nam nunquam era errans mea domo ecferret pedem Medea,
animo aegra, amore saevo saucia. *ut—in—am nay in nem—or—eh pay—li—oh*
seck—oo—rib—uss kye—sa ack—kid—iss—set ab—i—ayg—na ad tehr—ram
trab—ace . . . nam nun—quam eh—ra ehr—rahnce meh—a dom—oh eck—
fehr—ret ped—em maid—ay—a, an—im—oh eye—gra, am—oh—reh sye—woe
sow—ki—a.

[223]

If only in the forests of Pelion the fir-wood had not been cut by axes and fallen to earth (for the ship Argo) . . . For never then would my wandering mistress have left her home, Medea, sick at heart, wounded by a cruel love.
Ennius, Medea exsul 1.2.8.9.

Uxorem accepi, dote imperium vendidi. *ux—oh—rem ack—cape—ee, dote—eh im—peh—ri—um wen—did—ee.*
I have taken a wife, I have sold my sovereignty for a dowry.
Plautus. Asin. i. 1.

Vacare culpa magnum est solatium. *wa—cah—reh cull—pa mag—num est soh—lah—ti—um.*
It is a great comfort to be free from guilt.
Cicero. Ep. Book 6.3.

Vade mecum. *wad—eh may—cum/vay—de mee—cum.*
Go with me; be my companion.
Pr.

Vade Satana. *vad—eh sa—tah—na.*
Depart, Satan.
Vulgate. St. Matt. 4.10.

Vae misero mihi! quanta de spe decidi. *wye miss—eh—roe mi—he! quan—tah day spay day—kid—ee.*
Woe to my wretched self! from what a height of hope have I fallen!
Terence. Heautontimorumenos ii. 3.9.

Vae victis! *wye wick—teece!*
Woe to the vanquished!
Plautus. Pseudolus, Act v. 2.19.; also Livy etc.

Valeat quantum valere potest. *wal—eh—at quan—tum wal—ay—re pot—est.*
Let it have such value as it is able to possess.
Pr.

Vare, legiones redde! *wa—re, leg—i—oh—nace red—deh!*
Varus, give me back my legions!
Suetonius. Augustus 22.

Varium et mutabile semper/Femina. *wa—ri—um et moot—ah—bill—eh sem—per fay—min—a.*
Woman is ever a varying and changeable thing.
Virgil. Æneid 4.569.

Vectigalia nervi sunt reipublicae. *weck—tee—gah—li—a nair—wee sunt reh—ee—pub—lick—eye.*
Taxes are the sinews of the commonwealth.
Cicero (adapted).

Vel caeco appareat. *well kye—coe ap—pah—reh—at.*
It would be apparent even to a blind man.
Pr.

Vel capillus habet umbram suam. *well cap—ill—lus hab—et um—bram su—am.*
Even a hair has its own shadow.
Publilius Syrus. From the Greek.

Vellem nescire litteras! *well—lem ness—key—re lit—teh—rahss!*
I wish I knew not how to write.
Suetonius. Nero 9. also Seneca.

Velox consilium sequitur paenitentia. *way—loaks cone—sill—i—um seh—quit—ur pie—nit—en—ti—a.*
Repentance follows hasty counsel.
Publilius Syrus.

. . . Venale pecus. . . . *way—nah—leh peck—uss.*
The venal herd.
Juvenal Sat. 8.62.

Venditione exponas. *wen—dit—i—oh—neh ex—poe—nahss.*
Expose for sale (a writ directing the sale of goods).
Law.

Veni, Creator Spiritus. *vay—nee, creh—ah—tor spee—rit—uss.*
Come, Holy Spirit, Creator.
Mediaeval Hymn.

[225]

Veni, vidi, vici. *way—nee, wee—dee, wee—kee.*
I came, I saw, I conquered.
Attr. to Julius Caesar by Suetonius, Divus Julius, 37, 2.

Vestigia nulla retrorsum. *west—ee—gi—a null—la re—tror—sum.*
No steps backward.
Horace.

Vetera extollimus recentium incuriosi. *wet—eh—ra ex—toll—lim—uss re—kent—i—um in—coo—ri—oh—see.*
We extol ancient things, regardless of our times.
Tacitus.

Vexilla regis prodeunt;/Fulget crucis mysterium. *vexil—la ray—jiss proh—deh—unt; full—jet crew—chiss mis—tay—ri—um.*
The royal banners forward go; The cross shines forth in mystic glow.
Venantius Fortunatus (tr. J.M. Neale.)

Vicisti, Galilaee! *wee—kiss—tee, gal—ill—eye—eh!*
You have conquered, Galilean!
Attr. to the Emperor Julian by Theodoret, Hist. Eccles. 3, 20.

Vis consili expers mole ruit sua. *weece cone—sil—ee ex—pairce moh—leh ru—it su—ah.*
Force without mind falls by its own weight.
Horace. Odes 3.4.65.

Vitae summa brevis spem nos vetat incohare longam. *wee—tie sum—ma bre—wiss spem noce wet—at in—co—hah—reh long—gam.*
Life's span forbids thee to extend thy cares and stretch thy hopes beyond thy years.
Horace. Odes, 1.4.15.

Vivamus mea Lesbia, atque amemus. *wee—wah—muss meh—a les—bi—a, at—queh a—may—muss.*
Lesbia mine, let's live and love.
Catullus. Carm. 5.1.

Vox populi, vox Dei. *vohks pop—ul—ee, vohks deh—ee.*
The voice of the people is the voice of God.
Alcuin, Epist. 127.

Finis Coronat Opus

Designed by Newbury Books
Edited by Virginia L. Ulrici
Type is 12 pt. Aldine Roman by
Technical Composition, Newburyport, Mass.
Printed on 60 lb. Ticonderoga Laid by Mohawk
Paper Company
Presswork by Bradford & Bigelow, Danvers, Mass.
Binding by Robert Burlen & Son
Norwell, Mass.